The Diplomatic Reminiscences of Lord Augustus Loftus ... 1837-1862, Volume 2

You are holding a reproduction of an original work that is in the public domain in the United States of America, and possibly other countries.You may freely copy and distribute this work as no entity (individual or corporate) has a copyright on the body of the work.This book may contain prior copyright references, and library stamps (as most of these works were scanned from library copies).These have been scanned and retained as part of the historical artifact.

This book may have occasional imperfections such as missing or blurred pages, poor pictures, errant marks, etc. that were either part of the original artifact, or were introduced by the scanning process. We believe this work is culturally important, and despite the imperfections, have elected to bring it back into print as part of our continuing commitment to the preservation of printed works worldwide. We appreciate your understanding of the imperfections in the preservation process, and hope you enjoy this valuable book.

THE
DIPLOMATIC REMINISCENCES
OF
LORD AUGUSTUS LOFTUS.

THE
DIPLOMATIC REMINISCENCES
OF
LORD AUGUSTUS LOFTUS,
P.C., G.C.B.

1837—1862.

IN TWO VOLUMES.

Vol. II.

CASSELL & COMPANY, Limited:
LONDON, PARIS & MELBOURNE.
1892.

[ALL RIGHTS RESERVED.]

~~I 4229~~
H778.92

Br 2212.24

Sumner fund.

CONTENTS.

CHAPTER I.

Russian Proposal for a Congress—Object of Prince Gortchacoff—Language of M. de Balabine—Curious Document Giving Outline of Emperor Napoleon's Policy—Reported Russian Projects in Danubian Principalities—My Disbelief in them—Supposed Views of Emperor Napoleon—Proposed Congress Accepted by Lord Malmesbury Conditionally—Interview with Prince Metternich—His Opinion of a Congress—Cause of Russian Proposal for a Congress—Improvement in Relations between Austria and Russia—Difficulties Raised by Austria to a Congress—Eulogium of Lord Malmesbury—His Letter to me on Resignation of Count Buol, and an Interview with Count Apponyi—Kammer Ball at Court—Dinner at the Palace—Conversation with the Emperor on Disarmament—Influence of Financial Question on Austrian Policy—Mission of Archduke Albert to Berlin—Summons to Sardinia to Disarm—Cavour's Reply Evasive—Orders to General Giulay to Enter Piedmont—War Declared—Manifestoes of Emperors of Austria and France, and of King of Sardinia—Count Cavour—Policy of Prussia and Germany. 1

CHAPTER II.

Emperor of Austria's Manifesto Declaring War against Sardinia—French Embassy leave Vienna—Count Buol's Resignation and Causes of it—Emperor's Interview with Prince Metternich—Appointment of Count Rechberg—Battle of Magenta—Allied Army enter Milan—Hungary—Russian Minister's Language—Change of Ministers in England—Lord John Russell Secretary for Foreign Affairs—His Policy in Favour of an United Italy—Count Karolyi's Mission to St. Petersburg—Battle of Solferino—Interview of the two Emperors—Preliminaries of Villa Franca — Retirement of General Giulay — Interview with Count Rechberg—Conference of the Three Powers to meet at Zürich to Conclude Peace—Opinion of the King of Würtemberg on the Peace 33

CONTENTS.

CHAPTER III.

Return to Vienna on September 10th—Negotiations at Zürich still Continued—Prince of Hesse's Mission to St. Petersburg — Conversation with Count Rechberg on the Restoration of the Archdukes—Conversation with the Russian Minister—Archduke Albert's Mission to greet the Emperor of Russia at Warsaw—Reconciliation between Austria and Russia—Prince Metternich's Cordial Reception by the Emperor Napoleon—Central Italy Question Achieved by the National Will—King of Naples' Flight to Gaeta—French and Russian Missions Recalled from Turin—"Le Pape et le Congrès"—Count Walewski Resigns—Is succeeded by M. Thouvenel—Austria Declines to go to Congress—Three Treaties Signed at Zürich, November 10th, 1859—Union of Moldavia and Wallachia—War with China—Peace Signed at Pekin—Intervention of Europe in Syria—Change of Dynasty in Servia—Visit of the Queen and Prince Consort to Coburg—Accident to the Prince Consort—Changes and Reform in Austria—The Imperial Patent in regard to Non-Catholic Confessions—Cause of its Rejection by Hungary 75

CHAPTER IV.

Opening of 1860 with Favourable Prospects—Count Walewski succeeded by M. de Thouvenel—Appointment of the Marquis de Moustier as French Ambassador—Ball at Court—Dinner at the Palace—Conversation with the Emperor—The Emperor's Conversation with the Marquis de Moustier—Suicide of Baron Bruck—The Proposed Congress—Its Collapse—Annexation of Savoy and Nice to France—Count Seebach's Secret Mission to Count Beust at Dresden—Its Failure—Success of Lord John Russell's Policy in favour of an United Italy—Memorandum of my Conversation with Count Rechberg given to Lord John Russell at Coburg—His Reply—Three Meetings of Sovereigns—Progress of the Italian Movement—Occupation of Naples by Garibaldi—Flight of the King—Surrender of Gaeta—Garibaldi Retires to Caprera—Unity of Italy Effected—Assumption by Victor Emanuel of the Title of King of Italy 109

CHAPTER V.

Baron Stockmar—Creation of an Embassy at Vienna—Appointment of Lord Bloomfield as Ambassador—My Transfer to Berlin—Arrival at Vienna of Irish enlisted for Papal Army—Some Hundreds passed through Vienna, totally destitute and penniless—Expenses of their Return to their Homes defrayed by Papal Government— Request for a British Steamer to convey the Empress to Madeira—*Victoria and Albert* placed by the Queen at Her Majesty's Disposal—Reforms and Reorganisation of the Empire—National Debt and Finances of Austria—Hungarian Question—Death of Baron Josika and Count Széchenyi—

Audience of the Emperor to deliver Letter of Recall—Offer of Grand Cross of Leopold declined—Baron Anselm Rothschild—Departure from Vienna 136

CHAPTER VI.

Arrival at Berlin—Audiences of the King and Queen—Conflict between the Government and Parliament on Army Reorganisation—Hohenlohe Ministry succeeds Hohenzollern Ministry—Conversation with Baron Schleinitz on Syrian Affairs—Interview with Prince Hohenzollern—Lord Breadalbane's Arrival to invest the King with the Garter: He receives the Black Eagle—Visits to Strelitz, Schwerin, and Dessau—Riots at Warsaw—Polish Question—Recognition of Kingdom of Italy refused—Duel between General Manteuffel and M. Twesten—Attempt on King's Life at Baden—Audience of the King to congratulate His Majesty in the Queen's and Prince Consort's Name on his Escape—Death of Count Cavour—Dinner with Crown Prince and Princess at Potsdam—Conversation with the King on Schleswig-Holstein Question Military Fête at Potsdam 160

CHAPTER VII.

The *Huldigung* or Coronation—Differences between the King and his Ministry thereon—Lord Clarendon appointed Ambassador—The King's Visit to the Emperor Napoleon at Compiègne—Life of the King of Prussia at Baden—The Queen's Receptions—M. de Bacourt—English Church at Baden—Last Interview with the Queen of Prussia in 1889—Death of my Eldest Daughter—Sympathy shown by the Queen of Prussia—Coronation of the King—The Act of Crowning Himself and Speech much Commented on—The Non-responsibility of Ministers in Prussia—Expenses of the Coronation defrayed by the King—Poland—Attempts to revive a Polish Question—Fruitless Diplomatic Action of England and France—Life of the Grand Duke Constantine attempted at Warsaw—The Marquis de Wielopolski—Schleswig-Holstein Question—The German Question—Death of the Prince Consort—Deep Sympathy evinced for the Queen 185

CHAPTER VIII.

The New Prussian Parliament—Overwhelming Majority of the Liberal Party—Continued Struggle between the Government and Parliament on Army Reorganisation Bill—Conversation with Bernstorff on Recognition of Italy—New Order of Knighthood—The German Question—Despatch of Bernstorff to Rechberg in reply to his Proposals for Dietal Reform—Sensation it Produced—Identic Notes of South German States protesting against Prussian Policy—Conversation with the King of Prussia—The Question of the Partition of Schleswig Suggested as a Means of solving Differences with Denmark—The Hessian

CONTENTS.

Question—Discourtesy of the Elector to General Willisen—Dismissal of Hessian Ministry Demanded—Rupture of Diplomatic Relations—Unsatisfactory Conduct of the Elector—Prussian Parliament again Dissolved—Change of Ministry—Bismarck appointed Minister at Paris—Conversation with Prince Hohenlohe—Strained Relations with Austria—The King's Opinion on the Appointment of Grand Duke Constantine—Mr. White's Letter—The Japanese Embassy—Bernstorff on Restoration of the Primate—Happy Delivery of the Crown Princess of a Prince 213

CHAPTER IX.

Baron Ricasoli's Visit to Berlin—Prussian Sympathy for Italy—Servia—Disturbances at Belgrade—Conference at Constantinople—Montenegro—Collision with the Turks—Commercial Treaty between Prussia and France signed August 2—Opposed by Southern States—Proposed Treaty of Commerce between Great Britain and the Zollverein—Austrian Proposal to enter Zollverein rejected—Dinner at Baron Budberg's—Conversation with him—His Language very conciliatory—Continued Conflict between the Government and the Chamber—Changes in the Ministry—Count Bernstorff succeeded by M. de Bismarck—The Queen's Visit to Germany—My Interview with Lord Russell at Gotha—His Proposals on Danish Question approved by Austria and Prussia—Fatal Effects of their Rejection by Denmark – Missions to Berlin and London raised to Embassies—My Appointment to Munich—The Order of K.C.B. conferred on me by the Queen—Relations between Austria and Prussia—Count Bernstorff's Explanation of his Resignation—His Appointment as Ambassador to England—Rejection by the Chamber of the Naval Budget—Christening of infant Prince 241

CHAPTER X.

Recall of Prince La Tour-d'Auvergne, French Minister at Berlin : his Appointment to Rome—Ministerial Change at Paris—Importance attached to the Appointment of Drouyn de L'Huys as Minister for Foreign Affairs—Close of the Prussian Session—No Compromise on Internal Questions—Conflict between the two Houses—Conversation with Bismarck : his Departure for Paris to present Letters of Recall—On Russo-Prussian French Alliance—Appointment of Sir A. Buchanan as British Ambassador at Berlin—My Audience of their Majesties to present Letters—Visit of the King to Lady Augustus Loftus, and to present to me a Magnificent Vase with His Majesty's Portrait—Character of the King—Bismarck—Moltke—Roon—Appointed Envoy to the King of Bavaria—Departure for Munich 268

APPENDIX 291

THE
DIPLOMATIC REMINISCENCES
OF
LORD AUGUSTUS LOFTUS.

CHAPTER I.

Russian Proposal for a Congress—Object of Prince Gortchacoff—Language of M. de Balabine—Curious Document Giving Outline of Emperor Napoleon's Policy—Reported Russian Projects in Danubian Principalities—My Disbelief in them—Supposed Views of Emperor Napoleon—Proposed Congress Accepted by Lord Malmesbury Conditionally—Interview with Prince Metternich—His Opinion of a Congress—Cause of Russian Proposal for a Congress —Improvement in Relations between Austria and Russia—Difficulties Raised by Austria to a Congress—Eulogium of Lord Malmesbury—His Letter to me on Resignation of Count Buol, and on his Interview with Count Apponyi—Kammer Ball at Court—Dinner at the Palace—Conversation with the Emperor on Disarmament—Influence of Financial Question on Austrian Policy—Mission of Archduke Albert to Berlin—Summons to Sardinia to Disarm—Cavour's Reply Evasive— Orders to General Giulay to Enter Piedmont—War Declared—Manifestoes of Emperors of Austria and France, and of King of Sardinia—Count Cavour—Policy of Prussia and Germany.

ON Lord Cowley's return to Paris he learnt that, during his absence in Vienna, Russia had suggested to the French Government a Congress of the Great Powers for the settlement of Italian affairs. The French Government acted on this suggestion, and supported the proposal in a despatch addressed to the Duc de Mala koff on March 18. The French Ambassador, in making this proposal to the English Government, added that the suggestion came from Russia.

It was singular that the Russian Government, which up to the date of Lord Cowley's mission had taken no part in the peace negotiations, should have chosen this moment to come forward with the proposal of a Congress. It was surmised that so long as there existed any hopes of peace, Russia was content to be a silent spectator of passing events, maintaining a complete reserve and freedom of action. But when it became apparent that the efforts for the maintenance of peace were likely to prove unavailing, and that war was imminent, Russia was fearful that if the war were not localised, and that a general conflagration were to ensue, she might be obliged to participate in it, and at a moment when she was neither financially nor militarily prepared for action.

At this time various reports of an offensive and defensive alliance between Russia and France were in circulation, and even official inquiries were made at Paris and St. Petersburg as to the truth of these rumours. There was also an ardent wish on the part of Prince Gortchacoff to figure at an European Congress, in the hope of finding an opportunity for bringing forward his long-cherished aim for a revision of the Treaty of 1856. M. de Balabine, the Russian Minister at Vienna, was known at this time to have said openly, " *Qu'il y a deux pays mal couchés—l'un par les Traités de* 1815, *l'autre par celui de* 1856. *Ma foi, si la France veut refaire les Traités de* 1815—*elle a raison; nous aussi, nous voulons remanier celui de* 1856, *qui a été humiliant pour la Russie. Notre temps arrivera."* *

The confidential mission of Lord Cowley to Vienna was also viewed as a probable prelude to a future alliance between England and Austria, and in conjunction later with the mission of the Archduke Albert to Berlin, may have been construed into the probability of a Triple Alliance, in which case a general European war would have been inevitable.

The Russian proposal of a Congress may also have been made at the instigation of France in order to gain time for completing her armaments.

A very singular paper was placed in my hands by a colleague who had arrived from Paris, and who was intimate with the *entourage* of the Emperor Napoleon. It bore no date, no signature, no address; but it was given to me as purporting to be the outline of the policy of the Emperor Napoleon, if not an instruction to one of his ministers. I reproduce it here as a remarkable document, but am quite unable to guarantee its authenticity. The document is as follows:—

Pendant la durée de la guerre en Italie, il faudra ménager et cajoler l'Angleterre pour gagner son inaction et pour nous assurer sa neutralité.

La guerre en Italie heureusement et victorieusement terminée, la grande action en Orient commençera *de concert avec la Russie,*

---

* "There are two countries badly circumstanced—the one by the Treaties of 1815, the other by that of 1856. Indeed, if France wishes to remodel the Treaties of 1815, she is in her right. We also wish to retouch the Treaty of 1856, which was humiliating for Russia. Our time will arrive."

et on attaquera l'Angleterre simultanément sur ses côtes et ses stations navales dans la Méditerranée.

Quant à la Prusse, on se moque de ses démarches diplomatiques, ayant pour bût d'obtenir une garantie de l'Empereur de ne pas attaquer l'Autriche sur son territoire appartenant à la Confédération Germanique, et de conserver aux petits Princes Italiens leur territoire respectif.

Quant à l'Allemagne, on affichera une certaine estime pour son organisation, sa civilisation, ses progrès; et on fera croire à Frankfort qu'il ne s'agit que de l'affranchissement de l'Italie, sauf à faire des promesses solennelles de ne jamais attaquer le sol allemand, mais à la rigueur on lancera les populations contre les Gouvernements, et on tiendra en échec la Prusse et la Diète par la Russie.*

This document, of whatever origin, and whether authentic or not, is worthy of the pen of Macchiavelli. Whether or not this paper was a true exposition of the Emperor's intentions, circumstances subsequently occurred which gave them an appearance of authenticity. The Emperor Napoleon was apt to act under

---

* "Pending the duration of the war in Italy, it will be necessary to keep back and flatter England in order to obtain her inaction, and to be assured of her neutrality.

"The war in Italy happily and victoriously terminated, the great operation in the East will commence in concert with Russia, and England will be attacked simultaneously on her coasts and her naval stations in the Mediterranean.

"As for Prussia, one laughs at her diplomatic measures, which aim at obtaining a guarantee from the Emperor not to attack Austria on her territory belonging to the German Confederation, and to preserve to the minor Italian Princes their respective territories. As for Germany, a certain esteem will be pretended for her organisation, her civilisation, her progress; and it will be given out at Frankfort that it is a mere question of the liberation of Italy, except making solemn promises never to attack German territory; but in reality the populations will be roused against the Governments, and Prussia and the Diet will be held in check by Russia."

sudden impulses. He was easily impressed by those
feelings for oppressed nationalities which he had imbibed in his early youth, and he was the more easily
seduced by those feelings when they harmonised with
his ambitious views of remodelling the map of Europe,
without at the same time taking any decided resolution
of carrying them into execution. He was a "fatalist,"
and as such indulged largely in halcyon dreams; but
when, guided by his penetrating sagacity, he foresaw the
dangers which might confront and defeat him, he
yielded to those dictates of reason and prudence which
are the pre-eminent qualities of genius. Thus it was
that his policy often appeared tortuous and inconsistent,
and his apparent want of sincerity was productive of
disbelief and distrust. There were two currents in the
direction of his foreign policy, viz.: that of the ordinary
official current through his accredited diplomacy, and
that carried on through the medium of secret agents unknown to his Cabinet, the result of which was that the
language of his ministers abroad was not always in harmony with the Emperor's views and with facts. Thus,
while negotiating for the pacific settlement of the affairs
of Italy, he had predetermined on war, and at the same
time was negotiating with Count Cavour, through a
secret agent, the arrangements for action.

At the time when the secret paper which I have
reproduced was placed in my hands, I was informed by a
friend in a high position, and conversant with European
affairs, on undoubted authority, that it was the
intention of Russia to erect the Provinces of Wallachia,

Moldavia, and Bulgaria into an independent Christian State, and to place the Duke of Leuchtenberg as sovereign of it under the immediate protectorate of Russia. He could not as confidently state what future awaited Servia, but he surmised that in the eventuality referred to, the plan, which was not of recent date, for restoring the former Kingdom of Servia would be resumed, in which Bosnia and part of Roumelia to Salonica, Montenegro and Albania would be included. In that case, Herzegovina would probably revert to Austria, and the remaining Provinces of Thessaly, Epirus, and Macedonia, with the possession of the Dardanelles and Constantinople, would fall to Russia. However wild and speculative the foregoing programme may appear, there existed at this time a very serious movement and agitation among the various races of the great Slavonic family, and a general expectation existed that Europe would be shortly surprised by events of a grave and astounding nature.

I attached little value to this reported programme from the fact that the Slav races were mixed up with others antagonistic to them. For instance, the Bulgarians with the Wallachians and the Moldavians, and the Bosniaks with the Roumelians, who are deadly hostile to each other, nor was I edified by it in other respects.

There can be no doubt that the primary intentions of the Emperor Napoleon were to foment insurrection in Hungary and in the Christian Provinces of Turkey, with what ulterior aim cannot be known. Russia was, as a Conservative power, opposed to the revolutionary propagandism of Italy, and it cannot, therefore, be supposed that she would have instigated or coalesced in a policy which she disapproved, and which might have created danger to herself in Poland and even in Russia, where the Democratic and Socialist element was beginning to raise its head. It can only be surmised that the Emperor Napoleon looked to utilise these violent means in the event of a defeat, and of his failure to carry out his policy in Italy. His object was to free Italy from the dominant influence of Austria, and to wrest Lombardy from her grasp. He had no wish to make Sardinia the head of a strong and powerful united Italy, nor to deprive the Pope of the estates of the Church. He wished to acquire for France, and for the interests of his dynasty, the Provinces of Savoy and Nice, and that object once accomplished, he was satisfied. It was probably on these grounds that he assented to the restoration of the Austrian Archdukes to their sovereignties in Tuscany and Modena. On the same grounds he favoured the creation of an Italian Confederation under the Presidency of the Pope, in which he looked to exercise a dominant influence; all of which expedients would have suited France, but were in no way satisfactory to Count Cavour or the Italian party, the moderate portion of which looked to an united Italy under a monarchical form.

But it is equally true that the Emperor Napoleon had formed in his mind very extensive projects for the "*remaniement de la carte de l'Europe,*" and that to carry out these schemes he was prepared to utilise all means, legitimate or illegitimate, to attain his ends. His reception at Paris of Klapka and Teleki; his summons to Kossuth to meet him at Genoa; the sending of arms and ammunition up the Danube to the Danubian Principalities; the project of Klapka and Kossuth (acting probably with the knowledge and assent of the Emperor Napoleon) to raise a foreign legion to be composed of Hungarians and Poles to seduce the Hungarian regiments from their allegiance; the proclamations of Kossuth (after his interview with the Emperor), which were distributed in Hungary, and in which he announced " that those who were against them in 1848–49 were now with them, and that money, arms, and ammunition were to be plentifully supplied "—(who was to supply them?); then again, the sending up a large French Fleet to Antivari to form, as it was said, a "dépôt for the French Fleet;"* the landing of a corps of 10,000 men on the Island of Lusino; the appearance of the French Fleet at Fiume, the seaport of Hungary; the support given to the Prince of Montenegro; and the intrigues of the French Consul in the Principalities, were all outward proofs that sinister intentions were entertained by the Emperor Napoleon in those parts, and they caused some anxiety to the Austrian Government.

The proposal of a Congress by Russia was accepted by England, France, Prussia, and Austria. It was

* This was an important fact—1. It was a violation of neutral territory. 2. It is a proof that French attention was turned in that direction.

accepted by Lord Malmesbury conditionally, viz., to be held in a neutral town; it being well understood that no question should be raised respecting the territorial possessions in Italy. Lord Malmesbury further formulated four points within which the discussion should be confined. These were notified to the Duc de Malakoff, the French Ambassador, by Lord Malmesbury in the following terms :—

Extract. *Foreign Office, March* 22, 1859.

I have the honour to state to Your Excellency that this morning a proposal (viz., for a Congress) has been made to Her Majesty's Government on the part of the Emperor of Russia, and that Her Majesty's Government is likewise disposed to agree to it, provided that the deliberations of the Congress are confined to the following four points, namely :—

1. The means by which peace may be preserved between Austria and Sardinia.

2. How the evacuation of the Roman States by the armies of Austria and France can best be accomplished.

3. Whether any, and, if any, what reforms can be made in the internal administration of those and other Italian States whose present administrative defects may obviously tend to permanent and dangerous discontent and disorder.

4. The substitution for the treaties between Austria and the Duchies of a Confederation of the minor States of Italy among themselves, for their mutual internal and external protection.

Her Majesty's Government further require, as a condition of their acceptance of the Russian proposal, that it shall be distinctly understood that the Congress will not entertain any question of interference with the actual state of territorial possessions in Italy, nor in any way disturb the Treaties of 1815.

I have given the above *in extenso*, for they were the basis on which the subsequent negotiations were carried on. These negotiations were of so protracted a nature that I will not weary my readers with entering into their details. But as the despatches referring to them are of importance as portraying the action of Her Majesty's Government in their laudable efforts to arrest war, I have selected for the Appendix of this work those documents which will give the readers a clear insight into the policy and action of the European diplomacy, and the causes of the failure of these negotiations.

Neither the Congress nor the basis laid down were of a nature to fulfil the object Count Cavour had in view, although they might have served to ameliorate the Government of the Papal and other Italian States. Count Cavour, however, was obliged to accept the terms offered, but profited of every opportunity to thwart the meeting of the Congress. His great aim was not to forfeit the support of public opinion in Europe, and to throw all the responsibility of the war on which he had determined on Austria, who, by her stolid opposition to, and disregard of, the counsels of the European Powers, had played into his hands. It was a game of chess, in which Austria, by a false move, was checkmated.

A perusal of the official correspondence in the Appendix will enable the reader also to judge how far the Emperor Napoleon and Count Cavour were sincere in their professions in favour of peace, and whether they ever entertained hopes of attaining it by means of the Congress, or whether, by prolonging the negotiations, they wished to gain time in order to complete their armaments.

During the discussions in regard to the projected Congress, I visited the venerable Prince Metternich shortly before his death. I found him very depressed. He considered that war was inevitable. He observed that the Emperor Napoleon wished for the same object as his uncle—namely, to become the arbitrator and dominator of Europe—but that he hoped to attain his ends by other means than his uncle. He thought that the Emperor Napoleon wished both for war and peace. His *penchant* was for the former, and he cited the old proverb—" *On tombe toujours du côté vers où est son penchant.*"

In speaking of the projected Congress, Prince Metternich said, " It is like a priest who is invited to baptise a child. The party assemble, and when the child's appearance is called for, it is discovered that the child is not yet born. Never mind, it was said, baptise it all the same. But how, said the priest, can I know its sex? Oh, that is of no consequence was the reply. Baptise it Charles or Charlotte, either will do. So," said the Prince, "it is with the Congress which is to meet, and nobody knows for what object." Prince Metternich later expressed his disapproval of the moment chosen to address the summons to Sardinia, observing that it ought to have been sent two months earlier.

Some surprise was evinced by the diplomatic world

at the Russian proposal of a Congress to France, and the moment chosen for it, during the Confidential Mission of Lord Cowley to Vienna. Up to this moment Russia had remained quite impassive in regard to the Italian Question, and had maintained a complete reserve. The attitude of Prussia and Germany roused Prince Gortchacoff from his lethargic state. He foresaw that if there should be war, it might possibly become general, and not bear a local character as he had expected. In that case, his engagements to France might have called Russia into action, and she was neither financially nor militarily prepared for war. He hoped, therefore, by suggesting an European Congress, to avert war, or, at all events, to serve France and Russia by gaining time.

There was, perhaps, another cogent reason. As I have previously stated, Prince Gortchacoff, like other distinguished men, was not devoid of vanity. It was his great ambition to figure at an European Congress. His chief aim (and a very laudable one for a Russian statesman) was to obtain a revision of the Treaty of 1856, and the annulment of that Article stipulating the limitation of the Russian Fleet in the Black Sea. I am told that the question was mooted later, at the meeting of the Sovereigns of Austria and Russia at Warsaw. And when Count Rechberg was interrogated on the subject by one of my colleagues, he replied evasively, but admitted "*qu'elle* (*La Russie*) *avait envoyé un ballon d'essai dans ce sens.*"

This meeting of the Sovereigns took place in the

autumn of 1860. It was effected through the medium of Prince Alexander of Hesse (the brother of the Empress of Russia), who had made previous attempts, but unsuccessfully, to restore the friendly relations between the two Courts. The Prince of Hesse probably represented to the Emperor Alexander the dangers which would menace Europe if the Revolutionary Party in Italy were to gain the upper hand. And no doubt the liberal and democratic language of a certain party in Russia tended to give weight to his arguments. The change of Ministers in Austria (Count Rechberg having replaced Count Buol) contributed greatly to inspire a wish on the part of Russia to renew friendly relations with Austria, and greatly facilitated the efforts of the Prince of Hesse in effecting a reconciliation. Russia was further anxious to gain the support of Austria in regard to the revision of the Treaty of 1856.

After the interview of the Sovereigns at Warsaw during the autumn of 1860, and on the return to Vienna of M. de Balabine, a great change was remarked in his language. He openly said to a member of the Press that all *rancune* between Russia and Austria had ceased, and he added, "*Non seulement je vous le dis, mais je vous autorise à l'écrire, que le passé est tout à fait rayé.*"

Monsieur de Balabine was a clever, shrewd diplomatist—the confidant and *protégé* of Prince Gortchacoff. He was gifted with some wit, and a playful and satirical mode of expressing his opinions. I remember that on the publication of the constitution of the first Representative Assembly in Austria, M. de Balabine cynically remarked to me, "*Qu'il y avait beaucoup de choisis, mais peu d'élus.*" Had he lived he would have made a brilliant career; he died shortly after in the prime of life. The difficulties raised by Austria to the meeting of the Congress were various and injudicious. She refused to sit in Congress with a Sardinian representative. She insisted on the previous disarmament and disbanding of the Free Corps by Sardinia. She raised a futile objection founded on the Protocol at Aix-la-Chapelle in 1818. She claimed the participation of the minor Italian States in the Congress. She opposed a military commission to supervise and regulate the general disarmament of the three Powers; in short, she played the game of her adversaries (who, though accepting the principle of the Congress, were determined on war), and finally she incurred the censure of her friends, and the general blame of Europe, by addressing her summons to the Sardinian Government to disarm, which was the sure prelude to war.

In this crisis, and during the whole of these negotiations, Lord Malmesbury was unremitting in his efforts to harmonise the conflicting elements, and to avert war. His patience, his moderation, his impartiality were beyond praise, and were not sufficiently appreciated. Some years afterwards, in conversation with Lord Clarendon on the subject of Lord Malmesbury, he spoke in praise of his negotiations during this crisis, and of his efforts to maintain peace. His words, characteristic of him, were—"Hang me, if I think any of us would have done better." And no one was more capable of expressing an opinion on the direction of our foreign policy than Lord Clarendon, for he was the *beau idéal* of an English Minister for Foreign Affairs. He possessed all the qualities required to fill that important post. Courteous and dignified, with charming manners, he won the regard and confidence of all with whom he came in contact. Firm and courageous, with consummate judgment, he was neither open to flattery nor to the influence of fear. He had a remarkable perspicacity and knowledge of human character, which, blended with that chivalry and disinterestedness which marked his character, rendered him one of the most popular, as he was one of the most able, statesmen of the age. Having referred to him above, I could not introduce his name without paying this just tribute to his memory, although I shall have much to say of him later in this narrative.

Among the difficulties to which I have referred, raised by Austria to the meeting of the Congress, the two principal ones were—first, the *sine quâ non* condition made by Austria of her going to Congress, that Sardinia should previously disarm and disband her Free Corps. The second was her refusal to sit in the Congress with a Sardinian representative.

The latter was so far arranged that it was agreed that the Congress should be composed of representatives of the five Great Powers, Sardinia being excluded. But

Count Cavour saw that the former (for he refused categorically to disarm) would bring about the war he desired, and the material aid of France.

I warned Count Buol that, in insisting on this condition, he was playing the game of Count Cavour, and, by frustrating the meeting of the Congress, would bring about war, but all my efforts were unavailing. I received from Lord Malmesbury the following letter—full of good sense—which I partly read to Count Buol:—

Foreign Office, April 6th, 1859.

You seem to have done all that could be done to break through the stolid determination which your Court appears to have made not to be saved. I am sure, and you cannot repeat it too strongly, that this country will turn dead against Austria if she breaks off on the point of disarming Sardinia. People here are always for the "little one" against the "big one," and they will not understand how 150,000 men insist on the disarmament of 50,000 men! It is only looked upon as an attempt to *humiliate* Sardinia. Now, we are neutral, and will not "*humiliate*" anybody, and could only ask Sardinia to disarm if France would join us in giving a guarantee for her safety. France refused, and Cavour would not disarm. Austria, by asking impossibilities, and breaking off upon them, will be completely in the wrong; and you must tell Buol that if this happens, we shall retire and meddle with no one, leaving things to take their course.

I have just seen Apponyi, who talks of the "honour" of Austria being concerned in the disarmament of Sardinia. This is absurd, and as if Sardinia was a revolted dependency. The French are arming rapidly, and everybody believes in war; but again I say, this is a reason for having a Congress, and for

Austria putting herself morally in the right. Prussia is urging France to insist on the disarmament of Sardinia.

(Signed)
The Lord A. Loftus. MALMESBURY.

In regard to this question of disarmament, I reported to Lord Malmesbury that, in the treatment and decision of political questions by Austria, there were other influences independent of—and predominant over —Count Buol. Consequently, there was often a struggle between the respective parties. In ordinary questions of foreign policy Count Buol's opinion and advice were dominant, but in cases where the military cabinet of the Emperor and the Ultramontane Party were united against him his chances of success were, to say the least, very problematical.

Early in March there appeared an article in the *Moniteur* of a more peaceful and conciliatory character. Count Buol, on first hearing of this article, said, " I am accustomed to surprises, but I look for facts."

I attended with Lady Augustus a "Kammer Ball" at the Court. These balls were very exclusive, and even the Foreign Ministers were seldom invited. The Emperor came up to me most graciously and said, "*Il y a de bonnes nouvelles de Paris;*" to which I replied that they appeared satisfactory, and the more so as they confirmed the article of the *Moniteur;* to which His Majesty replied, "*Au moins c'est un fait.*" On the question of the participation of the Italian States in the Congress, Count Buol, with his characteristic pedantry, brought forward the Protocol of the Treaty of Aix-la-

Chapelle, in which "the contracting parties agreed that meetings or congresses on affairs specially connected with other of the European States could only take place on a formal invitation on the part of those States to whom these affairs referred, and on the express reserve of their right to participate herein directly or indirectly by their representatives," and he based on this Protocol the right of the minor States of Italy—excluding Sardinia—to take part in the projected Congress.

I reminded him that very large holes had been made in the Treaties of 1815—of which this Protocol was a consecutive part—and that Austria was not free from the charge of having contributed to them. "How so?" asked Count Buol. I replied that the incorporation of Cracow was of too recent a date to have escaped my memory. He remarked that "*Three* had participated in this act," to which I replied that this did not make the hole in the Treaties smaller. On the 4th of April Lady Augustus and I had the honour of being invited to dine at the Imperial Court. After dinner a Circle was held by their Majesties, and the Emperor was graciously pleased to address me. His Majesty at once referred to the critical state of affairs, and to the subject of the projected Congress, stating that he had accepted the proposal for the Congress and the four points which had been submitted by Her Majesty's Government on the condition that Sardinia disarmed.

I ventured to observe to His Majesty that this

condition, I feared, would prove one of great difficulty to achieve, and that, in delicate negotiations of this nature, it was desirable not to overstrain the means of arriving at the aim desired, if that aim could be attained by a conciliatory process. I observed to His Majesty that the meeting of the Congress with the exclusion of Sardinia was equivalent to a "political disarmament," and that no greater proof of this existed than the irritation displayed by Count Cavour, whose efforts would be directed to cause its failure. If, therefore, the Congress should be unhappily frustrated by the refusal of Austria to take part in it in consequence of the non-compliance of Sardinia with the condition required, I was extremely fearful that the blame, and the grave responsibility for its failure, would be laid on Austria, and that it might seriously affect the sympathies and good wishes which had been hitherto so largely manifested towards Austria both on the part of England as well as in Germany. I begged His Majesty to believe that, in venturing to express myself so frankly, I was solely actuated by the most friendly feeling and interest for Austria.

His Majesty replied that he most sincerely desired peace, and that to maintain it " he had already made great concessions, but that he could not yield the conditions named. Unless Sardinia disarmed, Austria could not take part in the Congress." His Majesty said that he was "afraid that the Emperor Napoleon had set his mind on war, and that it was but a question of time." His Majesty then stated that he "had been given to understand that the Emperor Napoleon had promised Lord Cowley that his Government, conjointly with Her Majesty's Government, would summon Sardinia to disarm if Austria accepted the Congress and the four points. It was now for the Emperor Napoleon to fulfil his engagement if he really desired peace. Austria could not enter into the Congress until there was some evidence of the sincerity of France."

In reviewing this decision, it must be borne in mind that Austria was firmly convinced that the Emperor Napoleon, under the pressure of Count Cavour, had determined on war, and merely sought, by procrastination and accepting the Congress, to gain time for completing his armaments. There was further, on the part of the Emperor Franz Josef and his Military Cabinet (at that time in considerable ascendency in the councils of the State), a strong feeling in favour of what was termed the "military honour," a feeling in the present instance that false motives might be attributed to any concession to Sardinia. It is generally known that the war might have been avoided if Austria had agreed to accept a large indemnity and a territorial compensation for a voluntary cession of Lombardy and Venetia, but the chivalrous Emperor Franz Josef scouted any such idea, which would have appeared in the eyes of his army and his people as a humiliation. A voluntary cession, moreover, would have been irrevocable, whereas if these Provinces were wrested from him by force of arms, they might be recoverable in future years. On the other hand, had the offer been accepted, the

Austrian Treasury would have been greatly enriched, and the political position of Austria in Germany would have been considerably strengthened. But one can but admire the honest and chivalrous feelings of a young monarch ruling an ancient empire, every inch a soldier, and at the head of a magnificent army, declining to abandon his sovereign rights for a financial compensation, and, as it were, to barter away his subjects for lucre!

There was another vital consideration which, in my opinion, was the principal motive of the injudicious and much-censured act of the Austrian Cabinet, I refer to the question of finance. At that time the state of the Austrian finances was deplorable. History proves that the question of finance has rarely, if ever, prevented a country from engaging in war. In the present instance the Austrian Government were convinced that the Emperor Napoleon intended war, but that France was not prepared for it, and required time to complete her armaments. Austria was prepared, and her army in Italy then amounted to 150,000 men. The delay, therefore, was to the disadvantage of Austria. It was felt impossible that Austria could again make the military efforts and the financial sacrifices she had lately made ; nor could she then afford to maintain for any lengthened period the expenses of her army on the war footing which cost the Treasury half a million of florins per day. Under these circumstances she had but two alternatives—that of "bleeding to death" (the term used to me by the Minister of Finance) or of at once incurring all the risks of war by entering on an immediate contest.

Baron Bruck, the Finance Minister, at a public dinner on the 13th of March, when a toast was given to the army in the following terms: "May God maintain the Army," replied that his "fervent prayer was that He would, for he should not be able to do so much longer."

Count Cavour was on the point of resigning on learning the news of the projected Congress, and on telegraphing this intention to Paris the Emperor begged him to repair to Paris at once, saying that he would be able to "reassure" him (*de le rassurer*). On his returning to Turin he said that he was quite satisfied, and that there would be no change in his policy. This was known to Count Buol, and it certainly did not increase his confidence in the peaceful intentions of the Emperor Napoleon. Count Cavour was then said to have in his possession certain letters from the Emperor Napoleon which, if published, would have greatly compromised the Emperor.

I am inclined to believe that Count Buol himself would have yielded on the question of disarmament, but that he was powerless, the Emperor and the Military Cabinet having made this point with Count Buol the condition on which His Majesty agreed to the Congress and the four points submitted by England.

On the 11th of April the Archduke Albert, Governor of Hungary, left for Berlin charged with a confidential mission from the Emperor of Austria to the Prince Regent of Prussia. He was accompanied by four officers of the staff in addition to his aide-de-camp. I was privately informed that he was charged by the Emperor to express to the Prince Regent his anxious and sincere wish for peace, and to state to His Royal Highness and his Cabinet, in the present serious and critical position of affairs, the urgency for Austria that a decision should be speedily taken as to the course which Prussia would pursue. The Germanic Diet had already, on the proposal of Prussia, passed a resolution that the Federal Army should be placed in *Kriegsbereitschaft*, or readiness for war. The Archduke Albert, being destined to command the Austrian contingent to the Federal Army, was further charged to confer generally with the Prince Regent on the subject of military co-operation with Prussia and Germany in the event of war.

The Archduke Albert met with a warm reception from the Prince Regent, and I was told by one of my German colleagues that Count Buol had expressed himself as generally satisfied with the reports that His Imperial Highness had made to the Emperor. A few days after his arrival at Berlin the Austrian summons to Sardinia was despatched. His Imperial Highness may not have known on his leaving Vienna that there was any intention to address a summons so precipitately to Sardinia, but no mention was made of it to the Prince Regent, and it was only known after His Imperial Highness's departure. It fell like a thunderbolt on the Regent and his Cabinet, and produced a very unfavourable impression.

On the 13th of April I wrote to Lord Malmesbury that it "was reported that Austria, having exhausted her patience and forbearance towards Sardinia, was on the eve of taking some decisive step; I sounded Count Buol on the subject, when he replied that, 'appreciating the "friendly acts" (*les bons procédés*) of Her Majesty's Government towards Austria, no change in her present passive and pacific attitude would take place without such intention being previously notified to Her Majesty's Government.'"

My surmise was not far wrong. On the 12th of April Count Buol addressed a despatch to Count Apponyi for communication to Lord Malmesbury, announcing that the Austrian Government were about to address a direct demand to the Cabinet of Turin to reduce the Sardinian Army to the peace establishment, and to disband the Free Corps. The text of the summons will be found in the Appendix, as well as the despatch of Count Buol to Count Apponyi, instructing him to communicate it to Lord Malmesbury.

It was only on the 15th of April that, in the course of conversation, Count Buol informed me that he had sent on the 12th a despatch to Count Apponyi, as mentioned above, notifying the intention of the Austrian Government to address a summons to Sardinia to disarm. I observed to him that this appeared to me a very grave and important step, but that much depended on the form and manner in which it was made. He said that it would be couched in very courteous terms, and that it would be in the form of a letter addressed to Count Cavour.

The position of Austria at this time may be summed up as follows: The Government saw that war with France, sooner or later, was inevitable. They regarded the projected Congress with distrust rather than with confidence; they considered that France was merely seeking to gain time to complete her armaments, and would endeavour in the Congress to establish a *casus belli*, rather than to confirm peace. They considered their position not bad; they considered that if in the first campaign they were victorious, they should not require aid, and the fruits would be their own. If they were beaten, they were confident that in the long run neither England nor Germany could sit still and see them swallowed up, with a certainty that their turn would come. They considered that there would be no repose or peace with the Emperor of the French, and they calculated that a war would be his downfall.

As events afterwards proved, all their hopes and calculations proved illusory.

In the meantime, Count Cavour, at the instance of England and France, had accepted disarmament unconditionally, but I ascertained that Count Buol had no knowledge of this acceptance when he despatched the summons.

The answer of Count Cavour was regarded as evasive, and the orders to General Giulay, the Commander-in-Chief of the Austrian Army in Lombardy, were carried out, and he crossed the Ticino into Piedmont on the 29th of April. The Marquis de Banneville, French Chargé d'Affaires, had already informed Count

Buol officially that the crossing of the Ticino by Austrian troops would be considered by France as a *casus belli*.

After all the laborious and tortuous negotiations in which the Great Powers had been engaged to avert war, the die was now cast. Europe was again exposed to the dangers of a war, the consequences of which, if not localised, were incalculable. Happily, in these days wars are short, and it proved so in the present instance. The strain of war on the commercial and financial world is too great to permit it to be of long duration, as in former times; and its costly nature, as well as the perfection of the present engines of war, tend greatly to open the avenue to peace after one decisive battle. I will here digress shortly from my narrative to review the original causes and motives of the war. They are shortly told. Count Cavour was the author and prime mover of it. He was a man of great ambition, of a daring and resolute character; a thorough patriot devoted to the interests of his country; of indisputable ability, and of that subtle, unscrupulous character which enabled him to overcome all obstacles, and to utilise every means at his disposal in order to attain the object of his ambition. That ambition, in which his sovereign wholly participated, was the expulsion of Austria from Lombardy, and the formation of an united Italy under the auspices of Victor Emanuel. He was prepared to make any sacrifices to the Emperor Napoleon for his support. He was prepared to cede to France the Province of Savoy (the cradle of the

Piedmontese dynasty) and the Comté de Nice; he was prepared to bring about the marriage of Prince Napoleon with his sovereign's daughter, which Count Buol humorously styled the "Rape of the Sabine." In short, he was prepared to make any sacrifices for the attainment of his ambitious aim. He cleverly allured the Emperor Napoleon into participating in his designs, and when once in his meshes, he allowed him no escape. The acquisition of Savoy and Nice held out to the French nation not only the acquisition of glory, so pleasing to that nation, but the aggrandisement of territory as compensation for the expenses of the war— and these terms were assented to by the Emperor. But the difficulty for Count Cavour was to carry out these designs in the face of Europe without disclosing the ambitious aims he had in view, and to arrive "*sur le champ de bataille.*" He described the sufferings of the Italian nation under a foreign yoke. He invoked the passions of the Italian people—more excitable and sensitive than any nation—under the garb of patriotism and nationality. He appealed to the Governments of Europe for sympathy on the grounds of civil and religious liberty, for which he had certain grounds based on political wisdom rather than on equity. He was aware that any hasty provocation of war with Austria would destroy his chance of European sympathy and support, for there then still existed in Europe a feeling in favour of "right against might," although of late years it has been supplanted by the principle of *Vox Populi*, *Vox Dei*. Having formally engaged the support of the

Emperor Napoleon, he brought into prominent notice the question of Italy, "*Le cri d'angoisse* of the Italian nation," as he termed it. This led to great agitation in Italy, in which the Mazzinist Party and the Patriotic Monarchical Party both joined for the union of Italy, but each differing in their object in view, the one aiming at a Republic, the other holding to Monarchy.

The precipitate act of the Austrian Government in addressing the summons to the Cabinet of Turin completely nullified all hopes of a peaceful settlement by means of a Congress, and gave the utmost satisfaction to Count Cavour, who had openly stated "that he would have war in spite of the Congress." It will be seen that, although protests were addressed to the Austrian Government against this act by England, Russia, and Prussia, all attempt to recall the orders to General Giulay to advance into Piedmont were fruitless.* Austria pursued her course heedless of the counsels of Europe, and of the grave consequences following on their rejection. Austria, by persisting in her independent line regardless of the interests of Europe, lost its moral support and all hopes of future material aid.

In regard to the reported Treaty, offensive and defensive, between Russia and France, Count Buol said

* In referring to the public opinion of England on the "Summons" to Sardinia, Count Buol said to me: "We are in the most embarrassing position, having to choose between 'une faute militaire' or 'une faute politique,' and under the pressing circumstances, and having to take into consideration the opinion of the public and of the army, we could but decide for the latter." He added, on my appeal to recall the order to General Giulay to advance, "What are we to wait for? English sympathy? English support?"

he did not believe in it, but thought that some engagement might have been taken for Russia not to join in any future coalition against France; M. de Balabine, the Russian Minister at Vienna, styled it "*un canard offensif.*" During this crisis the policy of Prussia was directed to maintain peace, which she did most zealously and loyally. Her position was one of great difficulty: she had to safeguard the security and interests of Germany, but she had neither the duty nor the wish to preserve to Austria her Italian possessions, nor to plunge Germany into a war with France. On the other hand, she had to take into account the public opinion of Germany, which was very excited against France, and more especially the Liberal portion of it. The French Emperor and Government were anxious to encourage Prussia to adopt a pacific policy, and to obtain her neutrality in the coming contest; and in these endeavours were strongly supported by Russia, who wished above all things not to be entangled in a general war.

In duly appreciating the attitude taken by Prussia, dictated alike by a laudable desire to avert, if possible, the miseries of war, and by that impartial spirit which appertains to a mediating Power, the public opinion of Germany became deeply moved as the certainty of war became more visible, and it looked to Prussia for a more decided line of action on the part of the Prussian Cabinet. A resolution was taken by the Germanic Diet to place the Federal Army in *Kriegsbereitschaft*—or readiness for war—the first step towards mobilisation.

The missions of the Archduke Albert to Berlin, and of General Willesen to Vienna, gave unmistakable proofs that the federal duties of Prussia for the defence of German territory and German interests would be faithfully performed, whilst her duties as a great European Power had been equally carried out in her endeavours to maintain peace. The Government of the Prince Regent had, in this latter respect, co-operated consistently with Her Majesty's Government, and had placed itself completely in unison with them. But when the Austrian summons was precipitately addressed to Sardinia—the issue of which was certain war—without previous concert with Prussia, and against which Prussia strongly protested, it could not be expected that Prussia would associate herself with the cause of Austria in Italy so long as no attack was made on German territory.

There was at this time a strong feeling of distrust and hostility towards France in the whole German nation. It had not originated with the Sovereigns, nor the Governments, but had sprung from the ranks of the people, and had been loudly proclaimed in the various Representative Chambers. This feeling was largely associated with a spirit of nationality, which, in many respects, although under a different garb, represented the same sentiments which evoked, in 1848-49, a general cry for German unity. It was generally felt that Germany would sooner or later be exposed to an invasion by France, and the painful reminiscences of former times, and the sad experiences which the

German nation then underwent, naturally excited a wish to avoid a recurrence of similar miseries and disasters.

The attempts that were made both by France and Russia to produce disunion in Germany were too patent to escape observation. It was obvious both to the German Government and to the nation that the object of France was to neutralise Prussia and the German States in her war with Austria, and that Russia was using her best efforts to hold back Prussia and Germany from taking any overt steps for the protection of the German territory.

Whether the fears of a French invasion were real or not, they were participated in by all the German States. They all armed, and made great military preparations. They felt that in face of a common danger all Germany should hold together for its common safety. Austria was viewed not as a great Power, but as a member of the Confederation. If Austria should be weakened and reduced by France, not only would it be a weakness and reduction of strength of the Confederation itself, but it was feared that a similar process of reducing Prussia would be resorted to—as history has proved— and that thus the two great military Powers of Germany, in lieu of holding together against a common enemy, would be vanquished in detail, and that Germany would thus be deprived of her independence and might.

The publication of the manifesto of the Emperor of the French augmented these fears. The public opinion of Bavaria, Würtemberg, Baden, Hanover, Hesse-

Darmstadt, and even the Rhenish Provinces of Prussia, assumed a tone of violence and ardour against France which their respective Governments were barely able to control. It is to the calm and prudent policy of the Prince Regent that this violent ebullition of public feeling did not lead to acts which might have gravely compromised the relations between Prussia and France, and have produced a general conflagration in Europe.

There can be no doubt that the Emperor Napoleon was fully cognizant of the feelings of the German nation, and that it operated largely with other motives in leading him to offer peace to the Emperor Franz Josef at Villa Franca.

CHAPTER II.

Emperor of Austria's Manifesto Declaring War against Sardinia—French Embassy leave Vienna—Count Buol's Resignation and Causes of it—Emperor's Interview with Prince Metternich—Appointment of Count Rechberg—Battle of Magenta — Allied Army enter Milan — Hungary — Russian Minister's Language—Change of Ministers in England—Lord John Russell Secretary for Foreign Affairs—His Policy in Favour of an United Italy—Count Karolyi's Mission to St. Petersburg—Battle of Solferino—Interview of the two Emperors — Preliminaries of Villa Franca — Retirement of General Giulay—Interview with Count Rechberg—Conference of the Three Powers to meet at Zürich to Conclude Peace—Opinion of the King of Würtemberg on the Peace.

On the receipt of Count Cavour's answer* to Count Buol's letter summoning Sardinia to disarm, a Manifesto † was published on the 28th April by the Emperor to his people, declaring war against Sardinia. Proclamations of a similar nature were issued by the Emperor of the French and the King of Sardinia.

Sardinian troops had already marched into Modena and occupied Massa and Carrara, and established there a Provisional Government. Whatever may be said of Austrian aggression against Sardinia, it was now patent that Sardinia had invaded the territory of an independent Sovereign without a cause and without a declaration of war.

Captain Edmund Mildmay, Aide-de-Camp to the

* See Appendix.   † See Appendix.

d

Duke of Cambridge, and for eighteen years an officer in the Austrian Service, was appointed British Commissioner to the Austrian Army, and left Vienna on the 13th of May to join the headquarters at Verona. Fears were entertained here for the safety of Cattaro and Istria. Count Buol told me that there was a French Corps already nominated "*l'Armée d'Istrie.*" It was feared that an attempt might be made to revolutionise Hungary, for it was known to the Austrian Government that General Klapka had been received by the Emperor Napoleon, and closeted with His Majesty for three hours.

The command of the army in Italy was given to General Giulay, and General Hess, who had been originally destined for it, remained with the Emperor, and was lodged at the Burg. Under his advice His Majesty directed the movements of the army.

The army in Italy was composed of the following corps:—

2nd Corps commanded by Prince Edward Lichtenstein.
3rd   „   „   „ Prince Edmond Schwarzenberg.
5th   „   „   „ Count Stadion.
7th   „   „   „ General Zobel.
8th   „   „   „ General Benedeck.
9th   „   „   „ General Schaffgotch.
10th „   „   „ General Wernhardt.

A corps of 60,000 men was stationed in Galicia as a counterpart to the Russian corps placed on the

Russian frontier. Count Buol stated to me that he had no fear of any aggressive act on the part of Russia, but that he considered that it would be wanting in due respect to Russia not to respond to her military demonstration.

Complete secrecy was preserved by the official authorities at Vienna in regard to the movements of the army, and the public was left in darkness of what was passing at the seat of war.

In consequence of the inundations of the Po and Sessia, the original plan of offensive operations was impracticable, and the Austrian general took up a strong defensive position, awaiting the enemy to advance.

On the 3rd May the Marquis de Banneville, French Chargé d'Affaires, communicated a despatch to Count Buol, in which Count Walewski, after reviewing the various phases of the negotiations, and portraying the peaceful wishes of the Emperor Napoleon, instructs him to ask for his passports. The Chargé d'Affaires and the whole French Embassy left Vienna on the 4th of May. The Russian Minister, M. de Balabine, and all the members of his Legation, accompanied the French Embassy to the railway station, with a line of carriages to mark the demonstration. He embraced each member of the French Embassy before the assembled crowd, much to the annoyance of the Marquis de Banneville, who, I was told, did not appear overpleased by this Russian effusion.

At the opening of the war the complete isolation

of Austria caused a general feeling of depression and insecurity, and was attributed by the military party— then in the ascendant—to the mismanagement of Count Buol, and to his known antipathy to Russia. Prince Windishgrätz and Count Grünne, the two most influential members of the party, were very anxious for a reconciliation between the Courts of Austria and Russia; both were in favour of a Russian alliance, and were devoted to Russian interests. Both also considered Count Buol as the chief obstacle to a renewal of friendly relations between the two Courts, and their object was to effect his retirement from office.

Prince Windishgrätz accordingly proposed to the Emperor, without the previous knowledge of Count Buol, to send him to St. Petersburg on a special mission to the Czar. He led the Emperor to believe that this mission might, at least, be so far successful as to induce the Czar to adopt a position of strict neutrality in the Austro-Franco-Italian War. The proposal was partially approved by the Emperor; but when it was referred to Count Buol, he represented to His Majesty that he could not counsel a step which he conceived would compromise the dignity of His Majesty and of his Empire. Thereupon the Emperor referred to Prince Metternich, and on this occasion visited him in person, and remained with him three hours. On leaving him, Count Grünne was charged by His Majesty to inform Prince Windishgrätz that he considered the proposed mission as inopportune, and that it should be deferred to a more favourable occasion.

There can be no doubt that at this prolonged interview of the Sovereign with the venerable Prince, other State subjects were treated of than the Windishgrätz mission, and that the advisableness of a change in the Ministry for Foreign Affairs was recommended by the Prince.

On the 13th of May Count Buol resigned his post as Minister for Foreign Affairs at the request of the Emperor.

From the secrecy with which are treated all official questions depending solely and directly on the will of the Sovereign, and from the silence of the Press, arising either from ignorance or necessity, it was extremely difficult to ascertain with positive accuracy the immediate causes of this important change in the Imperial Cabinet.

But it cannot be said to have been an act of impulse or a hasty decision on the part of His Majesty. For some time previously Count Buol had to struggle against a powerful party at Court, composed of the highest members of the aristocracy and the most influential military personages, having the ear of the Sovereign. Their opposition to the policy of Count Buol dated from the period of the Crimean War.

This party, of which Prince Windishgrätz was the leading member, openly denounced at the time the policy pursued by Count Buol towards Russia, which subsequently led to the cessation of the former friendly relations between the two Empires. They were envenomed also by the personal feelings between Prince

Gortchacoff and Count Buol, the former having been Russian Minister at Vienna during the negotiations on the Eastern Question.

The various attempts to effect a reconciliation between the two Courts (which I have previously mentioned) were frustrated by the *sine quâ non* condition of Russia, viz., the retirement of Count Buol. The Emperor Franz Josef persistently refused to dismiss his Minister, and on one occasion is reported to have said, "*Que ces choses se faisaient à Constantinople, mais pas ici.*"

The military influence of the Court party, seeking to return to the alliance with Russia, was consequently in continual antagonism with Count Buol; and although Count Buol had on most occasions successfully counteracted its agency, yet on other occasions decisions were taken on matters of political importance without his advice or knowledge, and of which he was subsequently obliged to take the responsibility. Thus it was that a want of confidence, and a difference of opinion resulting therefrom, gradually sprung up between the Sovereign and his Minister, which, it was evident, could not long continue without inevitably leading to the result which now occurred.

But other circumstances also concurred to give effect to the efforts of those who had been so long striving to displace Count Buol. There was a general feeling among the aristocracy, the army, and even among his own colleagues that the policy pursued by Count Buol had been signally disastrous; that it had isolated

Austria, and had placed her without an ally in Europe. "If," it was said, "Count Buol had thought it necessary and politic for Austria to break off her alliance with Russia, and to enlist with France, he should, at all events, have taken care to maintain cordial relations with his new ally, and to have formed a strong link in the chain of alliance between England and France; but it was now proved that he had sacrificed an alliance which had rendered, and could render, important services to his country for one of an ephemeral and doubtful nature."

The policy pursued by Count Buol during the negotiations on the Italian question was likewise severely criticised and blamed, and there is reason to suppose that, in his interview with the Emperor, Prince Metternich expressed his disapproval of it.

It was the opinion of the Prince that Count Buol should, in the first instance, have declined the Congress, stating that the good offices of England had been already accepted to bring about a more friendly understanding with France; and if later a Congress had been urged by England, that then Austria should have accepted it without conditions.

The demand " of the disarmament of Sardinia " was disapproved by Prince Metternich, on the ground that it was ill-advised and impossible; and, secondly, that the decision of the question was thereby placed in the hands of the Sardinian Government.

All these various causes tended to render the position of Count Buol extremely difficult, if not untenable, and prepared the mind of the Emperor for the decision he took. He was a sovereign of noble and generous feelings, and was incapable of doing a harsh or ungracious act, but he was governed by a strong sense of duty to his country, and must have felt that there was no other course to take. The opportunity only was wanting, and it soon offered itself. It was the projected mission of Prince Windishgrätz to St. Petersburg. The idea of a mission first originated with the Emperor in a wish to send Prince Windishgrätz to Berlin to conclude some military arrangements with the Prussian Government which had been commenced during the residence there of the Archduke Albert.

Prince Windishgrätz, on his arrival at Vienna from Prague, submitted to His Majesty the proposal that he should extend his mission to St. Petersburg with a view to renew friendly relations with Russia, and to obtain, if possible, from the Czar an assurance of his neutrality during the war. Some publicity was given to this projected mission, and Prince Windishgrätz even mentioned it to the Russian Minister, M. de Balabine. Count Buol, to whom the subject had never been mooted, appealed to the Emperor for a confirmation of the rumours which had reached him. The Emperor told Count Buol that he had had such an intention, but had taken no final decision, and, therefore, had not mentioned it to him. As I have previously stated, Count Buol expressed his disapproval of the mission as compromising to the dignity of the Emperor. The Emperor then sought the advice of Prince Metternich, and it is presumed that the impressions produced by the opinions of the Prince on the general state of affairs induced His Majesty to take the resolution of confiding to other hands the direction of foreign affairs.

Count Buol, as I have previously stated, resigned, and his resignation was accepted by the Emperor. He accepted his retirement from office in a noble and loyal spirit, without one word of resentment or reproach, merely observing in regard to the future line of policy, "*Qu'on sera plus mou à l'extérieur, plus raide à l'intérieur.*"

Count Buol was certainly the most liberal element of the Ministry, and was always desirous of a cordial understanding with England. He was succeeded by Count Rechberg, then Austrian Minister and President of the Diet at Frankfort, on the recommendation of Prince Metternich, to which I have previously referred in the early pages of this work. I had been personally acquainted with Count Rechberg for many years, and our official relations commenced on the most cordial terms. He was clever and energetic, with great shrewdness, and of a firm and resolute character, but he was quite under the influence of the Military and Ultramontane Party.

I received the following characteristic letter from Lord Malmesbury on the fall of Count Buol, dated May 24, 1859:—

I beg you will say something amiable from me to Buol in his distress. If I am turned out next month, I beg you will address me in the contrary strain, and wish me joy.

(Signed) MALMESBURY.

The retirement of Count Buol naturally gave rise to rumours of an entire change of policy, and of a future alliance with Russia. At first sight, these rumours might have appeared plausible. But Count Buol confirmed to me the assurances given by Count Rechberg, that the change of persons would not produce any change of system. He said that the line of foreign policy he had laid down had been entirely approved by the Emperor, and that he was fully convinced that His Majesty would not change his convictions. Count Buol even went so far as to say that it was the greatest satisfaction to him to feel assured that his system would not be abandoned. "For," said His Excellency, "however great may now be the difficulties of Austria, I am fully persuaded that in the course of time the system which I have laid down will develop itself, and that I shall then have the satisfaction of feeling that I am entitled to my share of its success."

His Excellency stated that, in his conviction, the basis of the policy of Austria should be an alliance with England, and a cordial understanding with Prussia and Germany, and that this combination was the surest guarantee for the peace and independence of Europe. In a conversation I had with Prince Metternich, His Highness took especial care to assure me—with a view to counteract any erroneous impressions—that the change of Minister would not produce a change of policy, adding that, in this respect, he would answer for Count Rechberg, who was a pupil of his own school.

At this time General Willisen was sent to Vienna by the Prince Regent on a military mission of the following character: 1. To restrain any precipitate act on the part of the Diet which might unnecessarily compromise the relations of Germany with France; 2. To concert with the Austrian Government as to the moment when a joint action of Prussia and the Diet with Austria should be deemed necessary for the protection and safety of Germany, and to arrange that the initiative at the Diet should be taken by Prussia; and 3. To arrange the military distribution of forces should the Diet be called upon to resort to active measures for the protection of the German territory.

These negotiations, which were of a conciliatory character, were carried on very secretly by General Willisen with General Hess. In the meantime war was commenced, and on the 25th of May General Willisen returned to Berlin, his mission having terminated without any result.

The news from the seat of war, though very scanty and somewhat confused, was not satisfactory to the Austrian arms. At Palestro an action took place which proved unsuccessful to Austria, and at Montebello an Austrian corps was taken in ambush, and incurred heavy loss in men and of ten guns. Nine of these guns were recaptured later. This action was merely a reconnaissance to ascertain the position and strength of the Allied Armies, which, having been effected, the Austrians retreated, and the Allies crossed the Ticino. But the most serious engagement took place at Magenta, where victory at one time appeared to declare itself in favour of the Austrian arms, but, like at Marengo, finally turned against them. The Emperor Napoleon was in danger of capture during the battle of Magenta, and was saved by Marshal McMahon, whose arrival with a large reinforcement at a critical moment turned the scale, and decided the battle in favour of the French. The Austrians fought magnificently, and were well led by their officers; but the generalship was much criticised, and the result of this action decided the Emperor to supersede General Giulay, and to appoint General Hess to take the command of the army. After Magenta, the Austrian army retreated to the Mincio, having at its back the famous Quadrilateral. The Allies entered Milan, and advanced rapidly to the Adda. The French army had suffered severe losses since the opening of the campaign, and fever and ophthalmia from the extreme heat were thinning its ranks. The commissariat was also very deficient, which acted banefully on the health of the troops.

Count Rechberg informed me that the accounts which the Government had received from Hungary and the Border Provinces were satisfactory. Great loyalty and patriotism were exhibited, not in words only, but in deeds, and the enrolment of volunteers had far exceeded their expectations, or even the necessity of the moment. He mentioned to me an interesting incident which had come to his knowledge. The Emperor Napoleon had lately given audiences at Paris to Kossuth, Klapka, and Teleki, the most prominent chiefs of the Hungarian Rebellion in 1849. His Majesty likewise sent for an Hungarian refugee of the name of A——sy, and made certain proposals to him relating to Hungary. A——sy not only refused the Emperor's offers—whatever they may have been—point-blank, but stated that he should now, when his country was in danger from a foreign foe, avail himself of the Amnesty Act and return to his country for the purpose of seeking active employment in the cause of his sovereign and his country.

These satisfactory assurances of Count Rechberg were, however, not confirmed by private reports I received. I learnt from several sources that there was great agitation in the Slav Provinces and among the Slav Races. In Hungary general discontent prevailed. I was informed that a Bosniak had appealed to the Russian Minister at Vienna to know whether the Christian population should make a demonstration, to which the Minister replied that they should for the present keep quiet, and await events. The same agitation existed in Servia, and it extended even to Poland. In short, all oppressed nationalities were looking for succour and support, but there seems to have been no organisation, and both money, arms, and ammunition were wanting. In speaking of Italian affairs, M. de Balabine gave expression to curious language for a Russian Minister. He openly said to a colleague, "*On ne demandera point les Gouvernements, on appellera aux peuples: c'est la voix du peuple qui décide, comme a été le cas en Vallachie et Moldavie.*"

I was informed that the discontent in Hungary was increasing, and that a certain portion of the population was prepared to rise in arms against the Government;

but there was also a large party who were loyal to the Emperor, and there further existed a strong anti-French feeling. There was also a strong animosity between the Serbs, Croats, and Hungarians, thus rendering any fusion of those races unlikely. The Serbs are Slavs, have no affinity of race with the Wallachians and Moldavians, who are Roumans, although they have with the Bosniaks, who are also Slavs, and speak nearly the same language. The Magyars are not of the Slavonic race, and are supposed originally to have come from Cashmere.

The Austrian Government were much alarmed for the safety of Istria and Dalmatia, and more especially of Cattaro, a most important strategic and naval position; but whatever may have been the schemes and primary intentions of the Emperor Napoleon in regard to these parts, they were completely frustrated and "nipped in the bud" by the preliminaries of Villa Franca.

In the middle of June, 1859, a change of Ministry took place in England. In the new Ministry, of which Lord Palmerston was Premier, the Secretaryship for Foreign Affairs was conferred on Lord John Russell. The change was not very pleasing to the Austrian Cabinet, as it was felt that Lord John Russell's sympathies were wholly in favour of Italy, and of its complete independence, dating back from his early youth. Nor did the antecedents of Lord Palmerston, whose antipathy to Austria was well known, inspire the Austrian Government with much confidence. The publication of the Blue

Book on Italian affairs laid before Parliament produced a good effect at Vienna, and on presenting Count Buol with a copy I received his personal thanks for the correct and truthful manner in which I had reported my interviews with him.

Prince Paul Esterhazy, for nearly twenty years Austrian Ambassador in London, paid a visit to England in the summer of 1859. He told me that he had no official character, he went as a private individual to see his old friends, and to revisit a country where he had passed so many happy years, and for which he felt a true affection. He was a *grand seigneur* of the old type, a thorough man of the world, an acute observer, very sagacious, and with that conciliatory spirit and those courteous manners so needful and successful in diplomacy. He had immense possessions, which, on his death, were found to be greatly embarrassed, partly owing to mismanagement, and partly to his own extravagance and that of his predecessors. However, under careful management, I am happy to say that they are coming rapidly into order. He was, he told me, greatly pleased with his reception in England, and was quite surprised—and apparently not much edified—by the vast changes, political and social, which had taken place since his departure. It must be borne in mind, however, that he was of the school of Prince Metternich, who remained stationary since 1815, and he was therefore wedded to the spirit of that epoch, and true to the principles of the Holy Alliance. In the present day, the policy of that age, and the opinions to which

it gave birth, have been swept away with the Treaties of
1815; the landmarks of Europe have been changed,
and treaties in the present day are repudiated and
broken before the ink is dry which recorded them !

Previous to the commencement of the war, Count
Karolyi (afterwards Austrian Ambassador in London)
was sent by the Emperor Franz Josef on a special
mission to St. Petersburg. The report he made on his
return was not favourable, and he avowedly confessed
that the object of his mission had failed. That object
was to make known to the Emperor Alexander and the
Russian Cabinet the political position of Austria as
regarded the war in Italy; to explain that Austria had
taken up arms in defence of her rights and a just cause;
to show the dangers to Europe of the revolutionary
policy which Sardinia was pursuing; and to express a
hope that, deeply interested as Russia was in the cause
of order and legality, the Cabinet of Russia would at
least give assurances of maintaining a neutral attitude
during the contest in which Austria was engaged. Count
Karolyi reported that he found prevailing at St. Petersburg a deep feeling of animosity against Austria, but
that in this respect there existed a difference in the
sentiments which produced this feeling on the part of
the Emperor Alexander and those of his Minister. It
was easy, he said, to discern that the deep wounds
which had been inflicted on His Majesty's mind by the
political part taken by Austria against Russia during
the Crimean War had not healed, and that there still
existed a strong feeling of enmity towards the Sovereign

and the country to whom he attributed the reverses suffered by Russia during that war, and, still more, her humiliation at the peace. These feelings were also embittered by the conviction that the part taken then by Austria had been the death-blow to the Emperor Nicholas.

On the other hand, the sentiments of Prince Gortchacoff were those of private vengeance and of personal hatred to everything Austrian, and he made no secret of them, and lost no occasion of giving expression to them.

Being a man of the pen, and not addicted to the use of the sword, I am quite incompetent to describe military operations, and, therefore, I have confined this narrative to reporting the results of the great military encounters between the belligerent armies. Other pens more competent than mine will record in detail for future history the military operations of the campaign.

After occupying Milan, the Allied Armies advanced rapidly to the Adda, when the Austrian Army crossed that river, and took up their position, under the immediate command of the Emperor, on the Mincio, where it was evident that a decisive action would be fought. This action took place at Solferino on the 24th of June. The Imperial Army crossed the Mincio on the 23rd in four places to take the offensive against the enemy. They encountered the Allied Army in superior force, and, after an obstinate contest of twelve hours, were compelled to retreat behind the Mincio, which was effected in perfect order. The entire force of the Austrian

Army then concentrated within the circle of their fortresses amounted to eleven Corps d'Armée, which might be estimated, in round numbers, at 250,000 effectives. The total loss of killed, wounded, missing, and disabled since the opening of the campaign amounted to about 30,000 men. The number of the Allied Army exceeded the Austrian forces.

On the receipt at Vienna of the reply of the Prussian Government to certain proposals of Austria, conveyed through General Willisen, Count Rechberg left Vienna for the headquarters of the Emperor Franz Josef at Verona. The Prussian reply was conveyed in a despatch to Baron Wertha, the Prussian representative at Vienna, who was instructed to read the despatch to the Minister for Foreign Affairs, but not to leave a copy in his hands. The reply was not wholly unsatisfactory, but it did not fulfil the hopes of the Austrian Government. It did not indicate the period of any active co-operation with Austria, but the mobilisation of six Army Corps by Prussia was regarded as a step in advance, and from it was augured that Prussia would not abandon Austria in so far as German interests were concerned. The chief object at which Prussia aimed in this despatch was to ascertain the terms on which Austria would agree to accept peace, with a probable view of interposing her good offices to bring about peace at the first favourable moment. The Austrian reply, I am told, expressed a wish to know more distinctly the views of Prussia and the basis of the proposed " armed " mediation.

I was informed later, after the preliminaries of peace had been signed, that the Emperor of Austria was mainly induced to accept the terms of peace offered by the Emperor Napoleon on learning from him that the neutral Powers supported the cession of Lombardy, and on being shown a proof in black and white that Prussia had engaged not to move a man to the assistance of Austria either in Lombardy or in the Venetian Territory. Further, the state of Hungary, as reported by the Archduke Max, caused His Majesty some alarm, and greatly shook his confidence in the fidelity of the Hungarian regiments in Italy. Lord John Russell took up a more active policy than his predecessors in favour of Italy. He was fully imbued with the feelings for Italian unity and independence. "He was anxious that all foreign troops should be withdrawn from Italy, and that the people should be consulted as to their rulers." It was at this time that he wrote that famous despatch—which was so criticised and censured—opposing the return of the Austrian Archdukes to Modena and Tuscany, and claiming for every nation the right of choosing their rulers. This despatch produced considerable sensation in Europe, and was regarded as of a revolutionary character. But Lord John Russell was really no revolutionist. He was opposed, and justly so, to bargains being made by which a people, without being consulted, was to be handed over to a ruler for his own aggrandisement, thereby giving it the character of a mercenary transaction. It was evident that if provinces like Tuscany, Modena, Parma, Savoy, and Nice were to be handed over to another Sovereign, without their being consulted, in compensation for services rendered by that Sovereign, a precedent would be established which would endanger the independence of other States —for instance, Belgium or Switzerland—and it was from fear of a similar expedient being again resorted to, independently of his strong aversion to it on the principle of justice and right, that Lord John Russell protested so strongly against it.

Neither the restoration of the Austrian Archdukes, nor the institution of an Italian Confederation—in which Austria would be represented on behalf of Venetia—were pleasing to the Italian people. It was felt that the whole object of the war having been to free Italy from Austrian influence and interference in the internal affairs of Italy, her influence and interference, by entering the Italian Confederation, would be greatly increased, and Italy, instead of being fortified by forming one united nation, would be divided into separate States and governments, thus producing disunion instead of unity, chaos and confusion instead of order and cohesion. In the meantime, at a meeting of the Representatives of Tuscany, Modena, and Parma, a resolution was passed unanimously in support of annexation to Piedmont, and this wish was conveyed to Victor Emanuel by a deputation. Thus the policy of Lord John Russell was supported by the national feeling of the Italian people.

After the Battle of Solferino, the Emperor Franz

Josef is reported to have observed to General Reischak that the enemy appeared to know the country as well as they did. The General replied that in 1858 General McMahon had been at Magenta, and had examined all the positions. He also went to Verona, where he (General Reischak) had seen him.

Another circumstance had come to light—namely, that a person who had been apparently sent as an engineer for the railways under French administration was in reality a Colonel of Engineers in disguise, and was accompanied by eleven other engineers, who during their stay had made themselves thoroughly acquainted with the *terrain*. This same Colonel of Engineers had been employed with the French army in Italy.

The Emperor Napoleon was not desirous of a strong united Italy at his frontier. He had agreed in the preliminaries of Villa Franca to restore the Austrian Archdukes. He had also agreed to the creation of an Italian Confederation for Central Italy. But how was this to be effected? Both parties had agreed not to use force. The whole question, then, had arrived at a deadlock. During the various stages of the Italian question Lord John Russell held firmly to his policy in favour of an "United Italy," and he had later the satisfaction of seeing the realisation of his wishes and the crowning of his efforts. Accordingly, when Victor Emanuel took the title of "King of Italy," he unhesitatingly advised the Queen to recognise the new Kingdom.

I have rather digressed from the chronological order

of events, and I, therefore, now revert to the events
which succeeded the battle of Solferino.

Immediately on the retirement of General Giulay
from the command of the Second Army, the Archduke
Maximilian was summoned by the Emperor to Verona.
During the Viceroyalty of Lombardy by the Archduke
Maximilian, he was constantly thwarted in his views and
policy by General Giulay, then Commander-in-Chief of
the Army, which department was separated from the civil
government. The Archduke was represented by General
Giulay to be imbued with too Liberal ideas, and to
be too lenient in the exercise of his civil functions.
The General only thought of governing by the sword,
and of enforcing obedience and maintaining order by
fear and the severity of his military measures. These
two systems produced continual friction and disputes
between the civil and military governments. The
Military Cabinet, of which Count Grünne was the
head, sided with and defended the policy and acts
of General Giulay, while the Archduchess Sophie (the
mother of the Emperor) and a portion of the Cabinet
supported the Archduke. I have mentioned this rivalry
between the civil and military governments in order
to account for the great effect produced by the summons
of the Archduke at this critical moment to the headquarters of the Emperor. Much speculation existed
as to the cause of the Emperor's summons; but I
believe the motive of it was to consult the Archduke as to the best means of allaying the general
discontent in the Empire, and more especially in

Hungary, and of thus restoring confidence in the Government.

On the 24th of June the decisive battle of Solferino took place. It was a hard-fought and very sanguinary action, in which the Allied Armies—or, I should rather say, the French—bore the palm of victory. The Austrian corps under General Benedek, who, with 20,000 men, was opposed to the Piedmontese Army, repelled its attack, and bivouacked at night on the ground on which it had fought.

The events which followed after the French victory were of momentous import. They were as sudden as they were unexpected. I will give a short summary of the events as they occurred, with the dates, before entering more fully into their details, the causes which originated them, and their subsequent results. I can only liken them to the passing scenes of a magic lantern. On the 6th of July the French troops recrossed the Mincio and evacuated Villa Franca, which town, when the interview of the two Emperors took place, was not in the possession or occupation of either belligerent.

On July 5th General Robillant, aide-de-camp to the King of Sardinia, arrived at the Austrian headquarters under a flag of truce, but the object of his visit never transpired.

On July 6th General Fleury, on the staff of the Emperor Napoleon, arrived at the Austrian headquarters charged with an autograph letter from the Emperor Napoleon to the Emperor Franz Josef. His interview lasted a long time.

On July 8th an armistice for five weeks was signed by Field-Marshal Hess and Marshal Vaillant.

On July 10th a wish was conveyed from the Emperor Napoleon for a personal interview with the Emperor of Austria.

On July 11th the two Emperors met at Villa Franca. The preliminaries of peace were signed at Verona, and all hostile operations by land and by sea were stayed.

In regard to the sudden close of the war by the preliminaries of Villa Franca, I believe that it was neither the wish nor the object of the Emperor Napoleon to weaken Austria. It was rather his hope and intention to make her an ally and friend. The Emperor had no wish to raise Sardinia to a great Power by the annexation of the Central Italian States; neither was he disposed to sanction the spoliation of the States of the Church, fearing the effect it would produce on the clergy in France. He was in favour, therefore, of the idea of an Italian Confederation under the presidency of the Pope, in the expectation of exercising a controlling influence over it. An Italian Confederation did not, however, find favour with those who were struggling for Italian freedom and independence. If it were to include Austria (as representing Venetia), Sardinia, Naples, and the Papal States, there would have been a constant rivalry for power and domination among those States, and the Italian sovereigns, instead of contenting their subjects by free and liberal institutions and thus gaining their confidence and support, would have looked for foreign support for their own maintenance. Thus an Italian Confederation would have rather increased than remedied the evils which then distracted that ill-governed country.

But there were many considerations which moved the Emperor Napoleon to close the campaign on the one hand, and which equally moved the Emperor of Austria on the other to accept the offer of peace made by the Emperor Napoleon.

The French army had incurred great losses, and was suffering much from sickness and ophthalmia. It was not in a condition to continue active hostilities without a large reinforcement of fresh troops. The Quadrilateral would have been a hard nut to crack, and had the army suffered a defeat it must have retreated beyond the plains of Lombardy to the Ticino.

The Emperor Napoleon likewise foresaw that, if he continued the war, Prussia and Germany would have intervened. Six corps of the Prussian army had been mobilised, and Prussia, with the Germanic Confederation, was preparing at the time of the signature of the preliminaries at Villa Franca a military demonstration on the Rhine. The Archduke Albert had been to Berlin for the purpose of negotiating united action between Austria and Germany.

Although after the battle of Solferino the Emperor of Austria was at the head of a large army, a considerable portion of which had not then been engaged, and although the fortresses of Verona, Mantua, and Peschiera were intact, and offered a safe refuge in case of defeat, he was fully aware that the Hungarian troops, which formed a considerable portion of his army, were disaffected, and that he could not safely count on their support. He was also aware that General Klapka was in communication with Kossuth to raise an insurrection in Hungary. The Emperor felt, therefore, the necessity and prudence of not continuing a war which might have placed him in a very serious dilemma; and on these grounds he accepted the offers of peace made by the Emperor Napoleon as the lesser of two evils.

When the intelligence reached Vienna, as may be conceived, wild rumours of every kind were circulated with reference to the terms of peace, the causes which had led to it, the possible secret arrangements between the two Emperors, the reported cession of Savoy to France, the transfer of the Danubian Principalities to Austria, the future alliance of Austria, etc. etc. These speculative rumours were circulated, and produced intense excitement among the excitable population of Vienna. But the motives by which the two Emperors were actuated were so apparent that they did not require any extravagant explanation or interpretation. The campaign had been marvellously successful to the French arms, and a result greater than could have been anticipated had been gained in an incredibly short space of time. The French Army had suffered great losses, and sickness—malaria and ophthalmia—were thinning its ranks. An attack on the fortified Quadrilateral would, even if successful, which is very doubtful, have required a very great sacrifice of human life. Further, there could be no doubt that the late revolutionary events in Italy under Garibaldi had somewhat alarmed the Emperor Napoleon, and had induced him to modify the programme he had promulgated at Milan.

Then, again, it was confidently reported that a coldness had sprung up between the Emperor Napoleon and the King of Sardinia, and that the late acts of Count Cavour had not been approved by the Emperor Napoleon, who had the sagacity to foresee that he would incur both danger and unpopularity in France were he to ally himself completely with the Revolutionary Party, and to lend his aid to the spoliation of the Papal Dominions. Nor, finally, would it be just not to attribute to the Emperor Napoleon higher motives and nobler aspirations for peace than mere interested views. He had been painfully impressed with all the sufferings and horrors of war which he had witnessed, and was deeply imbued with the grave responsibility which devolved upon him, with whom the power rested of putting an end to such a frightful effusion of blood. All these various causes, among which we may hope that the latter has been the most forcible, no doubt greatly influenced His Majesty in making the first advance towards a reconciliation, the result of which will gain for him a far higher renown in the page of History than the glory and laurels he might have acquired on the battlefield.

The position in which the Emperor of Austria was placed, and the part he took in these events, were of a different character, but not less creditable to His

Majesty's honour, loyalty, and humanity. He had courageously made a good fight for the maintenance of his just rights. He had nobly sustained the honour of his army and of his country, and when he found that the tide of war had turned against him, he wisely and courageously accepted the advances of the Emperor Napoleon, and signed the preliminaries of peace at the cost of a province in order to save a further and useless sacrifice of human life.

Other causes may have stimulated the Emperor to accept peace, namely, the abandonment of Austria by Europe, and her complete isolation. The animosity of Russia at any moment might have assumed a more active form had the war continued and become general. The danger and imminent risk of troubles in Hungary, fomented and supported by foreign aid, the lamentable state of the finances, and the feeling of discontent which was beginning to make itself heard generally throughout the Empire, forced themselves on the Emperor's attention. In addition to these causes, His Majesty had been deeply moved by the severe losses experienced by his army, and the misery which the war had entailed on his people. His Majesty had at least the consolation of feeling that he had acted the part of a wise and considerate Sovereign, who had been guided by the dictates of humanity and of love for his people rather than by the influence of a passion for military glory.

At my first interview with Count Rechberg on the 18th of July, on his return from Verona, I found him much embittered against England for having abandoned, as he stated, her oldest and most natural ally. "He bitterly reproached Her Majesty's Government for their unfriendly disposition towards Austria, especially alluding to a speech of Lord John Russell, in which he had openly avowed the wish of Her Majesty's Government that Austria should cease to hold any portion of the Italian territory. He observed that this inimical feeling of Her Majesty's Government towards Austria was not in conformity with the policy of severe neutrality which they had adopted. Neither was it in accordance with the Treaties in which England had taken part, nor was it in strict observance with the law of nations, and still less was it a friendly part towards an ancient ally, adding that it was not an act of justice or good faith to urge on an enemy to spoliate and rob the possessions of a friend." I replied that I had no knowledge of any such part having been taken by Her Majesty's Government, who had openly and avowedly expressed themselves in favour and support of a strict neutrality. We had from the beginning done all in our power to prevent war. The British nation was intent on peace, and did not wish to be dragged into a war in which their interests were not directly concerned, and which was not of their seeking. Austria had, unfortunately, acted against the counsels of her friends and allies, and had rashly entered on the contest. She must, therefore, incur all its responsibilities, its risks, its losses.

I inquired of His Excellency whether he did not think that if the neutral Powers had taken part in the contest, and if thereby a general conflagration—

which would have been inevitable—had ensued, far greater dangers would have menaced Austria, and that she might not have come so advantageously out of the contest as had now been the case. If so, I said, our neutrality, of which you complain, will have proved profitable to you rather than the reverse.

Count Rechberg replied, "Certainly not. We should never then have been obliged to sign this peace."

I observed to Count Rechberg that he had used the terms of "England having abandoned Austria." Now he must be aware that we had never held out any hopes to Austria of an active support or co-operation, and that, at the opening of the war, we had frankly announced our intention to preserve a severe neutrality.

He replied, "That although, perhaps, Austria had no right to expect the material support of England, still she had not expected that England would have taken an adverse line, for he must candidly declare that our policy of late towards the Imperial Government had been of the most unfriendly character." I expressed to Count Rechberg my surprise and regret both at the tone and nature of his observations, the more so when I remembered that, at our last interview, he had stated to me that he was much satisfied with the reports he had received, both from Count Apponyi and Prince Esterhazy, of their interviews with Lord Palmerston and Lord John Russell. I did not, therefore, understand this sudden change of language on his part, and the bitter reproaches he had made against Her Majesty's Government.

"It is true," Count Rechberg replied, "that at that time I had received satisfactory reports from London, but it is since then that the change has taken place."

During this interview Count Rechberg evinced much irritation and vehemence. Feeling that allowances should be made for the painful position in which he was placed, and bearing in mind that a great sacrifice had been made by Austria for the attainment of peace, which, however advantageous under the circumstances, could not be otherwise than galling to the feelings of a patriotic Minister, I maintained a calm and passive bearing, and, wishing to avoid any recriminations, I confined myself to the observations recorded above.

Count Rechberg was very reserved on the incidents which had taken place at Villa Franca and on the question of the preliminaries of peace. I had, consequently, to obtain my information through a private channel, which was from an authentic source, and to the following effect.

The first communication between the two hostile armies originated from inquiries made concerning Colonel Prince Windishgrätz, who had fallen at Solferino gallantly leading his regiment into action. Courteous messages were exchanged on this occasion, and this opening was profited of on both sides to express the concern felt at the severe losses which this war had entailed.

General Fleury was then sent by the Emperor Napoleon to the Austrian headquarters at Verona, charged with an autograph letter from His Majesty to the Emperor Franz Josef, in which he proposed an armistice of three months, and expressed a wish for a personal interview with the Emperor of Austria, to ascertain, if possible, whether an understanding might not be come to in order to put an end to this sanguinary war.

General Fleury, it appears, had verbal instructions from the Emperor Napoleon explanatory of the terms on which he was ready to conclude a peace. These terms (to which I shall refer later) were not of a nature to prove acceptable to the Emperor Franz Josef, and he replied to the Emperor Napoleon's letter in that sense, declining also the proposed interview on the grounds that, notwithstanding the satisfaction it would afford His Majesty to meet the Emperor Napoleon, it would be extremely embarrassing to both Sovereigns if, unfortunately, after the interview, peace should not be concluded, and that the war should be renewed. His Majesty further stated that he could not agree to an armistice for so long a period.

It appears that an idea was suggested—whether by General Fleury, at the desire of the Emperor Napoleon, or at the instigation of the Emperor Franz Josef, I am unable to state—that Prince Alexander of Hesse (brother of the Empress of Russia, who had greatly distinguished himself by his bravery during the late engagements) should be charged, on the part of the Emperor of Austria, to convey to the Emperor Napoleon the reasons which rendered His Majesty's proposal unacceptable, and with a view probably to discover whether there existed any possibility of bringing about a pacific arrangement.

Prince Alexander of Hesse was further charged to inform His Majesty that the Emperor Franz Josef could not agree to cede the fortresses of Venetia extending to the Mincio, and that His Majesty could not assent to any terms which did not stipulate the restoration of the Grand Duke of Tuscany and the Duke of Modena to their respective territories.

The proposals, of which General Fleury had previously given an outline, were on the occasion of Prince Alexander of Hesse's mission renewed to him by the Emperor Napoleon. They were: The cession of Lombardy, Venetia, and the four fortresses; Modena, Parma, and Lombardy to be annexed to Sardinia; Venetia to be erected into an independent State; and Tuscany to be given to the Duchess of Parma.

It was stated to Prince Alexander of Hesse, and subsequently repeated by the Emperor Napoleon himself to the Emperor Franz Josef, that these proposals had been made known, through Count Persigny, to the English Government, who had offered no objections to them, and that they had been communicated at the same time to Count Bernstorff, in London, who had expressed his belief that they would meet with the approbation and concurrence of his Government.

The Prince of Hesse, in fulfilment of his instructions, declared that these proposals could not be accepted by the Emperor Franz Josef, and after a personal inter-

f

view with the Emperor Napoleon of considerable length he returned to Verona.

In his report to the Emperor Franz Josef, the Prince of Hesse stated his opinion that there existed a great wish for peace on the part of the Emperor Napoleon, and that probably His Majesty would agree to a great modification of his original proposals to attain that end.

Acting on the report thus made by the Prince of Hesse, the details of which I was not able to learn, the Emperor Franz Josef was reported to have said, "*Eh bien, je sais que les difficultés sont graves. J'irai 'moi-même, et je tâcherai de lever les obstacles.*"

His Majesty accordingly wrote to the Emperor Napoleon, stating that he should be happy to have an interview with him, leaving it to the Emperor Napoleon to name the day and hour for it to take place. I can give no details of the interview, which took place at Villa Franca on the 11th July. I can only say that nothing could exceed the courtesy, the respect, and the great delicacy which the Emperor Napoleon evinced on this occasion towards the Emperor Franz Josef.

Soon after their Majesties' arrival at Villa Franca Count Rechberg was summoned from Verona to the conference of the Sovereigns.

I am informed that, in his presence, on the question being raised of the re-installation of the Grand Duke of Tuscany and the Duke of Modena, the Emperor Franz Josef stated that, as far as he was personally concerned, he was ready, in the interests of peace, to make the sacrifice of Lombardy, and that he could bring himself to bear the humiliation, but that he could never consent to sacrifice the smallest portion of the interests of those of his allies who had placed themselves under his protection.

The Emperor expressed this with so much feeling, sincerity, and nobleness of character, that the Emperor Napoleon was deeply moved, and I was informed that His Majesty from that moment made no further objections or difficulties.

It was also told to me that, on touching the question of territory, the Emperor Napoleon had said, "*Il me faut une indemnité pour la Sardaigne*" and that later, on the Emperor Franz Josef declaring that he could make no further sacrifice of territory than to the line of the Mincio, retaining the fortresses, the Emperor Napoleon replied, after some seconds of thoughtful reflection, "*Si votre Majesté ne peut pas céder, c'est moi donc qui dois céder.*"

The terms of the peace were then agreed to on the following basis, namely : The cession of Lombardy, the restoration of the Sovereigns of Tuscany and Modena to their States, the maintenance of Venetia by Austria to the line of the Mincio, including Mantua, Borgo-Forte, and Peschiera.

The Emperor Napoleon expressed a wish that the preliminaries should be drawn up at once, and proposed to Count Rechberg to accompany him to Vallegio, his headquarters, to arrange the remaining points (of which I was told there were eleven), in order that the documents might be signed, if possible, that evening.

Count Rechberg accordingly returned with the Emperor Napoleon that evening to Vallegio. Immediately on his arrival there the conference was resumed. The Emperor took the pen in hand and drew up the various articles. So anxious was he to meet the views and wishes of the Emperor of Austria, that His Majesty left to Count Rechberg almost entire liberty of dictation, whilst he with his own hand drew up the several articles in accordance with the views and wishes expressed by the Austrian Minister. One of those articles imposed on Lombardy a portion of the debt, and a further charge of the obligations of a financial establishment known under the name of "the Monte."

On the same evening, and before even Count Rechberg had time to reach Verona, Prince Napoleon was sent by the Emperor of the French to the Emperor Franz Josef to learn His Majesty's approval of the preliminaries agreed upon by the Emperor and Count Rechberg; and at the same time to state to the Emperor Franz Josef, on the part of the Emperor Napoleon, that if His Majesty desired to make any change or modification, he was most desirous to meet his wishes.

I was told that the Emperor Napoleon stated to the Emperor Franz Josef that he was very anxious for peace; that the war was a serious charge to him both in men and money, "*Qu'elle était au delà de ses forces,*" and His Majesty stated at the same time that at the battle of Solferino he had 750 officers *hors de combat*.

The great tact, the considerate delicacy and attention, and, above all, the conciliatory disposition shown by the Emperor Napoleon towards the Emperor Franz Josef produced a very deep impression on the mind of the latter, and also on Count Rechberg, who is eloquent in praise both of His Majesty's urbanity and dignified bearing, as well as of his great clearness of view and precision in matters of business.

The Emperor Franz Josef was more successful in his personal relations with the Emperor Napoleon than he was in arms. It was reported to me that when Prince Metternich was presented to the Emperor Napoleon, His Majesty observed to him, "*J'ai eu bien raison d'avoir redouté l'entrevue avec sa Majesté votre souverain, car j'étais bien sûr qu'elle me subjugerait.*"

The Emperor Franz Josef expressed a desire that the negotiations should be carried on directly between the belligerents, without the interposition of the neutral Powers. To which the Emperor Napoleon is said to have replied, "*Je ne demande pas mieux.*"

The Emperor Francis further requested of the Emperor Napoleon that he should treat directly with His Majesty for the cession of Lombardy without being brought in contact with Sardinia, and that the cession should be made to the Emperor Napoleon, and not to the King of Sardinia. The Emperor Napoleon fully entered into the feelings of the Emperor Franz Josef, and immediately assented to the request, and was no doubt flattered by this distinction paid to him. The cession, therefore, bore the character of a gift from the Emperor Napoleon, and not that of a conquest made by Sardinia.

There was some discussion in regard to the title of "King of Lombardy." The Emperor Napoleon, with great consideration towards the King of Sardinia, would not take upon himself to decide the question without referring to the King of Sardinia. The Emperor accordingly during the discussion wrote a few lines to King Victor Emanuel, to which he immediately replied, "That whatever the Emperor Napoleon decided would be agreeable to him."

I believe it was finally decided that the territory ceded should have the name of "The Cisalpine Province," whereby all difficulties with respect to the Kingdom of Lombardy were solved, and the title of King of Lombardy, and the right of conferring the Iron Crown, were retained by the Emperor of Austria. The Kingdom of Lombardy thus ceased to exist but in name, and the proud Lombards and Milanese, who had sighed for independence and to be delivered from Austrian rule, were handed over to their new ruler under the provincial denomination of "Cisalpines."

I was privately informed that at the interview of the Emperor Franz Josef with Prince Napoleon reference was made to the return of the Grand Duke of Tuscany and of the Duke of Modena to their respecpective States, and to the necessity of providing for their safe re-installation and future protection. The Emperor Franz Josef, I was told, expressed a wish that this duty should be performed by French troops, as he had no desire again to enter those Duchies. Prince Napoleon was reported to have replied that this subject need not cause any anxiety to His Majesty, as the Grand Duke of Tuscany would be received with open arms by his subjects, and that the experience which he (Prince Napoleon) had acquired during his passage through the Grand Duchy was that the party which was most detested there was the French. This very frank avowal of Prince Napoleon produced on the mind of the Emperor Franz Josef a very favourable impression of Prince Napoleon.

King Victor Emanuel was not present at the interview of the two Emperors at Villa Franca, nor was he or Count Cavour previously consulted by the Emperor Napoleon in regard to the preliminaries of peace.

When invited by the Emperor Napoleon to sign them as a co-belligerent, His Majesty evinced his disapproval and disappointment at the sudden termination of hostilities without the fulfilment of the pledge to free Northern Italy "from the Alps to the sea." Having placed his signature to the preliminaries, he added, "*En tant que cela me regarde.*" Count Cavour was so disgusted that he immediately resigned office as Minister-President and for Foreign Affairs of King Victor Emanuel, and was succeeded by M. Ratazzi.

It was agreed that the Plenipotentiaries of the three Powers, Austria, France, and Sardinia, were to assemble at Zürich at the earliest moment to conclude the treaty of peace on the basis of the preliminaries signed at Villa Franca. Zürich was specially selected for the Conference as having nó Diplomatic Corps residing there.

Count Colloródo,* Austrian Ambassador at Rome, was appointed Austrian Plenipotentiary, and France was to be represented by Baron Bourqueney. The 26th of July was the day named for the Conference to meet.

M. de Balabine, the Russian Minister at Vienna, on being told that the preliminaries of peace had been signed at Villa Franca, replied, "We," meaning the Russian Government, "are glad that peace is restored. The result has been what we all along have desired—the cession of Lombardy by Austria. We were always opposed to the revolutionary propagandism in Italy, and to the dethronement of the Grand Duke of Tuscany and the Duke of Modena. We deprecate war, and we require peace, for we are too deeply occupied with our internal reforms to have either time or disposition or means to engage in war." This language was very sensible and just. How far it was sincere is a question into which I will not enter.

The Emperor Franz Josef is said to have promised the Emperor Napoleon to advise the Pope to secularise his Government, but the advice did not prove of much avail.

Having been summoned to Baden on account of the serious illness of my youngest daughter, Lord John Russell kindly gave me leave of absence, and I left

* Count Colloródo died during the negotiations, and was succeeded as Austrian Plenipotentiary by Count Karolyi, afterwards Ambassador in London.

Vienna on July 23, having previously presented Mr. Fane as her Majesty's Chargé d'Affaires during my absence.

At Baden Baden I had two long conversations with the King of Würtemberg, the most enlightened sovereign in Germany. His Majesty looked on the peace of Villa Franca as a second "Campo Formio," and thought that it would be of a short duration. He said to me that Austria had always made war under the impulse of fear. It was so in 1805, in 1809, and in 1813. It was under the same impulse "that she acted on the late occasion—Austria had not changed her policy or her system." His Majesty was of opinion that one of two courses must occur. "There will either be a civil war in Italy, with Europe as spectators, or the war between Austria and France will be renewed; in the latter case, it must sooner or later become general."

Such was the opinion at that time of the most enlightened Sovereign and statesman in Germany. In regard to the former alternative, viz., civil war in Italy, if not all parties, the vast majority of the Italian people were united for liberty and independence, and there was only the difference between the Monarchists and the Republicans that could have produced any internal struggle. In regard to the second alternative, viz., a renewal of the war between Austria and France, the cession of Lombardy by Austria left France no further object to attain equivalent to the danger and risks she would incur by a renewal of the war. It was wisely agreed that the restoration of the Grand Duke of

Tuscany and of the Duke of Modena should not be effected by force, and the danger which otherwise might have resulted from foreign intervention was thereby removed. Time and patience alone were left to solve the Italian Question, which was finally effected by the Italian people and the strong current of public opinion.

CHAPTER III.

Return to Vienna on September 15—Negotiations at Zürich still Continued—Prince of Hesse's Mission to St. Petersburg—Conversation with Count Rechberg on the Restoration of the Archdukes—Conversation with the Russian Minister—Archduke Albert's Mission to greet the Emperor of Russia at Warsaw—Reconciliation between Austria and Russia—Prince Metternich's Cordial Reception by the Emperor Napoleon—Central Italy Question Achieved by the National Will—King of Naples' Flight to Gaeta—French and Russian Missions Recalled from Turin—"Le Pape et le Congrès"—Count Walewski Resigns—Is Succeeded by M. Thouvenel—Austria Declines to go to Congress—Three Treaties Signed at Zürich, November 10, 1859—Union of Moldavia and Wallachia—War with China—Peace Signed at Pekin—Intervention of Europe in Syria—Change of Dynasty in Servia—Visit of the Queen and Prince Consort to Coburg—Accident to the Prince Consort—Changes and Reform in Austria—The Imperial Patent in regard to Non-Catholic Confessions—Cause of its Rejection by Hungary.

I RETURNED to Vienna and resumed my diplomatic duties on the 10th of September, 1859. I found that the negotiations at Zürich for the conclusion of peace were not yet terminated; they were progressing slowly, but satisfactorily. The financial question relating to the amount of indemnity to be paid to Austria by Sardinia for the cession of Lombardy was the chief difficulty.

The Emperor Franz Josef instructed Prince Metternich, his Ambassador at Paris, to state to the Emperor Napoleon that as His Majesty was perfectly acquainted with the question, he (the Emperor Franz Josef) was content to leave the decision as to the amount in His Majesty's hands as arbitrator.

The Emperor then fixed the sum for the indemnity, the exact amount of which I was not told, but which was double the amount which the Sardinian Government had expressed their readiness to pay.

The Emperor Napoleon submitted to the Emperor Franz Josef the amount he had fixed in the form of a proposal, and not as his decision. Baron Brück, the Finance Minister, when consulted, evinced some disappointment, the amount being considerably less than he had expected. It was of importance to Austria to obtain a final settlement of this question by direct negotiations with France, who thereby became a surety to Austria without her having any negotiations with Sardinia.

On the 15th of September Lieutenant-General Prince Alexander of Hesse (brother of the Empress of Russia) left for St. Petersburg, charged by the Emperor of Austria to deliver the Grand Cross of the Order of St. Stephen to the Cesarewitch on the occasion of his attaining his majority. This attention was a further sign of the approaching reconciliation between the two Imperial Courts.

At my interview with Count Rechberg on my return to Vienna he received me with much cordiality. On the question of the restoration of the Archdukes to Tuscany and Modena, he said that there was no intention on the part of Austria of resorting to force to reinstate them. He trusted to time and patience alone to bring it about, saying that the Italian population were now under terrorism by the party in power. He was persuaded that if the public voice were appealed to, a large majority would declare itself in favour of their legitimate Sovereigns ; but he added that he did not mean, in saying this, to recognise the principle that the people had the right of appointing or electing their Sovereign.

I observed to Count Rechberg that, although he repudiated the principle, Austria had nevertheless, as far back as 1815, recognised the change of dynasty in Sweden; that in later times she had accepted the rulers *de facto* in France; that she had recognised the new Kingdoms of Belgium and Greece; and that only the other day she had put her signature to a Convention by which freedom of election of their rulers was granted to the populations of Wallachia and Moldavia. I added that, in the present case of the Italian Duchies, it was not a question of expelling, but of reinstating the Sovereigns of those Duchies. They had for the second time abandoned their people, leaving the country without a government. Was it, then, to be wondered at that the people now abandoned them?

Count Rechberg replied that Austria had obligations as well as rights. The former could not be violated; the latter could not be ceded. The Emperor of Austria could not, in justice to his heirs, abandon rights which were their legal inheritance, and which were confirmed by treaties. With respect to the Duke of Modena, he said that he had not been expelled by the population, but had retired with his army when his Duchy was invaded by a foreign army under the command of Prince Napoleon.

I replied that I did not presume to call in question the legal rights of Austria, but it was one thing to possess a right, and quite another question how far it was advisable or practicable to exercise it. For instance, I remarked that there had existed up to 1848 seigneurial rights enjoyed by the aristocracy in Germany, the legality of which could not be contested, but time and circumstances had worked great changes, and rendered them inapplicable in the nineteenth century. The aristocracy and feudal lords were constrained by their governments to abandon what they could no longer enforce. Thus in private as in public affairs circumstances are constantly occurring when individuals and Governments are called upon to yield to the force of necessity, and are obliged to recur to what is termed a "compromise" (*une transaction*) and to recognise "expediency" as obligatory in the general treatment of affairs.

Count Rechberg said that he considered the doctrine that nations were at liberty to expel their Sovereigns as most dangerous, and inquired whether we should admit it as applicable to India, Malta, or Ireland?

I replied that there was no analogy between Great Britain and her dependencies and the Italian Duchies. In India Great Britain had lately suppressed a formidable mutiny by her own strong arm without foreign intervention. If the Italian Sovereigns had remained at their posts, relying on the loyalty and affection of their subjects, and thereby maintained their authority, Europe, no doubt, would have applauded them; but, unfortunately, this had not been the case.

My interview thus ended, but not with any expectation on my part that Count Rechberg had been converted to the opinions I had expressed; but he was tolerant, and our conversation took place in the most friendly tone.

In a conversation I had subsequently with M. de Balabine, the Russian Minister, he told me that Count Rechberg had lately put to him the question whether the Russian Government assented to the "doctrine" that nations had the right to expel their Sovereigns and to elect their rulers? M. de Balabine replied that he could not view this as a "doctrine," but rather as a "principle;" but that as he had received no copy of Lord John Russell's despatch, in which this principle was laid down, and was not even aware whether his Government had received a copy of it, he was unable to reply to His Excellency's question; but that according to his own appreciation he might observe that, whether the principle was recognised or not, it had been acted upon in many instances, and he could not cite a more striking one than by reminding His Excellency that the Cabinet of St. Petersburg had recognised the Second Empire in France subsequently to its recognition by Austria.

The Archduke Albert, then Governor of Hungary, was selected by the Emperor Franz Josef to greet the Emperor of Russia on his arrival at Warsaw in His Majesty's name—on a previous occasion this complimentary mission had been confided to an Austrian general, Count Schaffgotsch. It was signified to the Austrian Government that the presence of a member of the Imperial family would be agreeable to the Emperor of Russia, and Count Rechberg accordingly considered the moment opportune to evince a more friendly disposition towards Russia. The language of M. de Balabine induced a belief that the feelings of the Russian Cabinet had undergone a change, and he openly stated that all feelings of rancour on the part of Russia had now ceased, and that there was a desire on the part of his Government to bury the past in oblivion, and to renew the former friendly relations between the two Governments. The mission of the Archduke Albert, which was purely a complimentary mission, was therefore a step in advance on the part of the Emperor Franz Josef towards a reconciliation between the two Sovereigns.

I was privately informed that, previous to the announcement that Baron Werner, the Imperial Under-Secretary for Foreign Affairs, was to accompany the Archduke Albert to greet the Emperor of Russia at Warsaw, Count Rechberg addressed explanations by telegraph to the French Cabinet in order to prevent any misapprehension as to the nature and object of the Archduke's mission; and so anxious was he that these explanations should forestall the announcement of Baron Werner's mission, that the departure of the Archduke was delayed for a day, and the customary notification to the Russian Minister of Baron Werner being included in the suite of the Archduke Albert was withheld until the day previous to his departure.

I was told that the explanations sent to the French Government represented the mission of Baron Werner

as with the view to induce the Emperor of Russia to
co-operate with Austria and France at any future Congress on Italian affairs; and to inform the Russian
Government that the object of his mission was one in
entire conformity with the policy and views of France.
I was also told that Count Rechberg had expressed his
fullest conviction that these explanations would prove
satisfactory to the French Cabinet, and that consequently the mission of Baron Werner would neither
give cause for umbrage at Paris, nor create any suspicion of the good faith or intentions of the Imperial
Cabinet.

It was previous to this that Prince Alexander of
Hesse had been working at St. Petersburg to bring
about a reconciliation between the two Sovereigns.
After a three weeks' residence at St. Petersburg, his
efforts, aided no doubt by the Empress, were successful in producing a more favourable disposition on the
part of the Emperor of Russia towards Austria, and a
letter was received from the Prince shortly before his
return to Vienna bearing testimony to the success of
his endeavours.

I was informed that the change in the language of
M. de Balabine was in pursuance of instructions from
Prince Gortchacoff, and these instructions were coeval
with the presence of Prince Alexander of Hesse at
St. Petersburg, and were addressed to M. de Balabine at
the very period when Prince Gortchakoff had remarked,
Ah, la mission du Prince de Hesse est bien importante. Elle a pour bût de chercher un successeur pour

moi." It was also reported to me that Prince Gortchacoff had further added, with reference to a renewal of friendly relations with Austria, "*Pourquoi est-ce que nous changerions envers l'Autriche ? Que vaillent ses phrases ? Nous voulons des faits. Si elle nous montre par ses actes que sa politique est changé envers nous, alors nous pourrion lui tendre la main.*"

It is therefore evident that Prince Gortchacoff, seeing the impression which Prince Alexander of Hesse had made on the Emperor Alexander, skilfully forestalled the decision of his Imperial master, and while appearing to treat the subject with indifference at home, had furnished M. de Balabine with instructions to meet what he foresaw would be the wishes and intentions of the Emperor Alexander.

No doubt *les faits* which Prince Gortchakoff alluded to on the part of Austria were her acquiescence in cancelling that article of the Treaty of 1856 limiting the naval forces of Russia in the Black Sea.

Count Rechberg told me, and it was confirmed to me afterwards by Prince Metternich, that they were on the best of terms with the Emperor Napoleon, and they both spoke in terms of eulogy of his good faith and friendly feeling towards Austria. Prince Metternich related that nothing could exceed his gracious reception at Biarritz (St. Sauveur), both by the Emperor and Empress. Their attentions were so overpowering that it was an embarrassment when they came to touch on political matters. "Well," said the Emperor to the Prince, on his return from Vienna, "you wish the restoration of the Archdukes?" "Very naturally," replied the Prince, "for they are Austrian Princes, and legitimate Sovereigns." "I know," said the Emperor, "Austria clings to her principles, but there are occasions when principles must be elastic and give way to circumstances. The difficulties in this case are great, and Austria has always proved herself so skilful, that she might now find a way to relieve us of this embarrassment."

I was told that Prince Metternich was asked to sound his Government as to whether they would be disposed to submit the question of the return of the Archdukes to a plebiscite founded on universal suffrage, and that he took back to Paris a decided negative. The Austrian Government of that day would never admit the principle of election in any shape, and held anything savouring of universal suffrage in horror.

But events proved more forcible and efficient than diplomatic negotiation, and the solution of the Central Italian Question was achieved by the national will, and presented to Europe as a *fait accompli*.

Tuscany, Modena, Parma, the Romagna, Umbria, and the Marshes all declared in favour of annexation to Piedmont. The Sardinian troops occupied those provinces, while Garibaldi delivered Sicily and the Kingdom of Naples into the hands of Victor Emanuel, who assumed the title of King of Italy. Thus the whole of Italy, with the exception of Venetia and Rome, became a united kingdom under monarchical rule, and thus *L' Independenza d' Italia* was an accomplished fact.

The King of Naples fled to Gaeta, and with the troops which had remained loyal to him was determined to defend that fortress. The Emperor Napoleon was much disconcerted by these events, and strongly disapproved of the course taken by King Victor Emanuel. He recalled Baron Talleyrand, his Minister, from Turin, ordered a division of his fleet to Gaeta for the protection of the King of Naples, and increased the French garrison at Rome for the protection of the Pope.

The deposition of the King of Naples by the Revolutionary Party caused alarm to the Northern Courts. The Russian Chargé d'Affaires and the Legation were recalled from Turin by the Emperor Alexander, and diplomatic relations were broken off as a mark of his disapproval of the acts of the Sardinian Government. The Prussian Government, although not suspending diplomatic relations with the Sardinian Court, addressed strong remonstrances against the policy of the Sardinian Government, but the *fait accompli* remained, and no attempts to reverse it were made by Europe. It must be admitted that the Italian people in their triumph behaved with great circumspection. No disorders took place, no act of vengeance or of cruelty was committed, and this bloodless revolution will be recorded in history as the opening of a new era, and of a brighter dawn to an enlightened but oppressed people.

The official correspondence of the several Governments of Europe during these emotional proceedings is well worth perusal, but it is too diffuse for me to present it to my readers in these pages. It will be found very succinctly given in the Appendix to this volume.

Towards the end of 1859 a pamphlet, "Le Pape et le Congrès," had been published at Paris, supposed to have emanated from the pen of the Emperor Napoleon, or been written under his auspices. The nature of it was of so advanced a character that Count Walewski required its disavowal, and, failing to obtain it, resigned his post as Minister for Foreign Affairs, and was succeeded by M. Thouvenel.

In consequence, also, of this pamphlet the Austrian Government declined to go to a Congress, the invitations to which had been issued and accepted conditionally by Lord John Russell, and which was to meet at Paris early in January. The Austrian Government, before going into Congress, required that none of the proposals or principles set forth in the pamphlet, "Le Pape et le Congrès," should be brought before or supported by the Congress. This being refused, the Congress died a natural death, and no more was heard of it.

The Conference at Zürich between the belligerents was protracted by the difficulties attending the financial question between Austria and Sardinia. But they were happily surmounted, and the political questions were regulated strictly in conformity with the stipulations of the preliminaries of Villa Franca. I will not weary my readers with the details of these negotiations, but briefly state that three treaties were signed at Zürich on the 10th of November, 1859, viz., a Treaty between Austria and France respecting the cession of Lombardy to

France; second, a Treaty between France and Sardinia regulating the cession of Lombardy by France to Sardinia; and third, a Treaty of Peace between the three belligerent Powers.

Although the diplomacy of Europe had been chiefly occupied with Italian affairs and the startling changes which had taken place in that Peninsula, other events of great importance in more distant parts had seriously engaged the attention of the European Powers. I will only touch cursorily on these events as a matter of history without entering into details, the more so as they did not come under my personal notice, and were beyond my diplomatic sphere. I will first mention the question of the Danubian Principalities.

By the Treaty of Paris in 1856 it was agreed that the Principalities of Moldavia and Wallachia should have separate Governments and rulers, the latter elected by the respective populations of those provinces.

A strong popular current had set in favour of the union of the two Principalities under one ruler. England and Austria were opposed to it; France, Russia, and Sardinia favoured it. When the elections, in conformity with the stipulations of the Treaty of 1856, took place, Colonel Couza was first elected for Moldavia on the 5th of January, 1860. The same personage was elected for Wallachia on the 5th of February following. Thus the populations of the two provinces elected the same individual with a view, by this act, to bring about their union. It gave rise to much diplomatic discussion, and, fortunately, more ink was spilt than blood, although at one time it was feared that it might produce serious friction among the signatories of the Treaty of 1856.

But the act of the double election clearly proved the wish of both populations for the union. The Porte was not edified by the transaction, but, after contesting the validity of the election, prudently gave way, and it was finally confirmed by the Conference of the Great Powers held at Paris.

No disturbance or disorder took place in the provinces, and thus was consummated an act which was the stepping-stone to the entire independence of the two provinces, and the forerunner of the future Kingdom of Roumania.

In this year also occurred a change of dynasty in Servia. Prince Kara-Georgievitch, who had displaced Prince Milosch, had become so unpopular that his deposition was pronounced by the Skuptchina (or Parliament), and Prince Milosch Obrenovitch was recalled by a vote of the same Parliament as ruler of the Principality. Among those Eastern races intrigue is their daily bread, and it was actively carried on under the Milosch rule. Russia has always had, or tried to have, a finger in those intrigues, even when not stimulated by her, her ambition being to unite Servia with Montenegro, under the present reigning Prince of the " Black Mountain," and thus to form the nucleus of a free Slavonic State under her immediate protectorate. But this is too large a question for me to enter upon in these pages. I will only, therefore, state that at Prince Milosch's death he was succeeded by Prince Michel Obrenovitch, who married Countess Julie Hunyadi, daughter of a Hungarian magnate. I was personally acquainted with them, but my preference was for the Princess, who was extremely handsome and charming.

The Prince was assassinated as he was walking in the park. Having no issue, the rulership of the Principality fell to a distant relation, Prince Milosch Obrenowitch. He married a Russian lady, was divorced from her, and shortly after, in consequence of that divorce, abdicated in favour of his son, then a minor. The Principality was erected into a Kingdom shortly after the termination of the war between Russia and Turkey in 1877.

I will now turn to the Chinese imbroglio. In 1860 peace with China was signed at Tientsin by the representatives of England and France. The war had been caused by the Chinese Government having obstructed the passage of the English and French representatives who had been sent to exchange the ratifications of the Treaty of Tientsin. The passage of the Pei Ho was forced, a considerable force of English and French troops was landed, marched to Pekin, and took that capital after ineffectual resistance. The Emperor and his Ministry fled, and the famous Summer Palace at Pekin was sacked and burnt.

In 1859-60 serious troubles arose in the Lebanon between the Maronites and Druses, where great excesses were committed. It was agreed by Great Britain, France, Austria, Prussia, and Russia to co-operate with the Sultan in quelling these disorders and in arresting a further effusion of blood. A Convention to that effect was signed by the representatives of the six Powers at Paris on the 5th of September, 1860, by which a corps of 12,000 European troops was to be sent to Syria, of which the Emperor Napoleon agreed to furnish immediately one half, and to supply the remaining half if required; England, Russia and Prussia consenting to supply the naval forces required for the restoration of tranquillity on the coasts of Syria. Six months were fixed for the occupation of Syria by the European troops.

A protocol was added to the Convention binding each of the contracting Powers neither to seek any territorial advantage nor exclusive influence, nor any commercial concession which could not be granted to the subjects of all nations.

Lord Dufferin was appointed the British Commissioner, and through his tact and judgment, ably assisted by his colleagues, complete pacification was obtained when the naval and military occupation ceased, and the French troops returned to France.

During the autumn of 1860 the Queen and Prince Consort visited the Duke of Saxe-Coburg at Coburg, attended by Lord John Russell as Cabinet Minister. I was summoned to Coburg to pay my duty to Her Majesty and His Royal Highness. On my arrival there intelligence had just arrived of an accident having occurred to the Prince. It appears that the horses to his light, open carriage had taken fright and bolted. The Prince, in endeavouring to get out of the carriage during their rapid course, fell on his head; his face was much cut, and the shock of his fall must have been severe. His escape from further injury was most providential, and our minds were greatly relieved when His Royal Highness returned to the palace. It was a most anxious moment of suspense till we heard that he was uninjured, except as regarded the cuts in his face produced by his fall on the hard macadamised road. His Royal Highness's calm and serene temperament showed itself on this as on all occasions, and no expression fell from him except of gratitude to Providence for his merciful escape.

I had the honour to be received twice by His Royal Highness. On each occasion the conversation dwelt on the internal position of Germany, of its future prospects and the craving wants of the German people. I was greatly impressed by the knowledge, the wisdom, and the marvellous foresight of His Royal Highness. He was fully convinced that a healthy constitutional system and union were the prevailing object and wish of the German nation, and that they could only be safely and practically carried out by Prussia through the Liberal and National Party. He foresaw with prophetic vision that the day would come, and was not far off, when this great change would be brought about; but he had little confidence in the Prussian statesmen of that epoch, and did not consider them equal to the task of bending to the national will. He trusted more to the efforts of the National Liberal Party.

His was a great, a noble mind. He was a distinguished scholar, deeply versed in all branches of literature. He was a deep thinker, but he never allowed himself to be carried away by the dreams of fancy, or to be enveloped by that philosophic and misty cloud of thought in which Hegel and other German Professors of great renown and learning indulged. His Royal Highness was endowed with that clearness of perception, that correctness of judgment, that rare appreciation of all that was pure and refined, and that sound and practical wisdom which never failed him and was never at fault, which governed all his actions, and gave to them an indescribable value. I feel that it may be a presumption in me thus to trace the character of a Prince of such exalted rank, and whose noble qualities have been delineated by abler pens than mine, and which are so widely known and so fully appreciated; but I could not refrain from expressing in these pages— too feebly and faintly I fear—my unbounded admiration of his noble and exemplary virtues and of the valuable services he has rendered to his adopted country, the grateful recollection of which will be handed down to future generations.

Countess Mensdorff (*née* Princess Dietrichstein), the wife of Count Mensdorff, a cousin of the Prince Consort, arrived on a visit to the Duke of Saxe-Coburg. It was her first presentation to the Queen, and she told me that she felt very shy and nervous. I said that she need not be the least nervous, for I felt sure that Her Majesty's gracious manner would at once put her at her ease. Count Mensdorff was afterwards Minister for Foreign

Affairs at a very critical moment before and during the Prusso-Austrian War. He was a distinguished man, a brave soldier, and thoroughly honest and straightforward in all his thoughts and deeds; but at that time Count Bismarck was intent on war, the hour for the struggle he had been preparing for years had come, and nothing could have averted it.

Before proceeding with my narrative, I must touch on the internal reforms and the change of system in the administration of affairs in Austria which were imperatively called for to allay the discontent arising generally throughout the Empire, and which was too patent to escape the Emperor's notice. To content and give confidence to the army was the first necessity. Great changes took place in the army, and a large retirement of superannuated officers in the higher ranks was effected to make place for younger and more active men. Count Grünne, the head of the Emperor's Military Cabinet, gave place to General Crenneville, retaining, however, the post of Grand Écuyer in His Majesty's household, and receiving the Grand Cross of St. Stephen, the highest decoration after the Golden Fleece in Austria, as a recognition of his faithful services to his Sovereign. Baron Bach, the Minister of the Interior, was also replaced by M. de Schmerling, and various changes of a similar character were made, thereby giving proof of the introduction of a new system, more progressive and more in harmony with the spirit of the age.

Nor were these changes confined to Austria proper—

they were extended to Hungary, Bohemia, and the other Provinces of the Empire.

But among the most notable changes in the administration of affairs, I may mention the relaxation of the laws which, since 1849 and subsequently to that date, since the Concordat with the See of Rome, had weighed so heavily on the Protestant and non-Catholic subjects of the Empire, including the Jews. As this question is one of great importance to Englishmen, who have always been the supporters of civil and religious liberty, I give the following details, which may be of some interest. For some time past there had been much discontent in Hungary, and generally throughout the Austrian States, at the spirit of intolerance evinced towards the various communities not professing the Roman Catholic faith, and more especially towards the Jews. This intolerance has been more actively in force since the Concordat, when the chief power of dealing with ecclesiastical matters was conceded by the State to the Catholic hierarchy.

In Vienna, where there are few Protestants, this intolerance was more specially exercised towards the Jewish community, who laboured under severe repressive laws of ancient date, which deprived them of the civil and religious rights enjoyed by their Roman Catholic brethren. These laws—which permitted Jews to settle only in certain stated parts of the Empire; which prevented them transferring their residence to another town or parish without the permission of the civil authorities; which precluded them from the right of possessing landed property; which closed the door to them of most of the Government inferior offices; which forbad them to hire Christian servants; and which were oppressive and humiliating in various ways—had been abolished in 1848. In 1852, however, Prince Schwartzenberg recalled and annulled the Act which had thus so justly emancipated the non-Catholic confessions in general as well as the Jews; and since that period the old laws were considered to be again in vigour, and no relaxation of them, although promised, had yet been granted.

On a report that the law forbidding Jews to hire Christian servants, which had been allowed to remain in abeyance, was again to be vigorously enforced, the influential Jews in Frankfort, Amsterdam, Berlin, and in various towns of Germany declared that, if this Act were to be carried out, they would henceforth cease to have any financial dealings with Austria, and that they would neither hold nor receive any Austrian funds or stocks. This declaration so alarmed the Ministerial authorities at Vienna that they decided not only not to enforce the law, but to take measures to relax the severity of the laws against the Jews and the other confessions, and to emancipate them from the unjust oppression to which they were subjected.

In order, therefore, to calm and tranquillise the fears entertained by the whole Jewish community, more especially at a moment when the exigencies of war might oblige the Government to have recourse to their services, and to appeal to their patriotism, a semi-official article was inserted in the *Vienna Gazette*, holding out hopes of an early and salutary change as regarded the position in the State of the non-Catholic confessions, which change, it was said, would be "conceived in that spirit of progress and humanity which characterises the civilisation of the age."

The Imperial Patent regulating the future position of the evangelical creeds in Hungary, Croatia, Slavonia, in the Servian Voivodine, in the Temesvar Banat, and in the military frontier districts, was published in September, 1859, and was received with much cordial satisfaction, not only by the populations of those provinces, but generally by the Protestants of the Empire, who no longer doubted that the same liberality would inspire the Ordinances destined to regulate the position and rights of the non-Catholic confessions of the Empire at large.

The new Ordinance, I was informed by Count Rechberg, had been already prepared by the late Ministry in the same large and liberal spirit, and the delay in its publication alone arose from difficulties, the nature of which it is my present aim to explain, and in doing so I shall endeavour to give a short narrative of the antecedent position of the Protestants in the various provinces of the Empire.

During, and in consequence of, the events of 1848, and previous to the conclusion of the Concordat, the equality of the confessions had been proclaimed, although at the time no definite basis on this principle had been laid down. These rights, however, were swept away with the annulment of the Constitution drawn up at Kremsir. It was, likewise, at the same time that the privileges accorded to the Jews—amongst others, that of acquiring landed property, of which they had been in the enjoyment during three years—were rescinded, but with an implicit promise that their civil rights should be regulated.

Since that period matters remained on their former footing, not only as regarded the Jews, but as regarded the Protestants.

The relief accorded to the latter by the Imperial Patent was, therefore, but the fulfilment—the very tardy fulfilment—of a promise antecedently given.

The position of the Protestant communities in Austria had been always different in the several Provinces. It was, for instance, more favoured in Hungary and Transylvania than in the other Provinces—Croatia and the Tyrol being those in which most intolerance was shown to Protestantism.

In general, the usage established since the Peace of Westphalia, and the tolerant laws of the Emperor Joseph II., had so far placed the Protestants in a position which, although not legally recognised as being on an equality with their Catholic brethren, yet, in practice, had been tantamount to it.

The publication of the Concordat, however, produced a change, and created serious disquietude in the minds of the Protestants. It appeared to confer on the Catholics not only a privileged position, but likewise a power, if they chose, of oppression over the other confessions.

The Protestants no longer considered themselves on a footing of equality with their Catholic brethren, although subjects of the same Sovereign.

The Concordat made it apparent that, as a religious body, they existed only on sufferance, and its stipulations breathed but one exclusive spirit in favour of the Catholics. By the Concordat the whole system of the Emperor Joseph II. was broken down, the principal aim of which had been to put a check on the spirit of Ultramontanism and the domination of its clergy. The extended power granted by the Concordat to the bishops restored to the Holy See the influence which Joseph II. had sought to diminish, and the restoration of this influence inspired the Protestants and other confessions with fears that the abuses which had characterised the Papacy of the Middle Ages would be again resuscitated.

It was against these abuses that the Gallican Church in France had raised her voice, and similar opposition was raised and precautions taken in other countries where the dissenting bodies were in sufficient force to enable them to provide for their own protection.

Thus, in Hungary and in Transylvania, where Saxon colonies had established themselves, the Protestants had been in the enjoyment of equal privileges. Thus, likewise, had been often evinced in the Hungarian Diets Separatist tendencies as regarded the Court of Rome, and petitions had been addressed to their King (viz., the Emperor of Austria) desiring to be declared independent of the Holy See.

With reference to Hungary, I will here observe that

the rights of the Protestants had been sanctioned and more especially defined by an Ordinance published in 1791 under Leopold II. This Ordinance had been, and was, in force until it was inconsiderately suppressed by General Haynau in 1849, who was then Military Governor of Hungary, although he himself was of the Protestant faith. As, however, his authority did not extend to Transylvania, the former legislation of 1791 remained in force in that province.

Before the publication of the new Ordinances, the Government inquired of the Protestants in Transylvania if they wished that the Imperial Patent should be equally applicable to them. They positively declined, saying that they preferred to be under the protection of the old legal rights, which quite satisfied their desires, rather than to be subjected to new legislation. This was the cause why Transylvania was not included among the provinces named in the Imperial Patent.

To return to the effect produced on the Protestants by the Concordat, it will be easily understood that that measure was justly calculated to cause alarm to the Protestant communities. At the moment of its publication, it must be borne in mind that usages legalised by time—ancient rights and even the Diets, which had been, till then, the protectors of the rights of all parties —had been swept away. The principle of political unity had been proclaimed, and it was hoped that this same principle would have been applied to religious, as well as to civil, legislation; but in lieu of it the Protestants found themselves exposed to the rigorous *régime* of intolerance.

At the time of the conclusion of the Concordat the Government, it is true, hastened to announce that special laws would regulate the position of the non-Catholic confessions, but the promise was not sufficient to calm the apprehensions generally felt, and three years had elapsed without the fulfilment of this promise.

It must not, however, be thought that this delay arose from any supineness or indisposition on the part of the Government to fulfil this promise. It proceeded solely from the difficulties arising from the interpretation to be given to the principle of unity proclaimed by the Emperor, who thought that he could not depart from the principle laid down by Prince Schwartzenberg.

That Minister had no administrative talent, nor was he a man to acquire by great labour and study that information and knowledge which the administrative details of an Empire so extended and so heterogeneous as that of Austria required. Although the principle of unity might have been the only practicable and safe internal policy, still its application need not necessarily have been absolute.

In France, the unitary system was not carried out in a day. The work commenced by Louis XI. was only terminated at the first French Revolution.

The great failure of Baron Bach, the Austrian Minister of the Interior, and the principal originator of the Concordat, holding extreme Ultramontane views, appears to have been in seeking too much to generalise. At each step he encountered obstacles—impossibilities. He found himself opposed by deeply-rooted prejudices and ancient customs. He was not sufficiently strong to overcome these difficulties and to carry out his will. The Emperor continually hesitated in his decisions, and, while supporting his Minister, took no definite resolution.

Baron Bach, devoted to His Majesty, was neither willing to harass him, nor was he possessed of sufficient influence to govern him; and thus the provisional state of things was indefinitely prolonged.

Count Buol in some measure contributed to this state of indecision and delay. Naturally indolent, he had, on accepting office, declined taking any active part in the administration of Home Affairs, with which he was little conversant. He had neither the energy nor the authority of Prince Schwartzenberg to carry out the system which that Minister had initiated, nor to smooth the difficulties which presented themselves in its general application. Among those difficulties, that of the equality of the religious confessions was indubitably the most prominent, and it is only since Count Rechberg and his Government succeeded in establishing the principle of "unity" without "uniformity" that the difficulties which had opposed the publication of this Ordinance have been overcome. Religious liberty had tacitly existed in reality since the Concordat, as it had existed before, but that ill-judged and unfortunate measure, which inspired fears on the one hand, gave rise to haughty pretensions on the other, which again led to an excess of zeal, to ambitious aspirations, and to many injudicious acts. The Italian bishops, for instance, considered themselves as censors over the Press; the German bishops intolerantly disputed the common use of the cemetery; the Archbishop of Vienna assembled a council, which passed intolerant resolutions, which were equally approved by the Episcopacy and sanctioned by the Holy See.

The object of the Government in 1859 was to conciliate the maintenance of the Concordat with full satisfaction granted to the non-Catholic confessions. They hoped to maintain the principle of "unity" in the State (as regarded the legislation on religious matters) by modifying the forms according to the wants and customs of the several nationalities. They tried to produce harmony with a due regard to divergent elements. They sought to create a future without taking account of the past.

It was in this sense that they proposed to act as regarded the communal laws, the organisation of the Provincial States, and the regulation of the civil position of the Jews. They thus commenced with those provinces where the Protestants had possessed the greatest privileges, and intended later to publish special Ordinances in the same large and liberal spirit for the Austrian Duchies, Bohemia, Moravia, Gallicia, Styria, and for all the provinces of the Empire.

The position of the Tyrol was exceptional. No Protestants were allowed to establish themselves in that province. The Government* then intended to

* I am referring to 1859. Having been transferred to Berlin in 1860, I am unable to state what took place later in regard to these religious questions.

submit the Ordinances to regulate the position of the Protestants in other provinces of the Empire to the Provincial States of the Tyrol, which province, in 1859, was the only one where the Provincial States still existed, owing to the circumstance that when a general armament was ordered during the war, by an old right enjoyed by the Tyrol the armament could only be ordered by the States, and not by the Sovereign. The Government, therefore, intended to submit to the States the Ordinances for the Protestants in the other provinces, leaving it to them to apply them in the measure they might judge advisable.

In regard to Croatia, I may observe that hitherto no Protestant had been allowed to possess landed property in that province. The Croats, however, raised no difficulties to accepting the Ordinance as applicable to their province.

In regard to the Jews, I was told (in 1859) that the Government intended to diversify the application of the liberal measures then projected. Thus, in the most enlightened parts of the Empire the Jews would be permitted to possess landed property, whilst a limitation would be imposed in this respect on those residing in other parts of the Empire, especially in the Polish districts.

I was also informed that full satisfaction would be given to the non-united Greeks, who are very numerous in the Slavonic and Polish Provinces.

By the Imperial Patent of September, 1859, the two evangelical confessions were permitted entire liberty and control over their ecclesiastical affairs. The right of superintendence, but not of interference, was reserved to the State, in accordance with the laws, but the head of the Department in the Ministry of Public Worship charged with the affairs of the evangelical confessions was to be henceforth a Protestant and not, as previously, a Catholic.

Special ecclesiastical courts were to be established, and the right of jurisdiction in matrimonial matters was to be confided to them. A supreme evangelical consistory was to be formed for both confessions, in accordance with the advice and wishes of their superintendents. The clergy were to be subject to the ecclesiastical authorities, but on matters of a civil nature they were to be referred to the civil tribunals.

The schools of both confessions were to be placed under the direction and superintendence of their own ecclesiastical organs, and the right of the Crown to superintend was to be exercised by members of one or other of the evangelical confessions.

In the Protestant schools no religious books were to be used without the sanction of the Protestant ecclesiastical authorities, with the concurrence of the Minister of Public Worship, and no school books were to be used unless authorised by the Minister of Public Worship, with the concurrence of the evangelical authorities.

The evangelical communities were granted the right of acquiring property, and all bequests, either to the Protestant churches or schools, were to be strictly devoted to their respective purposes. Both evangelical confessions were granted the unrestricted management of their own property subject to revision, if required, by the Ministry of Public Worship. The most remarkable concession, perhaps, was the right granted to each parish to elect freely its own rector, vicar, and schoolmaster.

Power was given to both confessions to hold synods for ecclesiastical matters, but all laws and regulations passed by them were to be submitted to the Imperial sanction.

The superintendents of both confessions were to receive their salaries from the Imperial treasury.

The foregoing were the principal features of the Imperial Patent, and it must be allowed that its provisions were dictated by a large and liberal spirit.

Hitherto the Protestant consistory had been presided over, both at Vienna and Pesth, by a Catholic. The inconsistency and injustice of this regulation has been recognised by the Imperial Patent, which decreed that the Protestant consistory would henceforth have the right of electing their own presidents. The State has regulated with the See of Rome, by means of the Concordat, all that concerns the hierarchy and the jurisdiction of the Catholic clergy. As regards the dissenting confessions, the Government apparently adopted the principle of their separation from the State—that is, they considered the dissidents merely as citizens, without making a distinction between the clergy and their flock —and consequently they abstained from appointing any Government commissary to their consistory. The independence, therefore, of the evangelical clergy and confessions is greater in Austria than in many Protestant States, especially in Prussia, where the Sovereign reserves to himself a supremacy over the hierarchy and clergy, and all high ecclesiastical appointments are vested in the Crown; whereas, by the Imperial Patent, the right of election of their clergy by the parishioners is accorded to the Protestant communities.

This wise and liberal measure caused great satisfaction throughout the Empire, with the exception of Hungary, which refused the measure, not on the score of the concessions to the Protestant communities being insufficient, but solely on political grounds, and declining to accept as a favour from the Imperial Government what the Hungarians considered to be a right and a privilege inherent in the Hungarian Constitution. The other parts of the Empire viewed the Imperial Patent with the greatest satisfaction, as a proof that the darkness of religious intolerance and oppression was passing away, and that the dawn of civil and religious liberty was about to commence.

In Hungary, on the other hand, it was viewed equally by the Catholics and Protestants both politically and religiously as a violation of their antecedent rights, the latter claiming their rights and privileges under the law of 1791, which, they asserted, had not been, and could not be, legally abrogated by the fiat of the Sovereign. They maintained that those rights and privileges were more securely held under a law than by an Imperial Patent, which could be rescinded to-morrow by the same hand which gave it to-day. They asserted that, by the law of 1791, their own Synod was the legal channel to resuscitate what had lain dormant, and that the right of the Crown, under the same Act, was restricted to a mere "veto," without any initiatory power. The Hungarians further maintained that if they were to accept the Imperial Patent it would be on their part a tacit recognition of the invalidity of the law of 1791.

On the other hand, the Emperor considered the Hungarians in the light of revolted subjects of a kingdom reduced to a province, and that whatever rights and privileges they possessed were forfeited by their act of rebellion, and that all that they now possess or may possess hereafter emanates solely from his will and pleasure.

The foregoing were the grounds on which the Hungarians refused the Imperial Patent. At popular meetings the Hungarians stuck to their colours, and at public dinners toasts were proposed, even in the presence of the Archduke Albert, the popular Governor, which were distasteful to him.

I refer to these as a matter of history, but since that period better counsels have prevailed. The old Constitution of Hungary—dating back for near a thousand years —has been recognised by the Emperor, with all its rights and privileges. Hungary has resumed her former state of autonomy. The Emperor has been crowned King of Hungary, and since the establishment of the dual monarchy there has been harmony and peace, and there is now no portion of the Empire more loyal or more devoted to the Emperor than his loyal Kingdom of Hungary.

In November, 1859, my sister-in-law, Lady Ely (one of her Majesty the Queen's ladies) paid us a visit at Vienna with her two children. On the occasion of Lady Ely's presentation to their Imperial Majesties, Lady Augustus and I were invited to dine at the Imperial Court, then residing at Schönbrünn. Nothing could exceed the gracious attention of their Imperial Majesties both to Lady Ely and ourselves. The Emperor received me in the most cordial manner. His Majesty expressed his thanks for the gracious reception which Her Majesty the Queen had given to Prince Esterhazy during his late visit to England. The Emperor did not refer to anything of a political nature. His Majesty inquired with some interest as to whether India was pacified, and whether the effects of the late mutiny had been entirely effaced. I was happy to assure His Majesty that the accounts from India were most satisfactory, and that peace and order were completely restored. Their Majesties inquired with warm interest after the health of Her Majesty the Queen and H.R.H. the Prince Consort, and it afforded me great satisfaction to be able to inform their Majesties that the Queen and His Royal Highness were in the enjoyment of the best of health.

In referring to the pamphlet "*Le Pape et Le Congrès*," I may state that the effect produced by this pamphlet on the minds of the Emperor and the Imperial Ministry was one of dismay and of distrust of the intentions of the Emperor Napoleon. In referring to it in conversation with Count Rechberg, he stated that the political doctrines it set forth were most dangerous to the principle of an hereditary monarchy, and that if the Emperor Napoleon, as he supposed, was anxious to consolidate his dynasty, he (Count Rechberg) could not conceive it possible that he could support any plan which would affect so deeply the prestige of hereditary monarchy as would the spoliation of the dominions of the Pope. To my inquiry as to whether he thought that this pamphlet represented the opinions of the French Govern-ment, he merely remarked that on a previous occasion a similar pamphlet had prepared Europe for events which subsequently took place.

Count Rechberg (I learnt from a private source) instructed Prince Metternich to inquire of the French Government whether, and how far, this pamphlet met with their approval; and in the event of their disapproval, to urge the desirableness of inserting in the *Moniteur* an official disavowal of its tenets. The Marquis de Moustier, the newly-appointed French Ambassador, professed complete ignorance of it, saying that it had been published after his departure from Paris.

CHAPTER IV.

Opening of 1860 with Favourable Prospects—Count Walewski succeeded by M. de Thouvenel—Appointment of the Marquis de Moustier as French Ambassador—Ball at Court—Dinner at the Palace—Conversation with the Emperor—The Emperor's Conversation with the Marquis de Moustier—Suicide of Baron Bruck—The Proposed Congress—Its Collapse—Annexation of Savoy and Nice to France—Count Seebach's Secret Mission to Count Beust at Dresden—Its Failure—Success of Lord John Russell's Policy in favour of a United Italy—Memorandum of my Conversation with Count Rechberg given to Lord John Russell at Coburg—His Reply—Three Meetings of Sovereigns—Progress of the Italian Movement—Occupation of Naples by Garibaldi—Flight of the King—Surrender of Gaeta—Garibaldi Retires to Caprera—Unity of Italy Effected—Assumption by Victor Emanuel of the Title of King of Italy.

THE year 1859 ended more peacefully than it had commenced. Although the question of Central Italy was still in suspense, the popular will had unmistakably declared itself in favour of unity and liberty, and notwithstanding the delay in the realisation of these hopes, the Italian people evinced great self-command and patience, not doubting for an instant that the dawn of their long-cherished ambition was nigh at hand, when their patriotic aspirations, so ardently felt, would be accomplished.

There were still many rocks and shoals ahead, and it required consummate skill for the pilot to bring the vessel safely into port, but that pilot was "Il Ré Galantuomo," in whom the whole nation placed the highest confidence. The return to power of Count

Cavour, that irresistible patriot, gave encouragement to the nation, who looked also to the invincible Garibaldi as their deliverer.

The maintenance of peace was so far ensured, as Austria, profiting by her dire experience, had fully accepted the principle of non-intervention, and had determined neither to assist the Pope nor the King of Naples, nor, indeed, to send a soldier across her frontier unless for self-defence.

The Austrian Government were too fully occupied with putting their own house in order—with reorganising the administration of the Empire on a more liberal basis, with introducing reforms and readjusting the finances, and also with preparing the measures to satisfy Hungary—to think of renewing the war. Count Rechberg was also deeply impressed with the necessity of relieving Austria from that state of isolation in her foreign relations in which she had been previous to the late war.

At the opening of 1860 Austria was on amicable terms with France, although distrustful of the policy of the Emperor Napoleon. Since the publication of the pamphlet " Le Pape et le Congrès," Count Walewski had resigned the Ministry for Foreign Affairs, and had been succeeded by M. de Thouvenel, a more pliant tool in the hands of the Emperor Napoleon. He was an able man, but less independent in character, and less compromised by his antecedents than Count Walewski.

The relations of Austria with Russia, since the

removal of Count Buol, had greatly improved, and a reconciliation between the two Sovereigns was in expectancy.

The relations with Prussia had not much improved. There existed between them an outward friendliness without sincerity, a frigidity without confidence.

The relations with England were friendly, if not cordial, on all European questions, except in regard to Italy, but the divergence of views on events passing in Italy did not prevent perfect co-operation and understanding with the English Cabinet on all other European questions.

Thus the new year opened with somewhat brighter prospects than the preceding one, and hopes in the maintenance of peace, for which all the European Governments were anxious, were generally and confidently entertained. It was felt that time and patience alone were required to consolidate the new order of things in Italy.

The Marquis de Moustier had been appointed French Ambassador at Vienna. I had been intimate with him at Berlin, where he was Minister during the Crimean War. He was a member of the old aristocracy of France, of ancient lineage, with large possessions, which he fortunately had preserved. He was a shrewd, clever man, and was afterwards for a short time Minister for Foreign Affairs. He made his *début* at Vienna at a ball at the Palace on the 18th of June, to which the Diplomatic Corps was invited. The Emperor and Empress were extremely gracious to me, but His Majesty did not enter with me, or with any of the foreign ministers, on political subjects.

These balls at the Palace are very striking for their magnificence. They represent the grandeur of an ancient Court. The jewels displayed by the ladies impress a stranger with a grand idea of the wealth of the Austrian aristocracy, and the beauty of the dresses and of their wearers could not be surpassed. It was a mystery to me how the thousands of wax candles, for there was no gas, which lit up the State apartments could be lighted. I learnt that it was all arranged beforehand by a prepared thread which was twisted around every wick, the end hanging down for ignition. This thread, when ignited from below, lit up the whole chandelier instantaneously, as if by magic. The same process is adopted at the Courts of Berlin and St. Petersburg.

Shortly afterwards a dinner was given by the Emperor to the foreign Ministers accredited to his Court. It was customary to divide the Corps Diplomatic into two series. I had the honour to be included in the first series with the Nuncio, the Belgian, Spanish, Dutch, Danish, Hanoverian, Würtemburg, Baden, and Hesse-Darmstadt representatives.

Their Imperial Majesties were most gracious and affable, expressing their sympathy and interest for Lady Augustus during her late severe illness.

In conversation, I profited of the opportunity to observe that Lord John Russell had expressed to me his satisfaction that Austria and England were perfectly agreed on one point—viz., on their mutual desire to maintain the peace of Europe. His Majesty replied :— "Most certainly; and I trust that there can be no doubt of my wish after the explicit declarations which I have given." I observed that, although the political horizon was somewhat clouded, yet the desire of all the Powers of Europe must be for the maintenance of peace, and that it might be consequently hoped that these clouds would be dispersed.

I ventured to remark to His Majesty that to maintain the peace of Europe no more efficient agency could be employed than the exercise of a moral power and influence, which would be of greater weight than any resort to physical force. To be effectual, this must be the united and unanimous expression of the Governments of Europe, and of public opinion. In the present day no one State could afford to stand up against the united moral influence of Europe. His Majesty fully assented to the justice of this observation.

There is a simplicity, a chivalry, and a dignity about the Emperor which is most attractive, and which cannot fail to win for him the love and respect of his people.

In April, 1860, I was informed by one of my colleagues of an important and interesting conversation he had had with the Marquis de Moustier, the newly-arrived French Ambassador at Vienna.

In referring to the policy of the Emperor Napoleon, the Marquis de Moustier stated that, previous to leaving Paris, he had had a long conversation with His Majesty. The Emperor had observed "that, when residing in

England, he had been struck by the enormous commercial wealth and industry of Great Britain, which was the foundation of her power and prosperity, and that he had often asked himself how it was that France, with equal elements for commercial greatness, still remained far behind England in commercial wealth and activity. His Majesty had at last come to the conclusion that the advantages enjoyed by Great Britain were entirely to be attributed to her insular position, and to the fact that Nature had given her a frontier which did not require, as in France, the maintenance of an enormous military force to protect. The military service in France, independently of the heavy cost for its maintenance, absorbed annually a very large portion of the male population, which could be lucratively devoted to reproductive labour. It was therefore necessary, in His Majesty's opinion, to rectify the frontiers of France in such a manner as to render her secure from attack, and thus enable her to diminish her army and the military expenses.

"The south-western frontier," His Majesty observed, "was fully protected by the natural frontier of the Pyrenees. She had now, on her south-eastern frontier, acquired the Alps as necessary for her safety. The neutrality of Switzerland assured her a safe frontier on the eastern side, and the neutrality of Belgium provided for her security on the north. There only then remained the frontier towards Germany," and His Majesty observed that "the present frontier on this side was imposed on France in 1815 in a spirit of distrust towards her. There were some portions on this frontier which it was necessary for France to acquire, in order to secure her from attack. He referred to the Palatinate, and more especially to the fortress of Landau, and to the Prussian districts of Sarrebruck and Sarre Louis." His Majesty considered that "this rectification of frontier, to satisfy the just exigencies of France, might be effected by means of negotiation and by an amicable understanding, without giving rise to any unnecessary fears of a desire for conquest and aggression. It was," said His Majesty, " in the interest of all Europe to satisfy the just wishes of France, as it would then enable France to disarm, and consequently all other countries, which were now keeping up large armies far beyond their means, would be equally enabled to reduce their military establishments."

The Emperor Napoleon disclaimed any intentions of aggrandisement or conquest. "If," said His Majesty, " France were to go to Mayence, she would also wish to go to Coblentz, and from thence to Cologne, and if once at Cologne, she would be further obliged to go to the Zuyder Zee, which would be committing over again the faults of the First Empire." His Majesty entertained no such ideas, but he wished to restore to France those frontiers which would enable her to feel secure and to disarm and to diminish her military budget. If this rectification of her frontier towards Germany were obtained, His Majesty did not see why France should require a standing army much larger than that of Great Britain.

This remarkable conversation was, some years later, verified by the proposals submitted by M. Benedetti to the Prussian Government in 1866; but the moderate intentions of the Emperor were not verified in the same degree, as he then claimed Mayence.

At this time the sudden resignation and death of Baron Bruck, the Finance Minister, caused great sensation at Vienna, following so closely on the suicide of General Eynatten, the Chief of the Commissariat Department during the late war, who was responsible for large defalcations in the administration of his department. It was first reported that Baron Bruck had died of apoplexy, but it was subsequently known that he had committed suicide. I was personally acquainted with him, and always found him very agreeable and obliging in any matters of business I had to transact. He was clever and an able financier, and was highly respected at Trieste, the city of his birth.

The European Congress to arrange the position of Central Italy, which had been convoked for the month of January, was indefinitely postponed to permit time for negotiations between France and Rome, which would enable the Pope to be represented at the Congress, as, since the publication of the pamphlet "Le Pape et le Congrès," it was evident that the Pope would not take part in the Congress unless he was previously assured that his rights and the integrity of his dominions would be respected.

I inquired of Count Rechberg whether the Congress would take place if the Pope declined to take part in it?

He replied that it might do so, provided that no question should be discussed relating to the affairs of the Papal States, as, by the Protocol of the Treaty of Aix-la-Chapelle, no affairs of an independent State could be treated in Congress unless the Sovereign of that State were represented at it; but in the present instance, as the object of the Congress was to provide for the stability of Central Italy, he did not well see how that object could be attained without the participation of the Pope. I gathered from his general observations that the Imperial Government would be entirely guided in their action by that taken by the Pope. They would follow in his wake without assuming a prominent position or placing themselves in the front rank.

The result was that the Pope refused to be represented at the Congress, and the Congress finally collapsed.

During the early part of the year the question of the annexation of Savoy and Nice by France occupied the attention of the European Governments.

The Emperor Napoleon had agreed to consult the Powers signatories of the Treaty of Vienna in 1815, on the subject of placing the 92nd Article of that Treaty in harmony with the 2nd article of the Treaty of Zürich. It was even proposed that negotiations should be entered into with the several Powers concerned in regard to the maintenance by France of the obligations incurred by Sardinia for the neutrality of Savoy, and that a Congress should then meet to record the agreement entered into, thus giving it a legal validity.

· The idea of this Congress was generally accepted, and the annexation, if assented to, would thus have become part of the public law of Europe.

I confess that I could never quite understand why Lord John Russell ever assented to any Congress. The Congress was simply to confirm the Treaty of Zürich, without any power to discuss it, and on the basis of that Treaty it was evident that no understanding between the Powers was possible. The Congress would have to treat of the affairs of Central Italy, and how could Lord John have harmonised his views for a united Italy with the terms of the Treaty of Zürich? France, on the other hand, was in favour of forming the Grand Duchy of Tuscany, with an extended territory, into a separate State—a kingdom of Etruria (said to have been intended for Prince Napoleon). Then again, in regard to the annexation of Savoy and Nice, the majority of the Powers would not have opposed it, and we should have been placed in the disagreeable alternative of having to ratify the annexation—which we thoroughly disapproved on principle—or of retiring from the Congress. As matters now stand, neither the Treaty of Zürich nor the Convention of the 29th March, ceding Savoy and Nice to France, form part of the public law of Europe.

On the collapse of the Congress, the Emperor Napoleon, foreseeing the inevitable unity of Italy in virtue of the popular will, and fearing that, if further delayed, serious difficulties might arise in regard to the cession of Savoy and Nice, hastened to exact from

Sardinia the fulfilment of her engagement, for which cession he assented to the entry of the Sardinian troops into Tuscany and the Duchies, and their annexation to Sardinia. Although he was much opposed to their absorption by Sardinia, he felt he was powerless to oppose it, and he abandoned all schemes of a kingdom of Etruria for Prince Napoleon and the possible restoration to Naples of the Murat family. It is true that a proposal was made by the French Government to act with Her Majesty's Government to prevent Garibaldi from crossing with his band from Sicily to the Neapolitan territory, but it was absolutely declined by Lord John Russell, as being opposed to the principle of non-intervention.

Under all these circumstances, the Emperor Napoleon claimed the fulfilment of the engagement taken by Sardinia, and a Treaty was signed by France and Sardinia on the 24th of March at Turin, ceding to France the "cradle of the house of Savoy," with the district of Nice.

At this time I received communication of a letter written to an influential person at Vienna from Paris, with the assurance that the information given was from an authentic source. It was as follows:—

"PARIS: LE 20 MARS, 1860.

"Monsieur Benedetti, Directeur Politique au Ministère des Affaires Étrangères, est depuis mercredi soir à Turin. Il a eu déjà deux longues conférences avec le Comte de Cavour, et les arrangements de détail pour notre occupation de la Savoie et du comté de Nice ne sont pas encore terminés. L'Empereur se montre assez impatienté de ces difficultés secondaires et de ces retards.

"Le Cabinet sarde s'oppose à ce qu'aucune troupe française venant de l'intérieur entre en Savoie et à Nice avant que tous les arrangements ne soient terminés. Les troupes venant de la Lombardie seront censées traverser seulement les deux provinces pour entrer en France.

"Les préparatifs de guerre ne cessent d'être pressés avec la plus grande activité par le Piémont. Le Gouvernement français fournit tout ce que le Roi de Sardaigne demande en chevaux, armes, munitions, etc. etc.

"Hier j'avais l'honneur de vous écrire que tous les plans étaient concertés entre l'Empereur et Victor-Emmanuel pour enlever la Vénétie à l'Autriche. L'armée française ne prendra pas l'initiative de la lutte—c'est l'armée italienne qui commencera l'attaque, puis quand l'action sera bien engagée—que les populations de la Vénétie auront été bien excitées, et chercheront à se soulever—que l'opinion publique en Europe aura été chauffée—Napoléon se présentera à l'Autriche comme médiateur, lui exposera l'impossibilité de conserver la Vénétie, et mettra le Cabinet de Vienne en demeure d'abandonner cette province en échange de certaines compensations sur le Danube. Pour préparer cette solution, des agents sont envoyés dans le Levant afin de hâter dans les provinces chrétiennes de la Turquie des événements qui puissent coincider avec ceux qui vont éclater en Italie.

"La semaine dernière un de ces agents bien connus qui a pris une part active à toutes les intrigues Napoléoniennes dans les provinces danubiennes, a quitté Paris pour se rendre dans la Servie, la Bosnie, l'Albanie, etc. Dans les plans attribués à l'Empereur, Venise ne serait pas donné au Piémont, et deviendrait une ville anséatique.

"L'entourage intime ne cesse pas d'affirmer que la guerre est toujours dans la pensée de l'Empereur." *

* Translation.—" Monsieur Benedetti, Political Director of the Ministry for Foreign Affairs, has been at Turin since Wednesday evening. He has already had two long conferences with Count Cavour, and the arrangements of detail for our occupation of Savoy and the county of Nice are not yet concluded. The Emperor is very impatient on account of these minor difficulties and of these delays.

"The Sardinian Cabinet is opposed to any French troops coming from the interior entering Savoy and Nice before all the arrangements are concluded. The troops coming from Lombardy will be considered as only crossing the two provinces to enter France.

"The preparations for war are unceasingly carried on with great activity by Piedmont. The French Government furnishes everything asked by the King of Sardinia in horses, arms, ammunition, etc. etc.

"Yesterday I had the honour to write to you that the plans were concerted between the Emperor and Victor Emmanuel for wresting Venetia from Austria. The French army will not take the initiative of the combat —it is the Italian army which will commence the attack, then, when the action is well engaged—when the population of Venetia shall be well excited, and will attempt to rise—when public opinion in Europe shall have been heated, Napoleon will present himself to Austria as mediator, will expose to her the impossibility of preserving Venetia, and will call on her to abandon that province in exchange for certain compensation on the Danube. In order to prepare this solution, agents are sent to the Levant to hasten, in the Christian provinces of Turkey, events to coincide with those which are about to take place in Italy.

"Last week one of those agents well known, who took an active part in all the Napoleonic intrigues in the Danubian provinces, left Paris for Servia, Bosnia, Albania, etc. In the plans attributed to the Emperor, Venice would not be given to Piedmont, and would become a Hanseatic town.

"The intimate entourage of the Emperor never cease declaring that war is always in the Emperor's thoughts.".

The negotiations preceding and succeeding the signature of the Convention were protracted, but they are of a curious and interesting nature.

A curious fact is mentioned by Count Beust in his "Memoirs" * which occurred at this time—

"At the moment when the Sardinian troops were preparing to invade the Papal territory and to support the unionist movement, Count Seebach, the Saxon Minister at Paris, suddenly visited Count Beust at Dresden on a secret mission from the Emperor Napoleon, who took this mode of hinting at Vienna (through Count Beust) that if Austria wished to oppose the invasion of the Papal States, he (the Emperor) would not intervene, provided no change was made as to the cession of Lombardy."

The Emperor Napoleon, Count Beust adds, was very fond of making these disclosures through indirect channels. He did not observe his Constitutional oath very strictly, but he was almost always to be depended on in negotiations, and Austria might have obtained guarantees. It might have been a great opportunity for Austria, for the articles of the Treaty of Zürich relating to the Duchies were still in force. "I received," said Count Beust, "for conveying this message a letter of thanks, which did not enter into details."

In regard to the above, I may here state that on January 30, 1860, I wrote to Lord Cowley as follows:—

"Of one thing you may be certain, that Austria has not the remotest intention of interfering by force of arms in Central Italy in behalf of anyone. She is totally unable to enter on any

* "Count Beust's Memoirs," Vol. I., page 20.

such struggle, and she will strictly confine herself to a defence of her own territory. She is quite decided to allow events in Italy to run their course."

The Austrian Government, profiting by past experience, and distrustful of the French policy, wisely paid no attention to these secret suggestions. They clearly perceived that the intention of the Emperor Napoleon was to curb the ambition and arrest the increasing aggrandisement of Sardinia, and that, fearing the opposition of the clerical party in France, he was anxious to prevent the alienation of the States of the Church.

Although Lord John Russell was unsuccessful in his attempts to prevent the annexation of Savoy and Nice, he was fully consoled by the success of his Italian policy, which finally resulted in the unity of Italy under Victor Emanuel, and in the realisation of the hopes of a liberal and constitutional Government under an enlightened Sovereign. "*Italia fara de se*" was the watchword, and it was patriotically carried out.

Before leaving Vienna for Coburg I had a long conversation with Count Rechberg, being desirous of learning his views and reporting them to Lord John Russell on various questions then engaging the attention of Europe.

Count Rechberg told me that he had received information confirming the report which had been for some time current at Constantinople that the Grand Vizier was to be recalled, and that on his return the present law of succession to the throne would be changed by which the Sultan's eldest son, and not his brother, would succeed him.

Count Rechberg was opposed to this change, fearing that it would produce disunion and discontent among the Turks, and eventually give rise to a struggle for the throne on the death of the present Sultan. It was in opposition to the Koran, and would certainly meet with strong opposition from the old Turks, for that same law ruled the whole Turkish social system.

I inquired of Count Rechberg whether he thought that Turkey would be benefited if Moldavia and Wallachia were to have their complete independence.

Count Rechberg expressed his entire objection to any separation of these provinces from Turkey, observing that the integrity of the Ottoman Empire would be thereby gravely violated, and that the precedent would affect the loyalty of all the other Christian provinces. In his opinion, the true policy was to maintain that integrity as long as possible. For Austria this was a vital question. She had a large Wallach and Rouman population, and these two races had in all times and difficulties remained loyal to the Imperial crown. No instance was on record of their insurging against Austria.

In referring to passing events in Italy, Count Rechberg said that he was sorry to see, by a despatch addressed by Lord John Russell to Sir T. Hudson which had been published, that he agreed with the Government of France in considering that, however aggressive might be the conduct of Sardinia towards

Austria, and however unfavourable to Sardinia the fate of arms might be, Lombardy should still remain attached to Piedmont. He considered this condition as a premium for wanton attack on the part of Sardinia, for she might gain Venetia, but could not lose Lombardy.

Lord John Russell, in answer to the memorandum I had placed in his hands, gave me a memorandum containing his replies, which, on my return to Vienna, I read to Count Rechberg, and of which the following is a copy:—

"The British Government agrees with Count Rechberg that an attempt to alter the law of succession in Turkey would meet with great opposition on the part of the Turks, and might even give rise to civil war. The Grand Vizier, since the project was first mentioned, has been recalled to Constantinople. It is to be hoped that he will be adverse to the project. At all events, Sir Henry Bulwer would be instructed to act in concert with the Austrian Internuncio in opposition to any change in the law of succession.

"Her Majesty's Government agrees with Count Rechberg that the Danubian provinces, if detached from Turkey, would establish a precedent tending to encourage disaffection in the other provinces. They entirely agree with Count Rechberg that the true policy is to maintain the integrity of the Ottoman Empire as long as possible."

In regard to Italy, Lord John Russell said "that Count Rechberg is mistaken in supposing that the British Government concurs with that of France respecting the fate of Lombardy in case of war. But they consider that the French Government would be supported by the national feeling of France in resisting the abrogation of the engagements of Zürich, which gave Lombardy to Piedmont, and which were the result and the trophy of French military successes. It would be, therefore, wise in Austria, in case of war with Sardinia, whatever might be the advantage of Austria in repelling an Italian aggression, not to bring France into the field by demanding the cession of Lombardy as the price of peace. It is to be hoped, however, that, for the present, the King of Sardinia will not make a wanton and causeless attack on Venetia.

"This respite should be employed by Austria in revising her whole system in regard to her Italian subjects. The Austrian Government has hitherto seemed to think that they could get rid of a truth by concealing and overlooking it. They should now look the real state of affairs in the face. If they do so, they will perceive that where a Treaty is confirmed by national feeling and opinion, it is easily upheld and maintained; but where it has no such sanction, it is like a decayed tree, that only waits for a gust of wind to be overthrown. Thus the Treaty of 1815, which secures the independence of Switzerland, is confirmed by the attachment of the Swiss people to their liberty and the integrity of their territory. Thus the Treaty of 1831, respecting Belgium, is strengthened and sanctioned by the attachment of the people of Belgium to their nationality, their King, and their institutions. It may be disagreeable to Austrian statesmen to remark the contrast which these facts present to the state of Italy, but the lesson is a useful one. The authority of the Pope, that of the Grand Duke of Tuscany, and, lastly, that of the King of Naples, having no root in the affections of their subjects, those Governments have fallen before the first blast.

"It is worth while for the Austrian Government to reflect on the position of Genoa and Venice.

"In 1815 one of these cities was given to Sardinia, the other to Austria. But while the annexation of Venice to Austria encountered little opposition, either from within or without, that of Genoa to Sardinia was strongly opposed. The ancient independence of the Genoese Republic, the principles of public law, the violent antipathy existing between the Genoese and Piedmontese, were urged in Liguria and invoked in the British Parliament as conclusive reasons against this union. But at the end of forty-five years what do we find? The dominion of Austria in Venice is precarious and unpopular, while the union of Genoa and Turin is cemented and confirmed.

"If we look for the reason of this instructive example, we shall find that, while the Austrian Government has done everything to depress, to irritate, and to humble the national feeling, the Piedmontese Government, on the other hand, has done everything to cherish, to flatter, and to exalt it.

"Something of the same policy may be observed in regard to Hungary. The aim of Prince Schwartzenberg was to centralise and to Germanise the Hungarian administration. How ill he succeeded the debates in the Reichsrath abundantly show.

"It would savour of the presumption of ignorance if the British Government were to attempt to point out the measures by which Hungary and Venetia might be made the strength, and not the weakness, of the Austrian Monarchy. But the most superficial observation enables them to see that it is by contempt and disregard of national feeling that the affection of Hungary and Venetia have been alienated, and they naturally conclude that by regard and respect for those national feelings a way may be found for regaining those estranged affections. Nor would the British Government say even thus much, were they not deeply convinced that the maintenance of the Austrian Monarchy is so bound up with European interests, and so conducive to the continuance of European peace, that they ought not to neglect any opportunity for urging on Austrian statesmen considerations which, in their opinion, belong to her peace, her prosperity, and even to her safety."

During 1860 there were three meetings of Sovereigns which engaged the attention of public opinion, and caused some sensation in Europe. The first and most notable one was that of the Emperor Napoleon with the Prince Regent of Prussia, which took place at Baden-Baden in June. The cession of Savoy and Nice to France had caused a feeling of alarm and distrust of France throughout Europe, and, coupled with the rumours in circulation of the wish of the Emperor Napoleon to obtain the left bank of the Rhine, had roused the fear and suspicion of the German nation. Another pamphlet had lately made its appearance at Paris, entitled "L'Empereur et la Prusse," supposed to have emanated from the same pen as that of "Le Pape et le Congrès," and it expressed similar views in regard to territorial changes. It was to allay these fears and the distrust of his policy that the Emperor Napoleon sought an interview with the Prince Regent of Prussia, in the hope of restoring confidence in his policy, and possibly also of coming to an amicable arrangement. But the Regent on this occasion was not alone. He was supported by the Kings of Hanover and Saxony and other German Sovereigns. The meeting, therefore, bore the character of a German political demonstration in favour of the integrity of the German territory. The Emperor Napoleon, surprised at finding himself in such a conclave of German Sovereigns, all united in maintaining the integrity of the German Fatherland, confined himself to reassuring them in regard to his pacific policy and denying *in toto* any intention on his part of extending his frontiers. But his aspirations for the aggrandisement of France, although greatly damped by this meeting, were not extinguished; they lay dormant for a time, but were resuscitated on various occasions and in various forms in 1866.

In July a meeting of the Emperor of Austria with the Prince Regent of Prussia took place at Toeplitz.

In the reply to the letter of the Emperor of Austria to the Prince Regent informing him of the details of his meeting with the Emperor Napoleon, the Emperor had expressed a wish to have a personal interview with his Royal Highness, leaving it to the Regent to name the place of meeting and the date which would best suit his convenience. The Regent accepted the proposal without hesitation, and immediately proposed Toeplitz as the most convenient place for both Sovereigns.

The Emperor of Austria left Vienna, attended by Count Rechberg and General Count Crenneville, for Toeplitz on the 26th of July. On his return, His Majesty visited the King of Saxony at Pillnitz, the Emperor Ferdinand (his uncle) at Reichenberg, and the King of Bavaria at Graeffenberg.

Count Rechberg attending His Majesty with M. Bigeleben, the Director of the German section of the Imperial Ministry for Foreign Affairs, gave rise to the opinion, on the part of the German public, that matters of great political interest were to be treated, but Count Rechberg informed me that it was not intended to revert to those minor questions of federal policy on which there had been a difference of opinion between the two great German Powers. On the present occasion, he said, the chief object was to restore cordial relations by means of a personal interview, and to lay the foundation of a thorough understanding between the two Cabinets on matters of general European policy.

I learnt subsequently that friendly assurances had been exchanged, but no engagement of a binding character had been taken. In the event of a common danger—such as an attack on Germany—community of action between the two Powers was agreed upon, but it was specially provided that, should Austria take the offensive without previous arrangement with Prussia, the assistance of Prussia could not be claimed.

The meeting itself had a salutary effect on Europe, as proving the solidarity of the two Powers for the defence of German interests and of German territory.

The third meeting of Sovereigns took place between the Emperor of Austria, the Emperor of Russia, and the Prince Regent of Prussia at Warsaw in October. I had some conversation with Count Rechberg in regard to this meeting. He expressed a great wish for a meeting between Her Majesty the Queen and the Emperor of Austria, for he said that "*Il tenait à cœur de donner par un acte le plus formel que la plus parfaite entente existait entre les deux pays.*"

He begged me to inform Lord John Russell that there was no engagement taken by Austria, and that the only object of Austria was "*De sortir de cet isolement et d'entretenir les meilleures relations avec toutes les Puissances.*" Mention had been made of diplomatic negotiations which had preceded the arranged meeting at Warsaw. Nothing of the kind, said Count Rechberg, had occurred. The simple facts were that Count Thun, the Austrian Minister at St. Petersburg, was told by Prince Gortschakoff that it was desirable, in the present state of European affairs, that there should exist a good understanding between Russia and Austria, and that the Emperor of Russia would be happy to meet the Emperor of Austria in fulfilment of this aim. Count

Thun telegraphed this message, and Count Rechberg communicated it to his Sovereign. The Emperor Franz Josef thereupon informed the Russian Minister at his Court that he should be happy to meet the Emperor of Russia, and that it would give him great pleasure to renew their former relations. A formal invitation was then addressed to the Emperor of Austria, and the place of meeting and date were arranged. This was all that had passed.

Of course, nothing could be known of the subjects discussed between the two Sovereigns, or at the secret councils of their Ministers, but I believe that the result mainly consisted in a perfect reconciliation and the renewal of the former friendly relations between Austria and Russia. The meeting passed off successfully, and produced a satisfactory effect in Europe, as proving the entire reconciliation between the two Sovereigns.

In the meantime events had rapidly progressed in Italy. Garibaldi, with a handful of men, left Genoa, landed at Palermo, and was enthusiastically received by the whole population. After taking complete possession of Sicily, he crossed with his band of followers into Calabria, and finally entered Naples without opposition on the 7th of September.

The King of Naples had fled to Gaeta with a portion of his army, with the determination to defend it to the last. The siege lasted for some months, but when the French fleet, which the Emperor Napoleon, with feelings of chivalry and compassion for the misfortunes of the King of Naples and his family, and for their protection, had sent to Gaeta, was withdrawn, the King of Naples, to prevent further bloodshed, surrendered the fortress and withdrew to Rome. Thus ended the reign of the Bourbon family over Naples, and Garibaldi placed the crown at the feet of Victor Emmanuel.

Garibaldi then threatened to march to Rome, and, having gained possession of that city as the capital of Italy—of the success of which undertaking he felt very confident—his intention was to attack Venetia, and thus to complete the union of Italy under the sovereignty of Victor Emmanuel. He was dissuaded from this foolhardy enterprise by the King of Sardinia. He then retired from the scene of his conquests to his Island of Caprera, having previously addressed an inflammatory appeal to his followers.* Sir Henry Elliott reported his departure to Lord John in the following terms :—

"NAPLES : Nov. 9, 1860.

"General Garibaldi left Naples this morning, and has retired to his Island of Caprera, carrying with him the personal respect and admiration even of those most opposed to his projects and loudest in their denunciations of the lawlessness of his enterprise; for although the corruption which has prevailed in every branch of the administration during his Dictatorship has far surpassed anything that was known even in the corrupt times which preceded it, he himself has to the last remained free from a suspicion of having shared in the plunder.

"After several months of the exercise of absolute

* See Appendix.

Dictatorship over Sicily and Naples, he is known to have been forced to borrow a few pounds to defray some trifling debts, and, refusing all honours and emoluments from his Sovereign, he has retired to his island, where he lives in a style but one degree above that of an ordinary peasant.

"A general opinion prevails that he has not received at the hands of King Victor Emanuel the consideration that his great services seemed to entitle him to, and this is said to have caused serious dissatisfaction among some classes of the population of Naples.

"I understand, however, that His Majesty has expressed his sense of his services in the most handsome language, and would willingly have conferred upon him the highest honours in the gift of the Crown; but, nevertheless, his Ministers and advisers cannot be entirely acquitted of a want of consideration or generosity, and there is no doubt that, after having bestowed two kingdoms upon his Sovereign, General Garibaldi's last days at Naples have been embittered by the sense of neglect and ingratitude."

No more honourable testimony could be borne of the pure and disinterested character of Garibaldi than the foregoing report of Sir Henry Elliott.

On the 11th of September the Sardinian troops entered and occupied Umbria and the Marches, the Emperor Napoleon having withdrawn his opposition to this measure on the conclusion of the Convention ceding Savoy and Nice to France.

Thus, towards the close of 1860, the unity of Italy

under Victor Emmanuel from the Alps to the Straits of Messina, and including Sicily, had been effected by the free and popular will, almost without bloodshed, and Victor Emmanuel assumed the title of King of Italy.

In the Grand Duchy of Tuscany and the Duchies a plebiscite was taken, with an enormous majority in favour of annexation to Sardinia.

A plebiscite was also resorted to in Savoy and Nice. Lord John Russell, writing to me, termed it a "farce." He said: "Persigny stated that it was got up to please us, but we are neither entertained nor edified by the spectacle."

CHAPTER V.

Baron Stockmar—Creation of an Embassy at Vienna—Appointment of Lord Bloomfield as Ambassador—My Transfer to Berlin—Arrival at Vienna of Irish enlisted for Papal Army—Some Hundreds passed through Vienna, totally destitute and penniless—Expenses of their Return to their Homes defrayed by the Papal Government—Request for a British Steamer to convey the Empress to Madeira—*Victoria and Albert* placed by the Queen at Her Majesty's Disposal —Reforms and Reorganisation of the Empire—National Debt and Finances of Austria—Hungarian Question—Death of Baron Tosika and Count Szechenyi—Audience of the Emperor to deliver Letter of Recall—Offer of Grand Cross of Leopold declined—Baron Anselm Rothschild—Departure from Vienna.

I HAD the great pleasure to see at Coburg—alas! for the last time—that distinguished, pure-minded statesman and thorough patriot, Baron Stockmar. I found him much aged, and depressed in regard to the affairs of Germany and of Europe in general. But he was calm as ever, and fully prepared, if not anxious, to change the cares and sorrows of this world for a better.

He was a wise counsellor, and gifted with sound judgment and a remarkable foresight into the future, with a serenity of mind that was never discomposed. He died shortly afterwards, and descended to the grave full of years and honours, amid the sincere respect and love of a large circle of friends and admirers.

Before leaving Coburg on my return to Vienna I had some conversation with Lord John Russell on our commercial relations with Austria, and I received his instructions in regard to negotiating a commercial treaty between England and Austria. He could only then speak in general terms, but he instructed me not to enter on the subject with the Austrian Government until the pending commercial treaty with France was concluded, when he would send me special and detailed instructions. He also asked me whether I should require a specialist from the Board of Trade to assist me. I replied that I thought it would be better to defer this assistance until the negotiations had reached that stage when technical knowledge was required.

A few days after my return I was surprised to receive the following letter, dated Pembroke Lodge, October 24, 1860, from Lord John Russell :—

"I write to prepare you for a change of post.

"With the Queen's approbation I shall write presently a private letter to Count Rechberg to propose to him that the Mission at Vienna should be raised to the rank of an Embassy. If this overture is well received by the Emperor, I think it right to recommend to the Queen that Lord Bloomfield, for his long and good service, should be offered the Embassy at Vienna.

"In case of his acceptance, I shall propose to the Queen that you should be her Minister at Berlin.

"I trust you will see in these arrangements every desire to consult what is due to the Queen's Diplomatic Service, and to provide for the continuance of your honourable career in public employment.

"I remain,

"Yours very faithfully,

"J. RUSSELL.

"The Lord A. Loftus."

The cause of this sudden change was that the relations between England and Prussia had become very strained in consequence of an unfortunate incident that had occurred at Cologne—Mr. Macdonald, a member of the Queen's household, had come into collision with the railway and police authorities, and had been roughly treated by them. In Prussia the authorities are always deemed to be in the right and to be incapable of doing wrong. The case was taken up by the English Government, and justice was claimed, but without any result. An angry correspondence took place. Lord Palmerston—who, during the absence of Lord John Russell with the Queen, was administering the Foreign Office—acting on his principle of *Civis Romanus sum*, proposed to Lord John, then staying at Coblentz, extreme measures. These proposals of Lord Palmerston reached Lord John Russell when the Queen and Prince Consort were staying at Coblentz with the Prince Regent and Princess of Prussia. To terminate this disagreeable affair, Lord John Russell proposed a change in the Mission at Berlin by the restoration of the Embassy at Vienna and by the appointment of Lord Bloomfield as the Ambassador there, and I was graciously appointed to the Mission at Berlin to restore harmonious relations with Prussia. This was happily achieved, and all reminiscences of this regrettable incident were obliterated. I was sorry to leave Vienna, but I felt that the affairs there could not be entrusted to better hands than to those of Lord Bloomfield.

In May there arrived at Vienna a batch of Irishmen

who had been enlisted by Papal agents, and were on their way to join the Papal army at Ancona. Two of them called at the Legation to complain of the act of the Papal agents, who had induced them, under false pretences (as they said), to join a party about to emigrate to Italy, and to express their wish, in consequence of the ill-treatment they had received, to return to their native country.

They were supplied with Papal passports, and being penniless, they applied to me for means to reach their homes. They positively declared that they were never informed that it was the object of the party who engaged their services to enrol them as soldiers for the Pope, but they conceived that they were to be employed in Italy in their several trades, when they hoped to better their position by the receipt of higher wages.

They informed me also that there were many of those engaged who had proceeded to Trieste, anxious to leave this motley band, and one of them stated that on his return to Ireland he would address a letter to the Press to caution his countrymen against being entrapped in a similar way. One of them—James McGarel—came to me on the following day to say that his companion, on receiving some money, had been induced to remain with the corps, consisting of above a hundred Irishmen; but he (McGarel) maintained his resolution of leaving it, and that nothing would induce him to rejoin it. No opposition was made to his leaving by the leaders, who told him that he was free to act as he chose. I consequently defrayed his expenses to Leipzig, and notified the circumstances of his case to Her Majesty's Consul-General at that town.

The Vice-Consul at Trieste a few days afterwards informed me of the arrival there of the first detachment of this Irish Papal brigade. Many of them evinced a great disinclination to proceed to their destination, and although no active compulsion appears to have been resorted to, they were taken before the police, and reminded of the oath they had taken, and informed that they were bound to abide by it. Partly under intimidation and partly by persuasion they were induced to embark.

On my suggestion, a gunboat was sent by the Admiral to Trieste to support Her Majesty's Vice-Consul in the event of British subjects, similarly circumstanced, appealing to him for protection, and also for the purpose of preserving order among the Irishmen themselves. Some hundreds passed through Trieste; and Paddy, with a blackthorn in his hand (for they were all armed with this weapon) and somewhat exhilarated by the "Mountain Dew," is an ugly customer—as was subsequently proved in June, when serious disturbances took place among the Irish at Ancona.

In June seven more Irishmen arrived at Vienna from Ancona. I applied for instructions how to act. These men, having violated the law by their enlistment in foreign service, had no claim on Her Majesty's Government, but they were utterly destitute, and could not be allowed to starve. I received instructions to assist them; but, foreseeing that several hundreds more would arrive from Italy under similar circumstances, and that the cost of their relief would fall heavily on Her Majesty's Government, I decided to take steps to render those persons who had engaged their services responsible for their return expenses to their homes. I therefore consulted Dr. Winnewarter, the legal adviser of Her Majesty's Legation, as to whether the agent who was acting for the Papal Government or, in his absence, the Nuncio who was the representative of the Papal Government, could not, by Austrian law, be legally called upon to provide for their return to their homes, they having been induced to emigrate under false pretences, and being provided with passports issued by the authority of the Papal Government. I instructed Dr. Winnewarter to act simply as the legal adviser of these emigrants, and not in any way as in connection with Her Majesty's Legation.

The result of Dr. Winnewarter's proceedings was that, after a consultation with Count Rechberg and the Papal Nuncio, the agent who had charge of these Irishmen undertook to defray their expenses forthwith to Ireland *viâ* Hamburg. The seven men returned to the Legation to express their thanks and gratitude for the successful efforts I had made in their behalf.

The precedent was a happy one, for within a short time a fresh shoal of these Irish emigrants reached Vienna. On returning to my house one afternoon, I found the whole street lined with them, evidently from the West of Ireland, with long frieze coats, breeches with no buttons on them, and very unquestionable Irish brogues and the usual blackthorn. They were waiting to see me. They sent a deputation to me to ask for assistance. I told them that, having violated the English law by enlistment in a foreign service, they had no claim on Her Majesty's Government, but that I would refer them to Dr. Winnewarter, who would take their cause in hand. As in the previous cases, application being made to the Nuncio, he defrayed their expenses to Ireland *viâ* Hamburg.

After the battle of Macerata most of the Irish left the Papal service. Several hundreds arrived at Vienna in a state of destitution, and were forwarded to Ireland by the Nuncio, thus saving several thousand pounds to Her Majesty's Government.

On the 29th of October Count Rechberg called on me, by the Emperor's order, to say that the health of the Empress rendered it necessary for Her Majesty to pass the winter in a warmer climate, and requested me to sound Her Majesty's Government whether—as at this moment the Austrian navy was required for home service—they would place at her disposal a steamer to convey Her Majesty to Madeira. The Empress's suite would be composed of three gentlemen, three ladies, and twenty-three servants. The Empress had been suffering for some time from a cough which had lately increased, and it was feared that her lungs were affected. Her Majesty would embark at Antwerp on the 20th of February, and would travel in the strictest *incognito*.

Baron Koller, who was administering the Foreign Department in the absence of Count Rechberg, was charged by the Emperor to request me to convey to the Queen his grateful thanks for the facilities which Her Majesty had so graciously afforded for the Empress's voyage, and for the kind solicitude which Her Majesty had evinced in her behalf.

The Queen had graciously placed her own yacht, the *Victoria and Albert*, at the Empress's disposal, and the *Osborne* was to accompany the *Victoria and Albert* as escort with her servants and baggage, which was of great bulk.

The Empress, before her departure, was graciously pleased to receive Lady Augustus and myself at Schönbrunn, when Her Majesty charged me to convey her grateful thanks to the Queen for Her Majesty's kind interest and solicitude, and for the facilities which Her Majesty had so graciously afforded for her voyage to Madeira.

The reorganisation of the Empire, and the reforms of the internal administration, proceeded slowly; but it was a work of great labour, from the heterogeneous nature of the laws in the several provinces of which the Empire was composed, each of which enjoyed local rights and privileges.

I will now give cursorily some of the reforms which were introduced; I will also refer to the measures proposed by the Government to effect a reconciliation with Hungary, and to solve the existing difficulties with that kingdom.

An Imperial edict was issued at the commencement of 1860 for the future regulation of "Guilds and Trades." This law had been anxiously expected by the nation, by whom it was received with great satisfaction. It abolished all the restrictions which had so grievously retarded the advancement of wealth and industry, and which had stifled the development of commercial energy. So great were the difficulties and annoyances caused by the old system in regard to all branches of trade, that it amounted to a system of monopoly, the depressing effect of which was equally felt in every branch of industry. It not only deadened and crushed the rising ingenuity and activity of the artisan, but it thwarted all healthy competition, and completely checked the useful application of scientific improvements and inventions. In April, 1860, an Imperial decree was published annulling the provisions of the Civil Code, according to which a foreigner who entered on a trade the pursuit of which rendered necessary a permanent residence in the country was obliged to acquire the character of an Austrian subject.

By removing the barriers which had hitherto obstructed the path of industry, a spirit of enterprise would, it was hoped, be awakened, which would give fresh impetus to trade, and stimulate the commercial and trading classes to increased energy and activity. By this wise reform the wealth and prosperity of the Empire would be promoted, and their concomitants, contentment and happiness, assured.

The next reform to which I will cursorily allude

was an Imperial decree, published in January, 1860, removing certain disabilities of the Jews. By this edict all persons not professing the Christian faith were permitted to give evidence in legal transactions, from which hitherto they had been excluded; and the testimony of Jews would hereafter be received on the same footing as that of their Christian brethren.

Members of the Jewish persuasion would also no longer be debarred from the exercise of certain legal functions, such as public notaries, etc. etc. Great opposition was raised by the Cardinal Archbishop of Vienna and the Clerical party to this measure on religious grounds, but the Imperial Cabinet carried their point with the Emperor, and the Imperial edict was published.

Two Ministerial decrees were published shortly afterwards, removing the restrictions which had hitherto prevented members of the Jewish persuasion from exercising certain trades and professions, and also granting them the right of residence in certain parts of the empire from which they had been hitherto excluded.

Two Imperial edicts were further published in February according to members of the Jewish persuasion the right of acquiring and holding land and real property in certain provinces of the empire. These edicts were not applicable to the provinces of Upper Austria, the Tyrol, Illyria, Carinthia, and Carniola, where the Jews were hitherto prohibited from settling.

A separate edict was published for the Provinces of Galicia, the Bukovine, and the Grand Duchy of Cracow, the object of which was to prevent the transfer of land in those provinces (much of which was mortgaged to the Jews) into the hands of a class who would not themselves become the cultivators of the soil, but would sublet, and thereby introduce a system which would ultimately impoverish the land and retard the improvement of agriculture.

In March an Imperial patent was issued, by virtue of which the existing Council of the Empire was transformed into a consultative body, and considerably enlarged and reformed by the increase of thirty-eight members, who were to be elected by the representatives of each provincial State, in addition to the nomination of other members by the Crown—the former to be elected for the period of six years, the latter to be named for life. This enlarged Council, which would consist of about seventy-six members, and which would be periodically convoked, was to meet at Vienna. They would not possess the right of initiating measures or projecting new laws, but they would be permitted a free discussion and expression of their opinions on the subjects submitted to them.*

Great difficulty and trouble had been experienced in framing this measure in consequence of the difference of privileges and systems existing in the several provinces of the empire. This Imperial patent thus gave proof of the intention of the Imperial Government to re-

* This was the dawn of constitutional government in Austria, and the Reichsrath has now become an important representative and legislative body.—Feb., 1892.

suscitate the provincial States, which had not been convoked for some time, and had been in abeyance.

This measure had been so long delayed, and so anxiously expected, that the hopes anticipated by those who looked for a more general representative system were somewhat disappointed; but at the same time it was regarded as the beginning of a constitutional system, and, consequently, of good omen.

The door, which had hitherto been closed to any species of representative system, was now opened, and, it was hoped, would gradually lead to a further development in a spirit of liberal progress.

The National Debt of the Austrian Empire, according to the Report presented to the Emperor by the Commission appointed to examine this subject, amounted in July, 1860, to 2,268,074,532 florins—about 220 millions sterling. This did not include the Lombardo-Venetian Debt, of which Sardinia had to pay three-fifths, nor the feudal charges on land (termed " Grund-entlastungs-schuld ").

The annual interest payable on the National Debt was computed at that time at 99,465,947 florins—or near ten millions sterling—of which forty millions of florins were payable in silver. I may here state that the financial embarrassments to which the State had been reduced may be attributed to the following causes: —(1) To the enormous, and even reckless, expenditure for the army and for military purposes since 1848. This expenditure has been doubly ruinous to the State. Independently of the vast sums required for its maintenance, the loss to the country of so many thousands of useful hands, which might otherwise have been devoted to reproductive labour, must be taken into consideration.

(2) Since the adoption of the system of centralisation a large increase has taken place in the number of officials in all the departments of the State, and I may add that the cost of collecting the revenue is unusually high in Austria.

(3) A very heavy annual expense is occasioned by having to remit in silver the interest due on the National Debt held in foreign countries. This additional cost may be computed at thirty per cent. on forty millions of florins.

(4) The financial difficulties were greatly enhanced by the absence of credit abroad, and the want of public confidence at home, under which the State is obliged to pay six or seven per cent. for loans.

(5) The general want of enterprise and of capital so urgently required to bring into cultivation vast tracts of lands now unproductive, neither yielding fruit to man nor income to the State. These lands in part belong to the Church and monastic institutions, in part also to the State—are ill-managed, and in many cases, by ancient privileges, are free from taxation. The want of roads and means of communication prevent any encouragement being given to proprietors to improve their estates.

The loss of Lombardy, and, later, of Venetia, has proved a great saving of expenditure to Austria, as the military budget and the administration of her Italian provinces was very costly. The good relations between Austria and Italy, thus substituting a friend and ally on the Italian frontier in lieu of an enemy, has been a great relief to Austrian finance.

The vast resources of the Austrian Empire are being largely developed, and, with the increased railway communication, if peace is preserved, Austria may be expected in a few years to become a wealthy and prosperous country.

The question of Hungary presented difficulties of adjustment which appeared almost insurmountable from the divergence of opinions between Austria and Hungary.

The Austrian Government took their stand on the assumption that Hungary had forfeited all her rights as an independent kingdom by the rebellion of 1848.

The Hungarians claimed the restoration of their ancient constitution, dating back a thousand years, with all its rights and privileges. Until that was restored, the Hungarians rejected all concessions from Austria, and would accept no law initiated by Austria. Thus the magnates, forming the whole aristocracy of Hungary, were in direct opposition to Austria, and would accept no place or favour from the Emperor.

In February, 1860, a memorial was addressed by the leading Hungarians to the Emperor, in which was given, with great clearness and moderation, the political grievances the Hungarian nation complained of, and in which was laid down the basis on which a perfect agreement and good understanding could be restored between the Imperial Crown and Hungary. The restoration of her Constitution was declared to be the first indispensable condition, and this act of justice was represented as the only means of preventing separatist tendencies. A further condition on the part of the Hungarians was that the Emperor should be crowned at Pesth as King of Hungary.

A numerous deputation—composed of magnates and of civil and clerical members of the various Protestant superintendencies in Hungary—arrived at Vienna in February, and requested an audience of the Emperor, to present a petition in the name of their Protestant brethren, praying His Majesty to withdraw the Imperial patent of the 1st September, 1859, and to permit the Convocation of the Synod, as stipulated by the law of 1791.

His Majesty declined to receive the deputation as a body on the grounds that, on account of the omission of certain forms, it could not be considered as a legally constituted deputation, but was willing to receive each member separately.

To this the deputation replied that they were only empowered by their co-religionists to act as a body, and that, consequently, they could not avail themselves of His Majesty's gracious will to receive them separately.

A committee of six members (three clerical and three civilians) were charged to confer with the Minister of Public Worship, with a view to effect an harmonious understanding between the Imperial Government and the Protestant body of Hungary. The deputation urged that the Hungarian nation claimed the rights and privileges of an ancient law passed in 1791, which could not be abrogated without their consent by an Imperial patent; and that, if they were to renounce this right, they would abandon the strong grounds of legality on which all their rights and privileges were based. They denied the right of the Government to deprive them of their legally acquired privileges, and to substitute for them the "fiat" of an Imperial patent.

The Minister declined to withdraw the patent or to suspend its execution.

I have mentioned the foregoing incident, as it embodies the whole principle of the political question between the Imperial Crown and Hungary. Unless the old Hungarian Constitution were restored in its entirety no final arrangement between Austria and Hungary seemed possible.*

The question of difference in regard to the Imperial patent on the subject of the Protestant Church in Hungary, to which I have previously alluded, was happily solved. The Emperor addressed an autograph letter to General Benedek, Governor of Hungary, in which His Majesty stated that, in consequence of the religious scruples which had induced a portion of his Protestant subjects in Hungary to refuse obedience to the Imperial patent, and as it was his desire to respect those scruples, His Majesty assented to the Convocation of a Conventicle in strict accordance with the law of 1791,

* No final arrangement was come to with Hungary till 1866, when, under the Government of Count Beust, the old Constitution was restored to Hungary, and the Emperor was crowned King of Hungary amid the enthusiastic loyalty and devotion of the nation.

which would take the affairs of the Protestant Church into consideration, and submit to His Majesty for approval their proposals for the convocation of a Synod to deliberate on the future organisation and regulation of the affairs of the Protestant Church.

Although the Imperial patent was neither withdrawn nor suspended, as desired by the deputation, it was virtually placed in abeyance.

A general amnesty was also given for all offences which had taken place against the Imperial patent.

This conciliatory concession of the Emperor produced little or no effect on the Hungarians. No concession, no spirit of conciliation would suffice to satisfy them unless they obtained a complete restitution of their civil and religious rights as enjoyed under their old Constitution. The continued separation of the Woivodine was likewise a grave matter of complaint, and no satisfactory arrangement could be made with Hungary until this portion of the former kingdom was restored to her.

The concessions already made by the Imperial Government, instead of satisfying the Hungarians, only proved a greater incentive to them to persevere in demanding the full measure of their rights.

Baron Eötvös, Baron Väy, and M. Somsich—three of the most influential leaders—respectfully declined the Imperial appointments to the Council of the Empire.

Baron Eötvös declined on the grounds that, having sworn to the Constitution of Hungary when Minister for that country in 1848, he could not conscientiously take office so long as that Constitution was repudiated by the Imperial Government.

Count George Apponyi, with much reluctance and at the earnest request of his Sovereign, accepted a seat in the Imperial Council, but he clearly signified to the Emperor and his Government his intention not to deviate from that political course with regard to Hungary which he had consistently pursued, and that he would be a staunch advocate in the Imperial Council of his country's rights and privileges.

At the opening of the Imperial Council, Count George Apponyi, in a speech of great interest, made use of the term, "Historical rights of Hungary." This could only apply to the *territorial* jurisdiction of Hungary, and would include the Woivodine, Croatia, and the Temeswar Banat, which, in 1849, had been separated from Hungary, and formed into separate provinces. The several members, representatives of those provinces, wished to refute Count G. Apponyi's observation at the next sitting, but were dissuaded from this course by the Archduke President stating that the Imperial Council was intended to produce union and not discord between the several nationalities, and that it was not desirable to raise a discussion which would inevitably give rise to much angry feeling and recrimination.

In 1860 the Hungarian cause suffered a severe loss in the death of two of its boldest and most distinguished advocates. The death of Baron Josika, an indefatigable labourer in the cause of his country, and a man universally respected, was followed by the death, attributed to his own hand, of the celebrated Count Stéphan Széchenyi. It was said that the death of Baron Josika, combined with the recent measure of seizing Count Széchenyi's papers, pressed so heavily on a mind already strained by misfortune, as to induce a fit of temporary insanity which led the distinguished patriot to put an end to his days. These melancholy events cast a gloom on the public generally, and especially on the countrymen of the illustrious men whose deaths I now record.

Count Stéphan Széchenyi, since his conviction of having participated in the Revolution, was permitted to live in a Maison de Santé at Döbling near Vienna. I visited him there with Count Edmond Zichy not many days before the sad catastrophe. I found him in bad health and very dejected. He seemed to despair of his country ever regaining its just rights, and spoke of the past with great sadness. I endeavoured to cheer him, but it was of no avail, for his mind was wrapped in gloom. He offered to send me two dozen of Tokay which had been in his cellar for years. I told him to reserve it for his own use, as it would tend to cheer him and chase away his despondent thoughts. But he said that he should not require it, and he sent it to me the day before his death. I was much shocked and grieved by this tragic event, for I had a great admiration for his noble character and his love for his country. He was a great man, and fascinated everyone with his distinguished, gentle, and winning manners. He was a great patriot, and had spent large sums for the benefit of his country.

The concessions made to Hungary were conceived in a liberal and impartial spirit, but they fell short of the restoration of the old Constitution. The National party repudiated anything in the nature of a concession from Austria which they claimed as a right under the old Hungarian Constitution, which gave to the Kingdom of Hungary absolute power, through the Diet, to govern Hungary distinctly and separately from Austria.

Nevertheless, Count G. Apponyi and others of the National party thought it prudent to accept appointments to the Reichsrath as a means of furthering their views, although some declined.

In regard to the other provinces, statutes were published for the convocation of the provincial States, by which bodies a certain number of members to the Reichsrath were to be elected. Thus the questions of reform progressed but slowly. The great object of the Ministry was to have the Reichsrath completed by the addition of the elected members, looking to it for their future support. At the commencement of December I was summoned to London to confer with Lord John Russell before proceeding to my new post at Berlin. During my stay in England, and when on a visit to Her Majesty the Queen at Windsor Castle, I was honoured by an audience of the Prince Consort, at which Lord Bloomfield, who was to be my successor at Vienna, was present. His Royal Highness was desirous of ascertaining the internal state of the Austrian Empire, and the reception which had been given by the nation to the various measures of reform that had been introduced, more especially as regarded Hungary. I stated to His Royal Highness that the reforms had been conceived in a liberal and impartial spirit, and evinced an anxious wish to meet the exigencies of the times, and to satisfy the just expectations of the people, but that it had been a work of great labour, and that what had been effected could only be regarded as a beginning to be extended and perfected as necessity required. A representative system had been introduced in the form of the Reichsrath, for the first time in the annals of the Austrian Empire, in which the whole empire was represented. This representative body was gradually acquiring the confidence of the nation, and, although in its infancy, had evinced great ability and remarkable power of oratory and debate.

The concessions made to Hungary had been most liberal and judicious, and though not received with satisfaction by the whole National party—who re-claimed the restoration of the old Constitution—yet were accepted by many of the leading politicians of that kingdom in a spirit of conciliation and loyalty. Time was required to prove the great value of the concessions granted, and I did not doubt that, with the political experience gained by all parties, progress in the extension of the representative system would be achieved.

As regarded Hungary, the appointments to the Reichsrath had been most impartial and judicious, the leaders of the National party—who had been the most strenuous opponents to the Government—having been appointed members of the Council. I augured well of that body, considering that it was the basis of a future constitutional system of government.

The Prince took the deepest interest in this question, as he did in the future welfare and prosperity of Austria, and expressed his satisfaction at the information I had given, hoping that the opinions I had expressed would be fully realised.

On my return to Vienna I had an audience of the Emperor of Austria to present the Queen's letter notifying my recall from the post of Envoy Extraordinary and Minister Plenipotentiary to His Majesty.

His Majesty was pleased to receive me on the 19th of January, when I placed in the Emperor's hands the Queen's letter.

His Majesty received me in the most gracious and affable manner. He was pleased to express to me his regret at my departure, and to add that he was fully sensible of the earnestness and sincerity which I had devoted to the maintenance of good relations between the two Courts.

His Majesty expressed to me the high value he set on a cordial understanding with England, and his anxiety that the happy relations now existing between the two countries should ever continue unimpaired.

His Majesty spoke with deep gratitude of the kind solicitude and thoughtful consideration which the Queen had shown towards the Empress on the occasion of Her Majesty's voyage to Madeira.

The Emperor then expressed his satisfaction at the

perfect understanding between England and Austria on Eastern affairs. Their mutual co-operation, His Majesty observed, would be the best surety against the dangers which were threatening the peace and tranquillity of the East.

In referring to my removal to the Court of Berlin, His Majesty took occasion to observe, and with evident marks of satisfaction, that the relations between Austria and Prussia were on the most friendly footing. His Majesty stated that the good understanding had not been confined to official communications. He had received the most cordial and friendly assurances from the lips of the King of Prussia himself, and the Emperor passed a high eulogium on the straightforward, chivalrous, and upright character of His Prussian Majesty.

In reply to the Emperor's inquiries after the health of Her Majesty the Queen, and His Royal Highness the Prince Consort, and the Royal Family, I took the opportunity to state that Her Majesty the Queen and the Prince Consort took the deepest interest in the welfare and happiness of their Imperial Majesties and of the Imperial Family.

On taking leave, His Majesty cordially shook me by the hand, adding his best wishes for my health and happiness.

On repairing to take leave of Count Rechberg, he informed me that he had been specially charged by the Emperor to convey to me his wish to confer on me the Grand Cross of the Imperial Order of Leopold as a mark of his esteem on the termination of my mission.

Count Rechberg was anxious to know whether I should be permitted to accept the honour which His Majesty was desirous of conferring.

I replied at once to Count Rechberg by requesting him to express to the Emperor my respectful and grateful appreciation of His Majesty's favour and gracious intention, but that I was obliged to decline the proposed distinction, as the regulations of the Queen's service did not permit any diplomatic servant of the Crown to accept a foreign decoration. I added that I should value His Majesty's gracious intention as highly as if it had been realised.

The Emperor graciously presented me with his portrait in oils, which I was allowed to accept.

I left Vienna on the 23rd of January, 1861, having dined on the previous night with Baron Anselm Rothschild, with whom I had been on intimate terms, and for whom I had a great regard. The Baron held to giving me a dinner of "adieu," to which he invited Prince Paul Esterhazy and a few personal friends. There never existed a more excellent, charitable, and beneficent couple than Baron and Baroness Anselm Rothschild (the latter died while I was at Vienna), who were highly respected by all classes.

The Baron was gifted with superior judgment and foresight, and was generally consulted by the Government on all financial questions, and he was thoroughly devoted to Austria. He would have been proud and delighted if he had lived to see the high position which his son, Baron Ferdinand, now holds in England.

CHAPTER VI.

Arrival at Berlin—Audiences of the King and Queen—Conflict between the Government and Parliament on Army Reorganisation—Hohenlohe Ministry succeeds Hohenzollern Ministry—Conversation with Baron Schleinitz on Syrian Affairs—Interview with Prince Hohenzollern—Lord Breadalbane's Arrival to invest the King with the Garter : He receives the Black Eagle—Visits to Strelitz, Schwerin, and Dessau—Riots at Warsaw—Polish Question—Recognition of Kingdom of Italy refused—Duel between General Manteuffel and M. Twesten—Attempt on King's Life at Baden—Audience of the King to congratulate His Majesty in the Queen's and Prince Consort's Name on his Escape—Death of Count Cavour—Dinner with Crown Prince and Princess at Potsdam—Conversation with the King on Schleswig-Holstein Question—Military Fête at Potsdam.

ALTHOUGH I quitted Vienna with regret, taking deep interest in the resuscitation of that Empire, where the first seeds of Constitutional Government had just been sown, it gave me great pleasure to return to Berlin, where, as unpaid Attaché and Secretary of Legation, I had passed twelve happy years of my early life, and where I had numerous friends. It was also at a moment of great political interest. It was the commencement of the struggle between the King and the Parliament on the reorganisation of the army and the military budget. At the time of the unfortunate Convention agreed to at Olmütz with Prince Schwartzenberg in 1850, the defective organisation of the army (the existence of which had been confirmed on the occasion of the mobilisation of the Prussian army) had greatly tended to this humiliation. From that time the attention of the Prince of Prussia—a true soldier—had been given to this subject, and the whole military organisation was revised and reorganised under his able administration. The Prince felt that the army was the backbone of Prussia and the monarchy, and he foresaw that at no distant date the issue of the struggle to give Prussia the predominant position in Germany would wholly depend on the army. The First Chamber supported the King, but the Second Chamber, on constitutional grounds, rejected the clause in the budget providing the cost of the reorganisation of the army. The King was firm and resolute in maintaining his military reforms. The Ministers were undaunted by the opposition of the Chamber. It was dissolved twice in 1862 and once in 1863, but on each occasion the opposition to the Government and the Army Bill retained its majority.

The reorganisation of the Prussian army nearly doubled the amount of the standing army by the augmentation of thirty-six regiments of infantry, by an increase of cavalry and of artillery, although in these two latter branches the augmentation was not proportionate to that of the infantry.

This augmentation was computed to increase the military budget by an annual amount of 7,030,000 dollars, or a sum exceeding 1,000,000 sterling.

The military budget with the increased cost was submitted to a Committee of the Lower House, which divided it into two separate portions—viz., the ordinary expenses of the army as existing before the reorganisation, and the extraordinary expenses since the reorganisation.

The former was voted as the normal military expenditure, the latter was only voted for one year, the Lower House thereby reserving to itself the power of an annual revision.

According to the Prussian Constitution, the Lower House has not the power of refusing the supplies or, in other terms, of intervening to prevent the levying of taxes once voted. Consequently, the Government were empowered to levy the taxes that had been, in the previous year, devoted to the army budget without a fresh vote of the Lower House.

On the rejection of the military budget for the reorganisation of the army, the Hohenzollern Ministry resigned. On the retirement of the Hohenzollern-Auerswald Ministry, the *Kreuz Zeitung* humorously remarked that the Auerswald Cabinet was absolutely in the position of a hen which had hatched duck's eggs. Prince Hohenlohe was appointed, by the King, President of the new Ministry. It was a weak Ministry, and not composed of elements strong enough to cope with a recalcitrant Chamber. It was doomed to a short existence, and on the resignation of Prince Hohenlohe in the autumn of 1862, the King placed M. de Bismarck at the head of affairs. He was not a man to be ruled by adverse majorities in the Second Chamber. He was ably supported by General von Roon, and they firmly supported the King in his military measures. The Progressist party had no cognisance of the ulterior views of M. de Bismarck, nor was it possible for him to give those explanations which might have induced the Second Chamber to forego their opposition. The subsequent successes of Prussia in the two campaigns of 1866 and 1870 are entirely to be attributed to the wise and effective measures taken by the Prince of Prussia (afterwards Emperor of Germany) for the reorganisation of the army in the teeth of Parliamentary opposition; and Prussia and Germany ought to be grateful (as I believe they are) for the patriotic and judicious foresight of His Royal Highness.

I may here add that, after the battle of Königratz, the Parliament unanimously voted an Act of Indemnity for the costs of the reorganisation of the army for the preceding years during which they had opposed it.

It was during this political crisis that I arrived at Berlin. I had audiences of the King and Queen on the 10th of February, 1861, to present the Queen's letters. It was nearly twenty-five years since I had been first presented to their Majesties, then Prince and Princess William of Prussia.

Their Majesties received me with gracious cordiality. I conveyed to the King, in the Queen's name, the assurances of Her Majesty's invariable esteem and regard, and of the deep interest which Her Majesty took in all that concerned the welfare and happiness of their Majesties and of their august family.

I stated to His Majesty how deeply I appreciated the high distinction conferred on me by the Queen, my gracious Sovereign and I begged to assure His Majesty that my constant efforts would be devoted to the maintenance of the harmony and good understanding which had so happily existed between the two Courts. I added that, in thus faithfully executing the instructions and wishes of the Queen, my Sovereign, I trusted that I should likewise merit the confidence and approbation of His Majesty.

The King was most gracious, and desired me to convey to the Queen the sincere expressions of his regard and esteem. He spoke in terms of the most affectionate interest in Her Majesty, in the Prince Consort, and in the Royal Family, and expressed his sincere desire to maintain a cordial and intimate union with Great Britain.

On taking leave the King expressed to me, in flattering terms, his satisfaction at my appointment as Her Majesty's Envoy at his Court.

I had, subsequently, an audience of the Queen. Her Majesty expressed her deep affection for the Queen, and how much she appreciated the many acts of kindness which Her Majesty had evinced towards her.

She further desired me to say how truly the King and herself had valued the affectionate sympathy and devotion of the Crown Princess during the mournful period through which they had passed, adding that Her Royal Highness had been of the greatest comfort and consolation to them.

I found Berlin very much altered and improved since I was last there. The Parliament had attracted many of the aristocracy and gentry to the capital, who had formerly resided entirely in the country, and thus added to the increase of social enjoyment. The interest taken in political questions was more general, and there was more life and activity in the various classes of society. The facility of communication by the railways had also brought the capital into greater connection with the provinces, and had also largely increased the number of European visitors. This had given life and vivacity to the capital. There was also more commercial activity, and, consequently, more wealth; and more luxurious habits had succeeded the former simple mode of life. The Court was very brilliant, and gave an impetus to society, which had greatly increased in numbers. The theatres had also greatly improved, and the ballets, under the direction of M. Taglioni, were most admirably given. The interest shown by the Crown Princess in the Fine Arts had produced also its effect, and proved to be a great encouragement to artists. In short, Berlin had risen to the position of a great capital, and, by the large increase of wealth, had exchanged the simplicity of former years for the luxury which had of late years become prominent in all European capitals.

It was a great pleasure to me to renew relations with my old friend, Baron Schleinitz, then Minister for Foreign Affairs. He received me very cordially. At my first interview with him I referred to the meeting of the Conference at Paris on the affairs of Syria. He said that he had informed Count Pourtales, the Prussian representative at Paris, that the Prussian Government could not consider that the state of the Lebanon was such as to preclude all fears of a renewal of disorders. He considered that if the foreign troops were removed, and that similar atrocities to those which had necessitated their presence should occur, a spirit of indignation would be raised against Turkey which might compromise its very existence, and possibly prove its death-blow. He thought a limit should be fixed for the occupation, which should be the period of the termination of the labours of the Commission, when a settled government would be installed. He fully agreed that no prolongation of the occupation of Syria should be permitted without the assent of the Sultan; that the unanimity of the Powers was requisite, and that the question could not be decided by a majority of the Conference.

This question was later finally arranged, and the occupation ceased on the establishment of a settled government, and peace and order were restored between the Druses and the Maronites.

I had, a few days afterwards, a long interview with the Prince of Hohenzollern. The conversation turned on the necessity for a perfect understanding between Great Britain and Prussia, and the desirableness for the two Governments, for their mutual interests, to pursue a common policy. I supported the principle of non-intervention—of not interfering in the internal affairs of other States. By this principle all collision between the European Powers would be prevented; without it, a collision might at any moment take place which would endanger the peace of Europe. There were, I said, three dangers which menaced the peace. First, the attitude which Germany had assumed towards Denmark in regard to the Schleswig-Holstein question. Secondly, the elements then at work among the Slavonic and other races tending to provoke an insurrection dangerous to the safety and integrity of Turkey. Thirdly, the consequences which might result from the inflammatory state of Italy, and the dangers which would menace Europe, if foreign intervention should take place in that country. With regard to the first, I observed a war on the Eyder might produce one on the Rhine. With regard to the second, the best means of preserving peace and the *status quo* in the East would be for Prussia to act in harmony with Great Britain and Austria. The Prince of Hohenzollern quite concurred in these views, and considered that on the basis which I had mentioned the interests of Prussia were quite in harmony with those of Great Britain.

In this year a great alleviation to commerce was effected by the abolition of the "Stade Dues" on the Elbe, for which an indemnity was paid to Hanover, very much in accordance with the principle which had regulated the abolition of the Sound Dues.

The Marquis of Breadalbane arrived at Berlin on the 1st of March, charged by the Queen to invest the King of Prussia with the Order of the Garter, accompanied by Lord F. Paulet, Viscount Hinchinbrook, and the Hon. Hussey Vivian. Sir C. Young, Garter King-at-Arms, with his suite, also arrived to conduct the arrangements for the investiture.

Lord Breadalbane and his suite were lodged by the Court, and provided with Court equipages during their stay.

The investiture took place on the 6th of March. The ceremony was solemn and imposing, and was admirably arranged.

Lord Breadalbane addressed the King in a short but impressive speech, to which the King replied in cordial terms. His Majesty did not much like giving up his sword, which is the perquisite of the Garter King-at-Arms, but he cheerfully assented, and was girt with that of the Order.

The ceremony was followed by a magnificent banquet in the Ritter Saal, to which two hundred persons were invited, and the members of Her Majesty's Legation. Before proceeding to dinner, the King invested Lord Breadalbane with the Order of the Black Eagle, having received a telegram from Her Majesty the Queen granting him permission to accept it.

At the banquet the King gave the health of Her Majesty the Queen, to which Lord Breadalbane responded by giving that of His Majesty the King, "Knight of the most noble Order of the Garter." During the banquet a selection of British airs was played, and amongst them that of "Rule Britannia." Everything passed off most satisfactorily, without a hitch or mistake, and the graceful and distinguished manner in which Lord Breadalbane and the Commission performed the ceremony was the theme of general approval.

Lord Breadalbane and his suite dined with me, and

knowing that he was a *bon vivant*, and had a *recherchée* cuisine, I was much puzzled to select a dish with which he was not acquainted. I consequently selected a saddle of wild boar with a Cumberland sauce, which he had never previously known, and with which he was quite delighted.

He was so pleased at receiving the Order of the Black Eagle that he told me that, on his return to England, he would have the star set in diamonds. He was surprised when I told him that he could not carry out his intention, as the star of the Black Eagle or any decoration in diamonds was the highest grade of the Order, and could only be conferred by the Sovereign.

I proceeded in April to Strelitz, to present the Queen's letter to the Grand Duke and Duchess of Mecklenburg-Strelitz, accrediting me as Her Majesty's Minister Plenipotentiary at that Court. I was lodged by the Grand Duke in a house not immediately adjoining the palace, but contiguous to it, and the apartments allotted to me were most comfortable.

I arrived in the early morning, having posted from Berlin during the night (there being then no railway). The country I traversed was a dead flat plain, interspersed with forest. The land was rich and well cultivated. The farmhouses appeared to me surprisingly good, and all in good order. The villages were well constructed, and the peasantry in good circumstances, and they appeared happy and contented. There was no appearance of want or poverty.

Many of the nobles had large estates, on which they

resided, and which they cultivated entirely themselves, and they entertained the best relations with the smaller occupiers and peasant class. The Grand Duke had large estates, and they were admirably administered. The Government was paternal, the taxation trifling, and the Grand Duchy then enjoyed that absence of political excitement, of speculative ambition, and thirst for money-making which was gradually overspreading Europe and causing discord and discontent among the several classes of society. It was a state of primitive contentment, and the population was satisfied to continue in the same groove in which their forefathers had toiled for generations.

Neu Strelitz was a clean, pleasant little town, with a good theatre — the only amusement it afforded. The ducal château — of commanding structure, and thoroughly comfortable in its interior — was adjacent to the town, to which was attached a large park and forest. There was the same amount of servants and retainers which exists in every German château. The Grand Duke had a very good table. There was a compromise between the Grand Duke and Duchess in regard to the cuisine. The Grand Duke liked the German cuisine, the Grand Duchess preferred the French cuisine. It was arranged, therefore, that the German and French cooks should have alternate days for the exhibition of their respective talents, and I confess that the superiority rested with the Frenchman; and the Grand Duchess was highly pleased with the verdict I had pronounced when invited to give my opinion by Her Royal Highness.

The arrival of a foreign Minister at Strelitz was an exciting event. On my arrival I was immediately invited to dine at the Palace at two o'clock. I had not yet given to the Minister for Foreign Affairs, Baron Bulöw (who was afterwards Secretary of State under Prince Bismarck at Berlin), as was usual, a copy of the Queen's letters, and, consequently, I could not presume that I was to present my credentials formally to His Royal Highness before the banquet. On arriving at the Palace at the hour of invitation, I was ushered through salons filled with the invited guests. Before being ushered into the Throne Room, I inquired of the Chamberlain whether the Grand Duke expected me to deliver the Queen's letters on that occasion. He replied, " Yes, it is your formal audience for that purpose." I then said that I had not brought the Queen's letters with me, having had no notification to that effect, and that I must consequently return to my apartment to fetch them.

The assembly in the salons, seeing that I had reached the door of the solemn audience chamber, and had then turned and passed through the salons, were in consternation, not knowing what calamity had happened, and fearing lest the happy relations between the two Courts might be broken off. However, all their anxieties and fears were relieved on my speedy return, and on my entrance into the Throne Room His Royal Highness, standing under a velvet canopy richly decorated, received me most cordially. I had been personally known to His Royal Highness for twenty-five years, when he was serving in the Prussian Army and quartered at Potsdam. He used to come over and dine with Sir George Hamilton, and accompanied us to the French play. I was then an Attaché, and now accredited as Minister at his Court.

I delivered my letter with the customary expressions of the attachment and deep interest of Her Majesty the Queen in the happiness and welfare of their Royal Highnesses. The Grand Duke, in reply, expressed his gratitude for the many favours the Queen had conferred on him. I was afterwards conducted to the Grand Duchess, to whom I delivered the Queen's letter. In expressing, in reply, her great affection for the Queen, she also expressed her deepest sympathy with Her Majesty in her late affliction.* Nothing could be more gracious or kind than the Grand Duchess, whom I had known for many years as Princess Augusta of Cambridge.

Early in May I proceeded to Schwerin to present my credentials to the Grand Duke of Mecklenburg-Schwerin, and to present the Queen's letter to the Grand Duchess. Their Royal Highnesses received me most graciously, and, in replying to the usual complimentary speech I addressed in Her Majesty's name, they charged me to convey to the Queen the assurances of their highest respect and regard, expressing their deep sympathy with Her Majesty in her affliction.

The Grand Duchess was in bad health, and I believe it was the last reception she ever gave.

A grand banquet was given in my honour, and very

* The Death of H.R.H. the Duchess of Kent.

magnificently done. The château, of great size, was built by the late Grand Duke at a great cost. It was a diminutive Versailles—the whole interior richly decorated and magnificently furnished. It is beautifully situated close on an extensive lake and near the town.

Schwerin is a clean, cheerful, pretty town, well paved, well lit, and prettily situated. There is some commercial activity, and trade has lately much increased. The Grand Duchy enjoys a species of constitutional government. The representatives meet every two years in conjunction with those of Mecklenburg-Strelitz at Malchin. In 1840, when I accompanied Lord William Russell on a visit to the late Count Hahn at Bassedow, I drove over to Malchin to attend a sitting of the Mecklenburg Parliament, and was much interested in it, observing especially the fluency and oratorical powers of some of the speakers.

There was an influential aristocracy in Mecklenburg-Schwerin, a very independent body, who lived at their châteaux dispensing hospitality as in England. They had large estates, in some instances cultivated under their own administration, in others by tenants. They were like the old feudal lords, and were much respected. The taxation was light, and the population was happy and contented till the wave of democracy flowed in upon it. The country was rich in pasture, and also in agricultural land. It resembled England in many respects, and specially in the hedgerows, which gave a picturesque appearance to the landscape.

My next excursion was to Dessau to present my

credentials to the Duke of Anhalt-Dessau. This Court
reminded me of the account given by Baron Bielefeld of
the minor German Courts in the last century. The
town appeared to me an old German mediæval town
—where no new ideas of the present age had pierced—
dull and uninteresting.

The Duke, a stately old gentleman, received me
alone most courteously. There was a small table in
the room, on each side of which a plain old-fashioned
arm-chair was placed. He invited me to be seated, and
entered into conversation on the topics of the day. He
made many inquiries as to the state of affairs at Berlin,
and the struggle between the King and the Parliament.

After the audience I was invited to a banquet at
two o'clock. It was quite in the old mediæval style,
and gave me the idea of what Court life was at a
German Court in the last century. Nothing could exceed the courtesy of the Duke and his Court. The
Hereditary Prince of Dessau, the Prince and Princess
Frederick of Dessau, and their daughters, Princess
Berthalde and Hilda of Dessau, to whom I was presented, were present at the banquet. There was a
simplicity, an ease of manner with dignity, in the Duke
which was very attractive. He possessed a large territory of the Duchy—a rich and smiling country, with
pretty hedgerows and fine timber—and is reputed very
rich. I consider that the position of the minor
Sovereigns—more especially since the restoration of the
German Empire—a highly favoured one, and far more enviable than that of the larger States. They are generally

wealthy, are free and independent, and relieved of all political cares and troubles. They have all the enjoyment of Royalty without its thorns, and occupy very much the position of the great magnates of our wealthy aristocracy. The life at Dessau cannot, however, be a lively one, although the railways have brought it into closer proximity with the larger capitals. Baroness Lehzen, who was so long at the Court of the Queen in the early part of her reign, on leaving England took up her residence at Dessau, and much interested the Ducal Court by relating the reminiscences of her previous life.

On my return to Berlin I found that the political struggle on the Army Reorganisation Bill had not advanced, and there appeared no hopes of a compromise between the Government and Lower House on that question.

The state of Poland, and the feverish excitement which then pervaded the Polish nation, caused some uneasiness at Berlin, and increased the suspicions very generally entertained of the Napoleonic policy.

Serious riots had taken place at Warsaw. The attitude of the Russian Government in Poland, and the conduct of Prince Gortchacoff, the Viceroy, was regarded at Berlin as weak and timorous, and I was informed that advice had been given at St. Petersburg from a high quarter to show more energy and firmness.

The events at Warsaw rekindled in the mind of the Prussian Government the fears of revolution, and a greater importance and a wider range was attributed to them than they apparently bore on their surface. The Government were under the conviction that a conspiracy on a large scale was being organised by the revolutionary party, of which Paris was the centre, and that when the propitious moment came the match would be set to the train, causing a general explosion which would encircle Germany.

Baron Schleinitz considered that it was in the interest of all Governments to join for mutual protection, and to put down the first germs of a revolutionary movement before the preparations for a general explosion should mature. He stated to me that he had no fears for the Grand Duchy of Posen, as half of the population of that province was German, and could hold its own against the Poles. He was impressed with the idea that attempts were being made to get up a Polish question, and that these attempts emanated from Paris.

I recollect that during the Crimean War, when the King, Frederick William the Fourth, was sounded in regard to Poland, he exclaimed with some animation, "Were I to march into Poland, I should find myself at the head of the 'Scythe men' (*Sensemännern*)."

A resolution was proposed by a Polish member of the Lower House inviting that assembly "to insist on the *status quo*, stipulated by the Congress of Vienna, being carried out." It was resisted by M. de Vincke, and rejected by a large majority. The object of the Poles was to bring before the notice of Europe the Polish question, and to set forth the grievances under which the Polish nation suffered. This aim was attained. A "cry of anguish," as in Italy, for "an oppressed nationality" was sounded, and the sympathy of Europe was claimed for its support.

The Prussian Government at this time was sounded by Count Launay, the Sardinian Minister, unofficially in regard to the recognition by Prussia of the Kingdom of Italy. Baron Schleinitz replied that, although Prussia was not prepared to recognise the new Kingdom, their diplomatic relations would be continued on the same footing as heretofore.

In conversation with me, Baron Schleinitz mentioned the Protocol of Aix-la-Chapelle, admitting, however, that it was not applicable to the present case of Sardinia. He said that the Protocol originated in consequence of the Elector of Hesse-Cassel desiring, in 1815, to assume the title of "King." It was also subsequently appealed to when some of the minor German Sovereigns wished to assume the title of "Royal Highness."

A good deal of sensation was created at Berlin by a duel between General von Manteuffel, chief of the King's Military Cabinet, and M. Twesten, in consequence of a pamphlet written by the latter, in which he treated with great disrespect, and in disparaging terms, the Military Cabinet of the King, as also the army. M. Twesten was slightly wounded; General von Manteuffel was unhurt. The King ordered a military inquiry, by which General von Manteuffel was sentenced to three months' arrest. M. Twesten was brought before the civil judicial authorities, and was likewise sentenced to imprisonment.

The King of Prussia paid a return visit to the Emperor Napoleon at Compiègne on the 8th of October. The reception of the King by the Emperor was very cordial, but, from what I could learn, there was nothing of a political nature referred to, and no mention made of any territorial changes. Of course, what may have passed between the King and the Emperor was not revealed, but the King had too much tact and prudence to touch on any question which could embarrass his illustrious host.

On the 14th of July a murderous attempt was made on the King of Prussia at Baden-Baden by a Leipzic student. At nine o'clock a.m., as the King was walking down the Lichtenthaler Allee, a young man, well dressed, passed His Majesty, saluting him in the most respectful manner. He then stopped, and the King passed him, when he again saluted His Majesty. Almost immediately afterwards, and close to the King, he fired with a pistol at His Majesty, the ball passing through the collar of the King's coat, and causing a contusion on the left side of the neck, but of no moment. The student was arrested by Count Fleming, the Prussian Minister who was in attendance on His Majesty, and given over to the Baden authorities. The King returned to his house on foot. I received a telegram conveying to me the Queen's commands to repair immediately to Baden to congratulate the King of Prussia in Her Majesty's name and in that of His Royal Highness the Prince Consort on his providential escape.

I arrived at Baden on the 17th, and, at an audience of the King on the following day, fulfilled Her Majesty's commands. The King charged me to convey to Her Majesty and the Prince Consort the expressions of his deep gratitude for the kind interest they had evinced on this sad occasion. His Majesty said that his escape had been most miraculous, and that he was truly grateful to the Almighty for his merciful interposition. The wound, he said, was a mere scratch—another hair's-breadth would have sufficed to render it mortal. He said that his health had not suffered, although the effect of the blow and the excitement of the nervous system had at first affected his head and had produced giddiness, but that it soon passed away, and His Majesty appeared in his usual health. His Majesty expressed himself as deeply touched by the universal interest and sympathy which had been testified by all ranks and classes of society, or, as His Majesty termed it, "from the greatest sovereign to the meanest cabin."

The assassin, Oscar Becker, was a native of Odessa, but of German extraction, born of highly respectable parents, well educated, and bearing a high character at Leipzic for industry and learning. He denied having any accomplices. His papers, found at Leipzic, confirmed this and all his other statements. He made no attempt to escape, expressed no contrition for his crime, openly avowing that, if at liberty, he would commit it again. He was a fanatic, whose fixed idea was that the life of the King of Prussia should be sacrificed for the unity of Germany.

Seldom has a political crime—if the atrocious act of Becker can be thus termed—produced so unanimous a feeling of horror and indignation, and so universal a sympathy, both in Germany and in Europe, as the late attempt on the life of the King of Prussia. It elicited a general expression of sympathy, of loyalty, and of admiration among all classes of the Fatherland for the noble and chivalrous character of His Prussian Majesty, and has afforded him the most convincing and consolatory proof of the affection of his subjects.

At the trial some difficulties were raised as to the charge for his arraignment. By the Baden law he could not be indicted for high treason, as that crime only applied to the Sovereign of the country, and was punishable with death. He was therefore tried on the count for attempted murder, and as no life was taken, he was sentenced to imprisonment with hard labour for a term of twenty years.

On the morning he committed the crime he wrote a letter, which was found on his person. It was as follows:—

"I have given in these lines the motives of my projected deed. I hold the conviction that the King of Prussia is not fitted, in present circumstances, to bring about the unity of Germany; I have therefore determined to put him out of the way.—Signed, OSCAR BECKER."

The death of Count Cavour in June, 1861, created considerable sensation in Berlin. It was feared that his loss in the present critical state of Italy, which required his strong mind to guide and lead it, might produce events of a nature to compromise the new order of things he had established. It was felt that, should a shock either from external or internal violence overturn the structure he had completed, then, and perhaps not till then, would Italy discover the great loss she had sustained.

On the 14th of June I had the honour to be invited to dine with the Crown Prince and Princess at Potsdam. Their Majesties were present on this occasion.

I had some conversation with the King on the Schleswig-Holstein question—that interminable web of complications.

I stated to His Majesty that we fully recognised that the question was one of a purely German character, and that we did not contest the legality of a military execution by the Confederation, but we rather looked to the consequences of it. It would give rise to a war between Germany and Denmark, and the question would then assume a wider sphere, and bear a European character.

His Majesty replied that Germany would strictly remain within its limits, that there was no reason that a Federal execution should be taken as a *casus belli* by Denmark, and that the Germanic Confederation could not refrain from enforcing obedience to its decrees in regard to a province appertaining to that Confederation. If, therefore, Her Majesty's Government were anxious to avert all dangerous consequences, they should press on Denmark the necessity of yielding to the joint reclamations of the Diet.

I stated to His Majesty that even if the German Confederation were determined, which I fully believed, to confine their action strictly within the limits of the Federal territory, still there was a portion of disputed frontier between Schleswig and Holstein. If, therefore, the Federal troops were to occupy any portion of that disputed territory—for instance, the fortress of Rendsburg—a *casus belli* would inevitably arise on the part of Denmark, and the quarrel would at once assume another character. I added that Her Majesty's Government was most anxious to avert from Europe the miseries of war, that it was difficult to say, if war broke out on the Eyder, what extension might be given to it, and it was their anxious desire to use their influence for the maintenance of peace. They counted on His Majesty's support to further their efforts.

The King replied that he most cordially concurred in their desire, and would most certainly contribute his support and assistance to this desirable end.

His Majesty was suddenly called away, and the conversation thus ended.

This interminable quarrel continued revolving in a stormy circle without leading to any result (the details of which I will not inflict on my readers), till at last war took place between Germany and Denmark, at the termination of which Denmark had to cede the Duchies of Holstein, of Schleswig, and of Lauenburg to Germany.

At the end of June I was graciously invited to a military fête at Potsdam in the expectation of the Grand Duke and Duchess of Mecklenburg being present.

This fête is given annually to the officers and men of what is termed the *Lehr battalion*, which consists of twelve men from every infantry regiment of the Prussian Army. The object of this military institution is to have a specimen of the clothing and equipment of every regiment in the service.

The fête commenced with Divine service in the garden of the Neu Palais, which was then the residence of the Crown Prince and Princess. A parade of the battalion was then held by the King. Immediately afterwards, a dinner was provided for the men, at which the King, Princes, and Princesses were present.

The opening scene was very impressive. The battalion formed a square. In the front an altar was placed. A semicircle was formed around it, where their Majesties, the Princes and Princesses of the royal house, attended by the officers of the Court, and the generals took their position. On one side of the altar were the choristers, on the other the band of the regiment, the two performing the vocal and instrumental portion of the service.

It was a religious service which could not fail to impress deeply all present, and to implant in the breast of every soldier that religious feeling and that faith and trust in the Almighty which was their stay and support in the hour of need. The participation of their Majesties in this service offered also a noble example, which left an indelible impression on the minds of all present.

The observance of the religious duties of the soldier

is strictly attended to in the Prussian army. Every soldier carries in his knapsack a copy of the New Testament, and in the late wars it was generally observed how deeply the effects of religious education permeated the Prussian Army.

A grand banquet was subsequently given by the King in the famous "Muschel Saal," which is all encrusted with shells. Nothing could exceed the attention shown to me on this occasion by their Majesties and every member of the Royal Family. The King especially expressed to me his satisfaction that Her Majesty's Minister had been present at this fête, although it was one of a purely military character, to which, in ordinary circumstances, the foreign Ministers were not invited. It was a proof to me that the susceptibilities which had been affected by the unfortunate Macdonald affair, and with no class so strongly as with the military, had not altered the friendly feeling of His Majesty towards England.

CHAPTER VII.

The *Huldigung* or Coronation—Differences between the King and his Ministry thereon—Lord Clarendon appointed Ambassador—The King's Visit to the Emperor Napoleon at Compiègne—Life of the King of Prussia at Baden—The Queen's Receptions—M. de Bacourt—English Church at Baden—Last Interview with the Queen of Prussia in 1889—Death of my Eldest Daughter—Sympathy shown by the Queen of Prussia—Coronation of the King—The Act of Crowning Himself and Speech much Commented on—The Non-responsibility of Ministers in Prussia—Expenses of the Coronation defrayed by the King—Poland—Attempts to revive a Polish Question—Fruitless Diplomatic Action of England and France—Life of the Grand Duke Constantine attempted at Warsaw—The Marques de Wielopolski—Schleswig-Holstein Question—The German Question—Death of the Prince Consort—Deep Sympathy evinced for the Queen.

For some time past a question had been under discussion between the King of Prussia and his Government on the subject of a *Huldigung* or the paying of homage to the Sovereign on his accession to the Throne—in other words, a "Coronation." I was present at the *Huldigung* of Frederick William IV. at Berlin on his accession to the Throne. It took place in what was called the "Lust Garden," a large open space in front of the Palace between the Palace and the Museum. A large estrade was constructed on the ground floor of the Palace, richly decorated, for the King and Queen, the Princes and Princesses, the Ministers of State, and the higher official functionaries. The various guilds, with their banners, took their position in front of the estrade, and a dense mass filled the remainder of the vacant space. Their Majesties and the Princes and Princesses attended Divine service in the Cathedral—a very unimposing structure, and not of that character which might be expected in a large capital. The King on his return took his place on the estrade, and there addressed his people.

On the occasion of the accession of King William I. it would appear almost incredible that a question of the *Huldigung* or coronation could lead to any discussion with his Ministers, or be converted into one of a political nature, still less, indeed, that it should give rise to a Ministerial crisis. The nature, however, of the ceremony, and the political importance attached to it by the King and by the Feodal party, will explain why the question assumed a political character, and why each party made it the battle-ground of their political faith.

In former times, when Prussia was an absolute monarchy, each Sovereign on his accession, in lieu of a "Coronation," received at Königsberg and at Berlin the homage of his people. Deputations were sent by each province, and, in the name of the province, swore fealty and allegiance to the King. It was an institution which belonged to an age which is past, and is no longer compatible with a Constitutional Monarchy.

The homage then paid, and the oath then subscribed, has been replaced by the oath which is taken by every representative of the people in the Lower House. Constitutionally speaking, the Government could not frame a fresh oath for the occasion without nullifying that which is taken to the Constitution.

The Feodal anti-Constitutional party profited of this incident to urge His Majesty to insist on having the same homage paid to him as was paid to his ancestors. The King, who was brought up in the school of absolute monarchy, and who held with a species of veneration to the traditions and prerogatives of his Royal house, could not divest himself of the idea that he held the same position as his forefathers, and that, as monarch of Prussia, the *Huldigung* was his right, his heirloom.

The Feodal party, who are opposed to all Constitutional forms, and who would gladly see the old system of absolute government restored, gladly profited of the opportunity to gain favour with the King by supporting his views, and by urging His Majesty to carry them into effect.

The Ministry, on the other hand, represented to His Majesty the impossibility of their assenting to a ceremony which was no longer in accordance with the principles of a Constitutional Monarchy, and after endless discussions, they stated to His Majesty that they should be obliged to tender their resignation should the King persist in carrying out his intention of having a *Huldigung*.

The result was that the King deferred having the *Huldigung* till the autumn, without taking any ulterior decision.

On the 6th of July the King issued a manifesto announcing his intention of reviving—in lieu of the *Huldigung* — the solemn act of coronation as first instituted by Frederick I. The coronation of their

Majesties was accordingly appointed to take place at Königsberg on the 18th of October, in the presence of both Houses of the Legislature, and of persons from all the provinces, to be summoned by His Majesty to attend. Lord Clarendon was appointed to represent the Queen at the coronation.

The King of Prussia, after the attempt on his life, remained at Baden-Baden, and prolonged his stay till the 15th of August for the purpose of taking a course of mineral waters. His Majesty then repaired to Ostend for a fortnight for sea-bathing.

During the month of July the Emperor Napoleon invited the King to the Camp at Châlons for the manœuvres of the French Army. The projected visit was much discussed. The King was disposed to accept it. The Prince of Hohenzollern, Baron Schleinitz, and the Ministry were in favour of it. It was judged that in the then existing state of Europe a meeting of the two Sovereigns, and an exchange of friendly courtesy, might act very advantageously, and could give rise to no false interpretations, whereas a refusal might produce disappointment and distrust. A Treaty of Commerce was being then negotiated at Berlin with France, and it was thought that a personal interview of the two Sovereigns might facilitate the conclusion of the treaty. It was urged that England maintained an amicable understanding with France, and that Prussia might well follow her example. England, Baron Schleinitz observed, above all things desired the maintenance of peace, and she would hail with satisfaction any step tending to a pacific object, and to a good understanding between the Great Powers of Europe.

The Emperor Napoleon gave evident proofs of his desire to conciliate Prussia, looking eventually to her alliance, and possibly to other objects. The neutrality of France, in the event of war with Austria, was also of great importance to Prussia (as was proved in 1866). Prussia had no object to gain by irritating France; but if France were to enter on an aggressive policy, Prussia would rally to England, and would consider the cause of England to be her own and that of Europe at large, or, to cite the words often expressed to me by Baron Schleinitz: "*Nous ne voulons pas une guerre de plumes avec la France, mais quand vous avez besoin de soldats, et que vous aurez tiré le premier coup de canon, vous pouvez compter sur nous.*"

The projected visit to Châlons was finally abandoned, the King's medical adviser having urgently counselled His Majesty to abstain from any fatigue or excitement immediately after finishing the course of Kissingen waters.

It was proposed that an interview should take place between the two Sovereigns on the King leaving Ostend, at some place contiguous to the frontier, and General Willisen was the bearer of a letter from the King to the Emperor to that effect, and explaining the causes which had prevented His Majesty from going to Châlons.

The interview eventually took place at Compiègne, to which I have already referred.

I had frequent opportunities of meeting the King at Baden. The King gave small dinners, and the Queen evening receptions, to which Lady Augustus and I had frequently the honour of being invited. I recollect at one of the Queen's *soirées* there were present the ex-King of Naples and the Crown Prince, which led me to observe to Her Majesty that there were represented in her salon, " The present, the past, and the future." The King represented the present, the ex-King of Naples the past, and the Crown Prince the future.

The ex-King of Naples appeared to me a young Prince of prepossessing manners—very unassuming, and very dignified in his deportment, bearing with calmness and resignation the misfortunes which had befallen him. I was presented at Munich to the ex-Queen of Naples, sister of the Empress of Austria. She was very beautiful and very fascinating, and, although the traces of inward suffering from all she had passed through were visible, she was calm and resigned.

Among the *habitués* at the Queen's receptions were the Princess Isabelle Gargarin, Princess Obolenski (who was the object of general admiration), Prince and Princess Wiasemski with their daughter—who was afterwards Grande Maîtresse to the Grand Duchess Vladimir, of Russia—Princess Kotchoubey, Count and Countess Chreptowitch, M. de Bacourt and Count Pahlen, and many others of the *élite* of the cosmopolitan society at Baden.

Nor can I omit my dear friends, Count and Countess Blücher, with whom the Queen was on intimate terms, and who were justly appreciated by Her Majesty.

M. de Bacourt was a man of considerable ability,

added to a great charm of manner. He was a devoted Orleanist, and had left the French Diplomatic Service on the fall of Louis Philippe. He had been secretary to Prince Talleyrand during his embassy in London, and was engaged in writing his memoirs from the Prince's papers, placed in his hands by the Duchesse de Sagan of which the Duc de Broglie has now undertaken the publication. He had been French Ambassador at Turin, and was conversant with the politics of Europe and personally acquainted with the leading statesmen of the day.

He was a strong anti-Buonapartist, and often foretold to me the destiny which awaited the Second Empire. In speaking of the Emperor Napoleon, he invariably used the term "*Ce Monsieur.*"

The King of Prussia led a plain, simple life at Baden. He took his early walk in the Lichthentaler Allée in the morning, gave audiences and transacted business till one or two, then took his drive, and subsequently paid visits or lounged about the promenade, conversing graciously with all alike with that *bonhommie* which was His Majesty's nature. One great trait of his character was his equanimity. He was always calm and benevolent, always ready to do a kind or charitable act, but he was firm and resolute in his opinions once formed on conscientious grounds. He was possessed of great perspicacity, of great shrewdness and foresight, tempered with prudence and justice, and of an irreproachable uprightness. He was truly a "*chevalier sans peur et sans reproche.*"

The Queen, with whom Lady Augustus and I had been on terms of intimacy for twenty-five years, was one of the most distinguished ladies in Europe. She had been brought up at Weimar (then the "Athens" of Germany) in the days of Goethe and the most enlightened professors of that epoch, and in that learned atmosphere she imbibed that love for literary culture which so highly distinguished her in after-life. She had a great deal of sentiment and poetry in her nature, and I recollect on one occasion, when talking of Venice, she quoted to me the lines of Byron, " I stood at Venice on the Bridge of Sighs." Happily I was enabled to repeat the second line, which pleased Her Royal Highness. She was very religious, and was very attached to our English service, especially to the Litany; and during her annual residence at Baden she always attended the English church, towards the erection of which she had so largely contributed.

The Queen was highly gifted. She interested herself in science, literature, and the fine arts. She took great interest in politics, and was always consistently anxious for a good understanding between England and Prussia. Scores of times this was the topic of the conversation with me, and she often expressed her great satisfaction at the marriage of her son, the Crown Prince, with the Princess Royal.

At Baden she made frequent excursions after dinner to take tea at the old château or other places in the neighbourhood. Servants were sent with all the paraphernalia beforehand, and we were constantly invited to accompany her. M. de Bacourt and Count and Countess Blücher were always of the party. I recollect once that I was seated on the box of her carriage with the Emperor, who was always most cheery on these occasions.

Nothing could exceed the humane and charitable spirit evinced by the Queen to the wounded during the wars of 1866 and 1870. She was indefatigable in visiting the hospitals (one of which she had built herself) and in attending to the wants of the wounded. In the latter part of her life she was wholly devoted to charities and good works, and has left a name endeared to the poor, as well as a noble example for others.

In October, 1889, we went to Baden on our way to Italy to pay our respects to the Queen, then Dowager Empress of Germany.

She was then very weak and suffering, but was graciously pleased to receive us.

I found Her Majesty greatly altered and very feeble, and greatly depressed. On leaving, I was deeply grieved, for I felt that it was my farewell visit to Her Majesty, who, during a period of forty years, had always been a kind and constant friend, and for whom I felt the greatest devotion.

The Queen interested herself much with the question of the building of an English church at Baden, the service being then performed in an old Catholic chapel, the use of which was generously granted by the Catholic pastor.

Lady Augustus and I were enabled at last to carry out this long-cherished idea, greatly aided by the generosity of Her Majesty. It was finally completed and dedicated by the Archbishop of Armagh in 1860. We gave the east window—representing the resurrection of our Saviour—and also the rose window. The design of the former was by the renowned Professor Hess, and the window was made at Munich. We also fitted up the whole of the chancel. The carved reading-desk was the gift of the Grand Duchess of Baden. It is a pretty church, and capable of holding about four hundred. There is a large congregation during the summer months, composed of English and Americans.

In those days the life of Baden was very gay and enjoyable. There was good society, and a very good theatre, at which, during the season, French plays were given by the first French artists.

There was music on the promenade twice a day—at three and at seven in the evening—when the society met and sat round tables reserved for them. There were balls twice a week, and a reading-room, with all the newspapers of Europe, free from charge.

All this is now altered, and Baden, since the abolition of the gambling tables, is no longer kept up in the same style. The picturesque shops in the Allee still remain, but the profits to their owners have greatly decreased. But it is, however, one of the prettiest spots in Europe, and must always attract many foreign visitors, from the beauty of the environs.

The Grand Duke and Duchess pass a portion of the summer there in their beautiful château before they proceed to Meinau, and we had the honour of paying our respects to their Royal Highnesses in 1890. At the invitation of the Grand Duchess we visited the house occupied by her mother, the late Empress of Germany, where the Grand Duchess exhibited, for a charity, various reminiscences of her late Majesty. It was a melancholy pleasure for us to revisit the salons where we had so often enjoyed the gracious hospitality of Her Majesty, and where, only a few months previously, we had taken our last farewell of that kind and beneficent Sovereign.

Having returned to Berlin from Baden on the 7th of September, I was suddenly again summoned there by the alarming illness of my eldest daughter, and I left Berlin on the evening of the 23rd.

I found on my arrival that she was in a most critical state, with scarcely a hope of recovery. She passed away peacefully on the 28th. I was grateful to have been permitted to pass the last few days of her life with her, and to receive her last embrace. It was a painful and a crushing blow to me. She was my favourite child, had been my constant companion, and was my idol.

We received the most gracious and sympathetic letters from the Queen of Prussia, the Grand Duke and Duchess of Baden, the Crown Prince and Princess of Prussia, Prince Furstenberg, Lord Clarendon, Lord J. Russell, and many others. The Queen of Prussia evinced the greatest sympathy. Her Majesty had known my dear child from her infancy, and used to call and take her to church when we were absent from Baden.

Her Majesty also graciously attended a Divine service held in my house before the funeral.

Never was there anyone who showed more deep feeling and sympathy for those in sorrow and affliction than Her Majesty the Queen of Prussia, and the many acts of gracious kindness shown to us, of which I shall ever retain a grateful recollection, have left that deep impression which time will not obliterate.

In consequence of my domestic affliction I was unable to attend the coronation of the King and Queen. I cannot, therefore, give any description of it. The King, in lieu of being crowned, took the crown from the altar and crowned himself. In the speech he delivered, he said that, " Mindful that the crown comes only from God, I have, by my coronation at the holy altar, manifested to Him that I have received it in all humility from His hands." After crowning himself, the King then placed the crown on the Queen's head. These words and this proceeding gave rise to many severe comments.

It was not a judicious speech, nor was it a prudent act; but it must be borne in mind that the King was a soldier, brought up from his early youth in the school of absolutism. He was strongly imbued with the duty —according to his view—of supporting ancient rights and traditions. But he was no despot or tyrant, and being of a most humane and kind disposition, he never imagined that the act he had performed and the words he had uttered could be misconstrued, and a false interpretation given to them. It was unfortunate, however, that the King did not previously consult and adopt the advice of his responsible Ministers.

I may here observe that the principle of the responsibility of Ministers to Parliament has never been recognised nor acted upon in Prussia. They are regarded as servants of the Crown, and bound to discharge their duties so long as the Sovereign commands them, and their resignation does not follow in the event of an adverse vote of Parliament. A Project of Law, providing for the responsibility of Ministers, was submitted to the Lower House by some independent members in the early part of the session, and was referred, as is the usual custom, to a committee, who declared against its being at present brought before the House. The amendment proposed by another fraction, namely, "To require the Government to submit a law for Ministerial responsibility on the basis of the 61st Article of the Constitution during the next session of Parliament," was agreed to. Only one voice was raised against the principle of the Bill on the plea of the restriction of the monarchical prerogative. This Bill has never yet been introduced.

Some difficulties having arisen as to the mode of defraying the expenses of the coronation, and to avoid any discussion or opposition if the question were brought before the Lower House, the King generously decided to defray the whole expense out of his privy purse. It was calculated that these expenses would amount to two millions of thalers (about £300,000). This gracious act of the King to relieve the country from so heavy a charge, at a moment when the increased expenses of the military budget, created by the reorganisation of the army, had caused violent opposition, produced a good effect, but it did not mitigate the hostile opposition of the Lower House to the Government in regard to that measure.

On my return to Berlin I heard from all sides general praise and admiration of Lord and Lady Clarendon and their two daughters (now Lady Lathom and Lady Ampthill). They were immensely popular, and won all hearts by their charming and prepossessing manners. The King and Queen showed great attention to Lord Carendon, who was a *persona gratissima* at the Court, and was duly appreciated. He had been personally known to their Prussian Majesties for some time, and in 1860 paid me a visit at Baden-Baden with his daughter from Wildbad expressly to pay his respects to the Queen.

At a *soirée* we gave to the Queen, at which were present Princess Obolenski, Princess Wiasemski, Ctsse. Edmond Pourtales, Princess Menshikoff, Lady Lothian, Princess Gargarin, and many others, Lord Clarendon told me that he had rarely seen a réunion of such beauty, and he was a good judge of the fair sex.

There was a large assemblage of German Sovereigns and Princes for the coronation, and they were all lodged and provided with Royal equipages. The "old palace" is very large and commodious, and as the King lived in his own palace under the Linden, there was ample room in the old palace to lodge the foreign Sovereigns and

Princes, who on all occasions are lodged there when visiting the Court of Berlin. It acquired from this circumstance the name of the "Hôtel de l'Europe."

Lord Granville, Lord Dudley, and the Duke and Duchess of Manchester also attended the coronation.

On my return to Berlin I had my first interview with Count Bernstoff, who had entered the Ministry as Minister for Foreign Affairs during my absence. We had been acquainted for many years, and he received me most cordially. I am glad of this opportunity to express my thanks for the many kindnesses which Count and Countess Bernstorff showed to Lady Augustus and myself during their official residence at Berlin.

As I have mentioned in a previous chapter, the serious riots which had taken place at Warsaw and the general agitation manifested by the Poles had caused some uneasiness at Berlin, and more especially as it was suspected that the direction of the movement emanated from the revolutionary committee at Paris, and was in connection with other revolutionary designs.

According to official information I received, the whole population of the Grand Duchy of Posen then amounted to 1,390,000 souls, of which 760,000 were registered as Poles, and 630,000 were registered as Germans. The Polish party do not accept this proportion—according to their estimate the population may be reckoned at the rate of eight Poles to five Germans. The rate hitherto adopted by the Government has been to consider as German those who speak German and are not of the Roman Catholic faith. It is, however, certain that the German population has been annually increasing, whilst the Polish population has been stationary.

At the Congress of Vienna Prussia, who had previously possessed Bialystock and a large portion of the Duchy of Warsaw, ceded to Russia all that was not necessary for her to retain for complete communication between Eastern Prussia and Silesia. The Netz district, of which Bromberg is the capital, was anciently possessed by the Teutonic Order, and was only ceded to Poland after the battle of Dannenberg in the fifteenth century.

Under no circumstances would Prussia be induced to give up the Grand Duchy of Posen. The military line of defence of Prussia on her eastern frontier is based on the fortresses of Thorn, Posen, Graudenz, and Dantzic, which combine strategically with the fortress of Königsberg.

The Polish representatives in the Lower House availed themselves of every opportunity to bring forward their grievances and to prove that their nationality was not extinct. A Polish member of the Lower House raised a question as to the desirableness of the civil authorities (who were all Germans) in the Grand Duchy of Posen being conversant with the Polish language. Count Schwerin, the Minister of the Interior, without contesting the point, observed that a Prussian patriotic feeling was even of more importance than a knowledge of Polish, and that it was comparatively a rare thing to find the two qualities combined. I refer to this to prove the agitation and irritation then existing among the Poles, and that the feeling of nationality on their part was as strong as ever.

Although the Czar and the Russian Government had never been better disposed towards the Poles, and ostensibly more anxious to pursue a policy of conciliation and forbearance towards them than at that period, all attempts in this sense proved abortive. The spirit of revolution, the cry of oppressed nationalities, the success which had attended the Italian patriots to free their country from foreign intervention and misgovernment—all aided in inflaming an excitable race like the Poles to attempt their own deliverance from the yoke of Russia.

In 1861 the Emperor Alexander appointed his brother, the Grand Duke Constantine, Viceroy of Poland. A Council of State was introduced, in which the Polish element was largely represented, and the Emperor placed at the head of the administration, under the Viceroy, the Marquis Wielopolski, a Polish nobleman who had ably and patriotically pleaded with the Emperor the cause of Poland. But the Poles aimed solely at complete independence, and nothing short of complete emancipation would have satisfied them. The life of the Grand Duke Constantine was attempted. He was wounded, and had a narrow escape. He retired from the Government, and the Marquis Wielopolski, who saw the fruitlessness of the conciliatory policy he had advocated, resigned his post; and this restless nation was doomed to undergo greater sufferings than it had previously endured.

"In conversation with Baron Budberg, then Russian Minister at Berlin (who had a great admiration for the character and abilities of the Marquis Wielopolski), he stated to me that the withdrawal of that statesman from his official post in Poland was not to be attributed to any misunderstanding between him and the Imperial Government, or any disinclination on his part to continue in the service of the Crown. According to Baron Budberg, the real cause to be assigned to the retirement of the Marquis Wielopolski was that, having been hitherto strongly opposed to the introduction of a state of siege and to the adoption of coercive measures in Poland, he considered that it would neither be consistent for him nor advantageous to the Government that he should continue to retain his official position under a state of things which he had always systematically denounced. Baron Budberg added that the retirement from office of the Marquis Wielopolski was, consequently, only to be considered as provisional during the continuance of the state of siege and the exceptional repressive measures then in action, and he considered that his decision had been a judicious one, inasmuch as he would be enabled to render more valuable services to the Imperial Government by resuming his former position at a later period, when it might be found practicable to govern without the aid of a state of siege or extraordinary repressive measures. Baron Budberg represented the Marquis Wielopolski as being perfectly satisfied with his reception by the Emperor and the Imperial Government, and he hinted that the decision taken by the Marquis had been with the full approval of the Imperial Government.

"How far the colouring of this incident given by Baron Budberg may be correct or not I am unable to say, but it is very probable that, although the explanation of Baron Budberg may be given by the Imperial Government as the grounds for the Marquis's retirement, there may be in the background other more cogent reasons, and that the Marquis had acted from an independent feeling, not wishing to be the executor of measures to which on principle he was opposed." *

* I may here remark that thirty years have now elapsed since the incident here mentioned occurred, and the Marquis Wielopolski has

The foregoing is an extract from a despatch which I addressed to Lord Russell in 1861.

The English and French Governments made feeble attempts to remind the Imperial Government of its engagements in regard to Poland under the Treaties of Vienna, but they were wanting in that mutual confidence and unity of purpose from which alone success could be expected.

Russia, Austria, and Prussia were bound to support each other in the event of their mutual interests in Poland being endangered. It was evident that if war had ensued between Russia and the Western Powers, it would have re-echoed on the Rhine, and the risks to which England would have been exposed, if such an eventuality had occurred, were equally apparent. It could not have been imagined that a statesman of the stamp of Prince Gortchacoff would be intimidated by a "homily," addressed to him by the Western Powers, on a question which he considered solely concerned the internal government of a Russian province; and all their threats and warnings produced no effect on Prince Gortchacoff. It was an unfortunate diplomatic campaign, which resulted in a triumph for Prince Gortchacoff, and in doing more harm than good to the unfortunate Poles.

In conversing with a Pole of some distinction, I asked him what Poland he wished to see restored. Was it historic Poland of 1772, or "a" Poland with a

remained in complete retirement, and has never been requested to resume his official post in the Government of Poland.

purely Polish population? The old historic Poland stretched to the sea at Dantzic, having the Vistula as the great tributary for trade. It stretched, I believe, also to Besserabia in the south, thus having two outlets to the sea. It appeared to me that " a " Poland without the command of a seaport would be impossible, and it would be equally impossible to retransform Dantzic into a Polish town, which had now become a German town. I did not, therefore, see how a restoration of Poland could be now effected with the necessary means of maintaining itself, or with advantage to Europe. My Polish friend was unable to answer my question, but confessed that my opinions were well founded, and that the restoration of ancient Poland, as existing before 1772, was quite impracticable.

The Slavonic question has now taken the place of the Polish question. The Poles are Slavs, and their freedom from Russia can alone be looked to by their association with their Slavonic brethren for the creation of an independent Slavonic State, either in the form of a Confederation or in that of a separate State. The aim of Russia, according to all appearances, would be to create an extended Kingdom of Servia under the Prince of Montenegro, which would include Bulgaria, Bosnia, and Herzegovina, and be placed under the protectorate of Russia. This scheme would, however, be strongly resisted by Austria, for it would be a death-blow to the Austrian Empire, which has a very large Slavonic population, and could not be brought about without a war. But this is too large a question to enter upon here.

The time has not arrived, although it may not be far distant, when the Slavonic question will engage the attention of Europe.

The question of the differences between Germany and Denmark, in regard to the Danish Duchies, continued its dilatory and shifting course, with no appearance of the pending negotiations leading to any satisfactory result. I will not inflict on my readers the wearisome details of this complicated and insoluble question. Suffice it to say that Prussia had cast her longing eyes on the Duchies, and by gaining delay only awaited the moment when she could carry into effect her ambitious views. The possession of Kiel, on account of its admirable harbour and the future construction of a canal between the North Sea and the Baltic, of which she would be mistress, were the allurements to her ambition, and her policy and action were governed by the intention not to be thwarted in the accomplishment of her ambition by any pacific arrangement with Denmark.

The activity of the *National Verein* in Germany for a reform of the Germanic Confederation, for the creation of a central Power, and the establishment of some representative system in connection with the central Power now engaged public atttention. Numerous plans were submitted by German statesmen for this end. Amongst them was one from Count Beust, the Saxon Minister, whose activity of mind far exceeded the limited sphere of his official action, and, being a man of considerable talent and merit, he assumed the character of a "roving politician." I had been personally acquainted with him for many years, having been his colleague at Berlin in 1837, when he was Secretary of Legation under Baron Minkwitz and I was attaché. Saxony was too narrow a sphere for a man of his large ideas, and it may justly be said that he felt himself as "*un géant dans un entresol.*"

I will give his plan in his own words :—*

"As the draft was made at a time when there was no pressure, either internal or external, on the Governments, it was conceived in a spirit of moderate and prudent reform. On the other hand, the character of a Confederation of States had to be maintained, as the establishment of a predominance of a 'Confederate State' would, in the view of its projectors, involve the exclusion of Austria. The practical result which I had in my mind was to make the machinery of the Confederation work more rapidly, and to introduce a mode of procedure more calculated to rouse public interest than the Assembly which sat during the whole year in the Eschenheimer Gasse at Frankfort. I accordingly proposed to leave at Frankfort only the members of the Federal Administration, and to fix biennial meetings of the Bundestag, each for a period of one month, on 1st May in a southern town (Ratisbon) and on the 1st November in a northern town (Hamburg), with the proviso that a representative Assembly of Delegates from the German Parliaments might be convoked from time to time, Austria presiding when the Assembly met at Ratisbon, and Prussia when it met at Hamburg."

This plan met with objections at Vienna. Prussia was certain to reject it. Count Bernstorff in his reply plainly indicated, as Count Beust states, that the Prussian plan was no other than Federal reform. I was

* See "Memoirs of Count Beust," Vol. I., page 199.

confidentially told that Count Bernstorff, on being asked his opinion on the subject of Baron Beust's proposal, observed that it was difficult for Prussia to enter into any such combination with Austria, as the *sine quâ non* condition required by Austria was always a guarantee for the Austrian possessions.

It was shortly after this time, in 1861, that Count Bismarck was unceasingly engaged in gaining the King in favour of his plans, and in impregnating his mind with the conviction that what was termed the German question could only be settled by the sword. In October, 1861, he wrote: "I have been active both at Coblentz and here in regard to the German policy, and not wholly without result."*

Count Beust was a strong upholder and defender of the minor German States, and a partisan of what was called the "Triade," or third Power in Germany. He was a strong opponent of Prussian hegemony, and a strong supporter of Austria.

The German question had become as insoluble as the Schleswig-Holstein question. The origin of it was the rivalry between the two great German Powers, and the general cry of the German nation was for a strong central Power, with a representative Assembly for the whole of Germany. This was the universal aspiration, and it could only be achieved by having one head, and that leadership could only be placed in the hands of Prussia.

In writing to Lord John Russell on November 16th, 1861, I stated as follows:—

* See Bismarck's *Merkwürdigkeiten*, page 265.

"There appears to be a general feeling that the present state of disunion and rivalry among the minor States of the Germanic Confederation cannot long continue without endangering the internal tranquillity, and even the external safety of Germany; but it is equally apparent that the divergence of opinions is so great, the separate interests so varied, and the power of initiative so weak, that there exists but slender hopes of the attainment of an harmonious understanding among the several States for the introduction of such reforms as would satisfy the nation, and as would give internal union and external strength. The evil which existed was too evident, too prominent not to be recognised by all, but no two States could agree as to the remedy to be applied.

"Prussia is ambitious of acquiring the leading part in Germany, and of centralising in her hands the entire direction of military and diplomatic affairs. Failing to obtain this position she will accept no other, and will prefer to leave matters in *statu quo* until external or internal events arise to promote the accomplishment of her views.

"Austria is solely desirous of maintaining the position she now holds in Germany and will not abandon the interests of her federal allies; she feels a distrust of Prussia, and that any concessions which she might be disposed to make to acquire her support would only be turned to her own loss and disadvantage.

"Bavaria pleads for what is termed the 'Triade.' She has an army of 100,000 men, and confides in the sturdy spirit of Bavarian nationality. She will never willingly accept a position under either of the two great German Powers, and least of all under Prussia. She will not separate herself from Austria,* and will continue as heretofore to make common cause with the minor States, struggling for the maintenance of their independent sovereignties.

"Saxony is in favour of a 'Triade'—a third Power in Germany, balancing between the two great German Powers and

* Bavaria and the Southern States proved this in 1866.

entirely antagonistic to the popular aspiration for unity. She will support Austria, and will endeavour by every means to guard herself against absorption by Prussia.

"Würtemberg is desirous that Germany as a whole should be strengthened by such a reform of the Diet as would produce greater unity in Germany. At the same time she will not willingly cede the exercise of her sovereign independence and rights, and least of all will she willingly place herself under the direction of Prussia.

"Hanover has been and is always the arch-supporter of the Germanic Diet, with all its cumbrous machinery and total want of vitality. She considers it the best anchor of safety to ensure the continued existence of the minor States. She will never consent to the abrogation of her sovereign rights, and will resist any attempts to weaken them by concession to the popular cry for unity.

"It is, however, more than probable, from the difficulties offered to the union of the several German Governments, that matters will remain in their present state until some external event shall awaken Germany to a sense of impending danger, and force a common understanding and a common action for mutual defence.* It is, I fear, scarcely to be expected that any initiative on the part of Germany itself will lead to any successful issue, however strong the necessity may appear, and however powerfully the national wishes may be felt and expressed."

It must be borne in mind that this despatch was written in November, 1861. It gave a cursory but correct account of the state of Germany on the accession of King William I. In the following year—1862— Count Bismarck was called to the Councils of the State and appointed Minister for Foreign Affairs. From that time a new era dawned on Prussia. He was a statesman of iron will, of daring but skilful action. His

* This was eventually brought about in 1870.

plans were already formed and he made no pretence of a concealment of them. He clearly saw that the Gordian knot with Austria could only be unravelled by the sword—that the union of Germany under Prussia could only be attained "with blood and iron." He saw at once that it was necessary for Prussia to abandon her hitherto lethargic policy, and to adopt a clear and decided line in lieu of that passive and neutral one which had neither gained her allies nor conciliated adversaries. Subsequent events proved how, with a strong and resolute will, backed by an efficient army, and aided by a skilful diplomacy, he successfully carried out the object he had in view. Prussia, since 1815, had been drilling and disciplining a large army and had brought it to a state of perfection. Count Bismarck was the first Prussian Minister who had the courage and daring to make use of it.

The close of the year 1861 was one of grief and mourning to the British nation. His Royal Highness the Prince Consort, who had been suffering from fever, caused, it is said, by a chill, passed away peacefully to his eternal home. He was only ill a few days, and no dangerous symptoms had appeared. On the 11th Lord Russell wrote to me "that the Prince had had two good nights and was going on well;" that he "had a kind of low fever, which might last ten days longer, and that there were no unfavourable symptoms; and that if I saw the Princess Royal I was to say everything most comforting and cheering." I received this letter on the 13th. On the morning of the 15th the sad news of the Prince's death reached Berlin. The suddenness of the shock, the feeling of grief and deep sympathy for Her Majesty the Queen and the members of her family, and the irreparable loss to the nation of this great and good Prince, filled me with sorrow. I went immediately to inquire after the Crown Princess. Her Royal Highness was deeply affected, but calm and resigned. The Crown Prince never left her after breaking to her the sad intelligence. Her wish was to accompany the Prince to England, but her physician dissuaded her, on account of her health, from undertaking such a journey.

Immediately on the receipt of the telegram announcing the mournful event, the King sent his aide-de-camp, Major Strubberg, to convey the expression of his sincere condolence, and of his deep sympathy for Her Majesty the Queen and the Royal Family. Count and Countess Bernstorff called to express how deeply they sympathised with the Queen, and how sincerely they felt for the irreparable loss which had befallen the nation.

This mournful event produced here the greatest sensation, and it was received by all classes of society with deep grief. Not only has there been manifested profound sorrow and regret for the loss of a Prince so distinguished for his virtues, for his matchless qualities, and his highly gifted mind—a loss indeed irreparable—but there was evinced a general feeling of the warmest sympathy for our gracious Queen under her severe bereavement.

In addressing Lord Russell, I expressed, in my own name and that of Lady Augustus, and of every member of Her Majesty's Legation, our profound grief and sorrow at an event which so deeply afflicted the Queen, and so grievously overshadowed the happiness of our gracious Sovereign; which deprived our Royal Family of a beloved parent, our country of its brightest ornament, and which plunged the nation in gloom.

I had an audience of their Prussian Majesties, who expressed their sincere and heartfelt sympathy at the severe affliction which had befallen the Queen, the Royal Family, and the nation. Their Majesties evinced deep emotion. During the many years that I have known their Majesties I have never seen them more deeply impressed with feelings of sorrow and sympathy as on the present occasion.

I caused an impressive service to be held in the British Chapel on the 23rd of December, the day of the funeral of the Prince Consort, which was attended by their Majesties, all the members of the Royal Family, the Diplomatic Corps, the Prussian Ministers and high Officials, and a large number of Generals, amongst whom was Field-Marshal Wrangel.

The Crown Prince had left some days before to attend the funeral in person.

CHAPTER VIII.

The New Prussian Parliament—Overwhelming Majority of the Liberal Party—Continued Struggle between the Government and Parliament on Army Reorganisation Bill—Conversation with Bernstorff on Recognition of Italy—New Order of Knighthood—The German Question—Despatch of Bernstorff to Rechberg in Reply to his Proposals for Dietal Reform—Sensation it Produced—Identic Notes of South German States protesting against Prussian Policy—Conversation with the King of Prussia—The Question of the Partition of Schleswig Suggested as a Means of solving Differences with Denmark—The Hessian Question—Discourtesy of the Elector to General Willisen—Dismissal of Hessian Ministry Demanded—Rupture of Diplomatic Relations—Unsatisfactory Conduct of the Elector—Prussian Parliament again Dissolved—Change of Ministry—Bismarck appointed Minister at Paris—Conversation with Prince Hohenlohe—Strained Relations with Austria—The King's Opinion on the Appointment of Grand Duke Constantine—Mr. White's Letter—The Japanese Embassy—Bernstorff on Restoration of the Primate—Happy Delivery of the Crown Princess of a Prince.

AT the commencement of 1862 the newly-elected Prussian Parliament met at Berlin. The result of the late elections had been signally triumphant to the Liberal party, which, although composed of different political shades, still, as a whole, formed an overwhelming majority of the Lower Chamber. The ultra-Conservative, or so-termed *Kreuz Zeitung*, party had been reduced to the very diminutive number of twenty-five or thirty representatives in the Lower House, while the fraction termed the Mathis party, which formed the nucleus of the Ministerial party, had been completely dissolved, the principal leaders, men of note, such as Mathis, Simpson, Beseler, etc., having failed to secure their re-election. From whatever cause, whether from the apathy of the Ministerialists or their unpopularity in the country; whether from the well-organised and active co-operation of all classes of the Liberal party, or whether from the special circumstances of the Prussian Electoral Law—by which the representatives are not elected direct by the people, but through the channel of electors who decide the election of a candidate (termed in German *Wahlmänner*)—it is a singular fact that the representatives to the Lower House should be principally selected from that class which does not form the landed aristocracy, and which may be said to represent the intelligence rather than the wealth of the country. It certainly does not appear of happy omen that one influential class of the nation, having a great stake in the country, should be, as it were, excluded from representation in the Lower House.

The great Constitutional struggle was between the Government, representing the Crown, and the Lower House on the question of the military budget, over which the Lower House claimed to exercise a discretional control. The Liberal party considered that an addition of eight or nine millions of dollars to the taxation annually for the army was too heavy a charge for the nation to bear in time of peace without any ostensible political object in view. Had the Government taken up a decided position on the German question, and been enabled to allege that the augmentation of the army was necessary to carry out their policy in Germany, this sum or any sum demanded would have been voted with alacrity. But neither the King nor his Government could have taken this course, or have made any declaration of their future policy satisfactory to the Liberal party without producing a rupture with Austria and the other members of the Confederation. Consequently, without a compromise there was no solution possible, and to this neither the Government nor the Liberal party seemed inclined. Thus matters drifted on in their usual unsatisfactory state, the military budget being sternly opposed by the Lower House and as sternly maintained by the Government.

I had a conversation with Count Bernstorff on the recognition by Prussia of the Kingdom of Italy. He was very reasonable on the subject, admitting that it was in the interest of Prussia to do so, but that there were many difficulties in the way. First and foremost, the principles of the King; secondly, the difficulties in regard to their relations with Austria, unless it could be accompanied with an assurance that Venetia would be preserved not only to Austria, but to Germany, for he remarked that it was generally recognised that the quadrilateral was the barrier of Germany; and thirdly, a fear of creating an ill feeling among the Catholic Rhenish population. All this, said Count Bernstorff, made it difficult for Prussia to take a formal step of this nature. But, he said, if the Roman and Venetian questions could be satisfactorily provided for, or if either could be finally solved, the recognition would be rendered more easy. He seemed also to doubt the possibility of detaching Italy from France. "If," said he, "you can procure any assurance that Venetia will not be attacked, you will greatly facilitate my endeavours." In speaking of the question of legitimacy, Count Bernstorff observed, "*Quant à la question de la légitimité il y a longtemps que j'en ai fait mon deuil. Il ne s'agit maintenant que de penáre en considération les intérêts du pays.*"

I wrote on January 11 to Lord Russell that "I did not think the time far distant when Prussia would consent to recognise Italy, and, from private information I had received, the action of the Catholic clergy in Poland and the dissatisfaction of Russia with the attitude of the Pope were working great changes in the mind of Prince Gortchacoff respecting Italy."

On the occasion of his coronation the King instituted a new order of knighthood, to which the appellation of the "Order of the Krone" was given, in imitation of the first King of Prussia crowned at Königsberg, who, on that occasion, instituted the order of the "Black Eagle," the motto of which is "Suum Cuique." After the partition of Poland, a humorous Pole took a secret opportunity of adding the word "rapuit," indicating the spoliation of his country by Prussia.

The King of Prussia also introduced a higher class of the Order of the Red Eagle, under the appellation of "Grand Cross of the Red Eagle," which will rank above the existing Order of the Red Eagle of the First Class.

The German question was beginning at this time to assume an important character. A despatch of Count

Bernstorff to Count Beust had very clearly proclaimed the policy of Prussia, and had struck alarm among all the members of the Confederation. In ordinary times no result might have immediately arisen, but behind Prussia there was a large party in Germany who were not inactive, who were largely represented in the Prussian Lower House, and would not easily be held back. Then, again, there was the Hessian question, which might at any time have produced a rupture and caused a collision, as in 1850 at Bronzell.

I have previously alluded to an important despatch addressed by Count Bernstorff on 20th December, 1861, to Count Beust in reply to his proposals for Dietal Reform. This despatch, which was published, created great sensation at Vienna and no small panic among the minor German States who clustered round Austria.

Count Bernstorff hinted at the formation of a "'Separate League' within the Germanic Confederation under the protection and leadership of Prussia." This clearly demonstrated to Austria that the aim of Prussia was to undermine her influence and position in Germany, and to acquire, at her expense, the general direction of German affairs. The other German States viewed it as the absorption of their Sovereignties, and their reduction to the vassalage of Prussia. Secret negotiations were entered into between Austria, Bavaria, Saxony, and Würtemberg, and it was determined to address identic notes to the Prussian Government protesting against the policy set forth in Count Bernstorff's despatch and against the Prussian interpretation of Art. II. of the

Federal Act, as being destructive of the Sovereign rights of the Independent States. The other German States were invited to adhere to the protest, and it was agreed to confide to Austria the drawing up of the identic note to be addressed to the Prussian Government.

Great secrecy was maintained on this subject, and the Prussian Government were completely taken by surprise by this unexpected and combined movement. These notes were presented to Count Bernstorff on the 2nd February by the representatives of Austria, Bavaria, Würtemberg, Hanover, Hesse-Darmstadt, and Nassau. The Saxon Minister conveyed to Count Bernstorff the adhesion of his Government to the action taken by his German colleagues.

These identic notes concluded with an invitation (though not in a formal manner) to Prussia to join a general conference to agree on the measures for a reform of the Diet.

In a long conversation I had with the King of Prussia His Majesty spoke with great interest and affection of the Queen, and inquired after Her Majesty's health with great solicitude. He spoke of the state of affairs in Germany and of the Austrian note. He said it was unheard of that a despatch not addressed to the Cabinet of Vienna should have been taken up in such a manner. His Majesty dwelt on the irritation and excitement which this incident would cause. I ventured to express my regret at the disunion of the two German Powers, observing that so long as this disunion existed no salutary and effective reform of the Diet could be hoped for, for which the German nation was yearning. I also observed to His Majesty that the publication of the notes exchanged between the two Governments appeared to me very regrettable, as disputes between Governments could be amicably arranged and forgotten, but when they became the property of the public they produced irritation, and envenomed the good feelings between nations, which was more difficult to obliterate. The King quite concurred in this view, observing that Austria had set the example.

His Majesty then referred to the Chambers, observing that he feared the discussion on the Hessian question which was to take place on the morrow. He evinced some irritation against the Lower House, saying, "*Ah, ces Messieurs désirent amener une guerre en Allemagne.*" I remarked that His Majesty had received lately proofs of the loyalty and devotion of his people, and I believed that there was an innate loyalty in the Prussian nation to their Sovereign. I could not therefore think that loyal subjects could be considered as dangerous. Opposition to the Government did not imply disloyalty to the Throne. A Government to be strong required also an opposition, and in England it was recognised, and even termed "Her Majesty's Opposition." Parliamentary Government in Prussia, I added, was as yet young and inexperienced; too much importance must not be attached to the speeches of young and ambitious orators. It was better, perhaps, that the gas should have free vent than be pent up and restrained. A great deal, I remarked, depended on the management of a Chamber.

By conciliation many might be gained; by repulsion, on the other hand, many who might be gained would be driven further than they intended to go. Time and conciliation would work a change and impart experience and judgment.

The King spoke in affectionate terms of the Emperor Franz Josef, and I told His Majesty that I could bear witness to the kindly feelings of the Emperor towards him, for that on several occasions the Emperor had expressed them to me. His Majesty said he knew it, but he repeated the phrase, "*Ces Messieurs veulent la guerre en Allemagne*," referring to the Second Chamber.

Thus ended the conversation. The King, who is always amiable and gracious, appeared depressed and careworn, and received my observations, as they were intended, in a consolatory light.

I again spoke to Count Bernstorff on the recognition of the King of Italy by Prussia, repeating the arguments I had previously used. He confessed that he was favourable to it, but that Austria would look upon it as a hostile act. I said: "Explain to her that it would enable you to exercise influence in Italy in her favour; that by recognising the present *status quo* you do not prejudge the question of Venetia, but rather confirm its present status, and will render it more easy for the Italian statesmen to keep the peace."

"*Ah*," he replied, "*que voulez-vous, l'Autriche ne veut pas qu'on lui rende des services.*"

Count Bernstorff then added: "Tell Lord Russell that if England will support us in the Schleswig-Holstein question, I can then carry the recognition of Italy. I am anxious for it; the difficulty is with the King."

I replied, "That if I urged the recognition on him it was solely for the interests of Prussia, and the maintenance of peace in Italy. It did not affect us and could do us no good. On the other hand it will cost you a sheet of paper and will place you in an advantageous position both at home and abroad."

The partition of Schleswig was now proposed for a settlement of the Schleswig-Holstein question by Count Bernstorff, and he told me that Prince Gortchacoff was not opposed to it.

"Therefore," said Count Bernstorff, "we have France and Russia, and we hope that England will not oppose it. Aid us in this and we will aid you in your affair." I asked him, "What affair?" "Italy," he said. I replied that "England had no authority to cut and carve portions of the Danish Monarchy."

The French Ambassador, Prince La Tour-d'Auvergne, told me that he saw no outlet for this interminable question but a partition of Schleswig. He said that M. de Thouvenel had not yet accepted this solution of the question, but that in this matter he was very much guided by him. He said that for the present he was quite passive, but he foresaw that a final solution of this question could only be arrived at by a partition. From Count Bernstorff's language to me it appeared that Prince La Tour-d'Auvergne had expressed an approval of the partition, whether by instructions or not I was unable to say.

It is unfortunate for Denmark that she did not at once accept this idea. Had she done so she would have maintained intact the entirety of the Danish Monarchy, and Europe would have been relieved of this tiresome and interminable controversy.

The Hessian question came now prominently forward. It was a contest between the Elector and his subjects. The conduct of the Elector was illegal and oppressive, and his subjects petitioned the Diet for redress. An understanding had been happily come to between the Austrian and Prussian Governments which precluded the possibility of any collision such as occurred in 1850, and was an intimation to the Elector that he could look for no support or assistance from Austria.

The question was brought before the Diet in the form of an Austro-Prussian proposal. Considerable delay had been caused by the necessary exchange of communications with Vienna. The Austrian Cabinet agreed to join Prussia in submitting the Prussian proposal to the Diet, but declined the proposal to send a special Minister in their joint names to remonstrate with the Elector on the course he was pursuing. Count Bernstorff informed Count Rechberg that in the event of the Diet not agreeing to their joint proposal, Prussia would, with Austria if she agreed, or without her if she declined, send immediately a special Minister to Cassel to obtain from the Elector the withdrawal of the proclamation he had issued, and to move him to abandon the Electoral Law of 1860 which had been promulgated for the election of the Second Chamber.

On the 12th of May General V. Willisen was sent on a special mission to Cassel charged with a letter from the King to the Elector. General V. Willisen was instructed in the name of Prussia to move the Elector to withdraw his proclamation of the 26th of April. In case of non-compliance a rupture of diplomatic relations would take place, and the Prussian Minister would leave Cassel.

At an interview I had with Count Bernstorff on May 16, I first congratulated him on the felicitous turn which the Hessian question had taken in consequence of the Austro-Prussian proposal having been agreed to by the Diet, and the reported intention of the Elector to conform to the wish expressed by that body. I presumed, therefore, that the difficulties which this question had presented might be considered as satisfactorily adjusted.

Count Bernstorff, to my surprise, said that although the Austro-Prussian proposal had been carried by a large majority of the Diet, and that the Federal question had so far been settled, a fresh incident had occurred which was of a serious nature, and likely to compromise the relations between Prussia and Electoral Hesse.

Count Bernstorff then related the following circumstance which had attended General Willisen's mission :—

He stated that he was the bearer of a letter from the King of Prussia to the Elector, written in friendly terms, which he was charged to deliver in person. As was usual in the case of a military mission of this character, General Willisen, immediately on his arrival at Cassel, had addressed himself to the Aide-de-Camp in Waiting to request an audience of the Elector, stating the object of it—namely, to deliver a letter from his Sovereign.

The Aide-de-Camp, with much embarrassment, replied that his audience could not be then granted, and intimated that he should apply officially through the Minister for Foreign Affairs. On the following day General Willisen was informed that the Elector was indisposed and could not receive him; but on the evening of that day, after a Council of Ministers had been held, General Willisen was summoned to the Palace.

On arriving there he found awaiting him the Ministers for Foreign Affairs and of Justice, the two members of the Electoral Ministry the most hostile to Prussia, and the most ardent supporters of the anti-constitutional views of the Elector. From their presence in the ante-room General Willisen foreboded no very agreeable or satisfactory result to his approaching interview, which subsequently took place in the presence of the above-named Ministers.

The Elector received General Willisen with marked discourtesy, and gave vent to his feelings of anger in terms of disrespect to the King and to his Government.

General Willisen, with calmness and self-possession, requested His Royal Highness to peruse the letter with which he had been charged by his Sovereign, observing that he would learn from the friendly expression it conained the object of his mission. The Elector, with a movement of disdain, threw the letter on the table and declined to open it in the General's presence, accompanying his act with expressions which Count Bernstorff designated as insulting.

The manner of his reception having been reported by General Willisen to his Government, a telegraphic instruction was sent to M. de Sydow, the Prussian Minister at Cassel, to complain of the want of respect shown to the King's special envoy, and to demand that the Elector should again receive General Willisen within twenty-four hours to apologise for his discourteous reception of him.

No answer to this demand having been given, and no notice having been taken of it within the time specified, General Willisen quitted Cassel and returned to Berlin.

Count Bernstorff remarked that the honour and dignity of Prussia were at stake, and demanded that this insult on the part of the Elector of Hesse should be atoned. He said the King was deeply wounded by the want of respect shown by the Elector to his special envoy and to his letter, and that Prussia could not submit to be treated with such indignity without claiming and, if needs be, enforcing due satisfaction.

Count Bernstorff stated that, after due deliberation by the Council of Ministers, it had been determined to instruct M. de Sydow to demand as reparation for the insult shown to the King's special envoy the immediate dismissal of his present Ministry; and that if this satisfaction should not be granted within two days

M. de Sydow was to break off diplomatic relations and to leave Cassel.

Count Bernstorff said it was time to put an end to a state of things in Hesse which had become intolerable, and that the Electorate was an *enclave* within the Prussian territory, which had always been, and continued to oe, the focus of intrigue against Prussia. He said that he had received information of preparations being made for an outbreak in Hesse, which would be followed by similar disturbances in Nassau and in Hesse-Darmstadt. "If," said Count Bernstorff, " a revolution should break out in Hesse, we should be obliged to enter and put it down. It will, therefore, be far better to enter beforehand to maintain order and prevent disturbance."

I observed to Count Bernstorff that this fresh incident which threatened to disturb the relations between the two States appeared to me fraught with the gravest danger, not only to the peace of Germany but to that of Europe. It amounted to an isolated action of Prussia, and must therefore be considered as bearing an international and not a federal character. It would no doubt be viewed by many of the States of Germany as a virtual withdrawal of Prussia from the Confederation, and what would be the consequences if, out of this untoward dispute, an open collision should be brought about between Prussia and the Diet? Count Bernstorff replied that Prussia had no intention of withdrawing from the Confederation, but she was determined to defend her honour and to maintain her dignity and position in Germany. He had duly reflected, as had also the Prussian Cabinet, on the consequences of the step they had taken, and he fully admitted the gravity of it. It was, however, high time for Prussia, whose patience had been exhausted by the antagonistic course of the Elector of Hesse during a period of twelve years, to put an end to a state of things intolerable in itself, and dangerous alike to the interests of Prussia and of Germany.

The Elector of Hesse refused to accede to the Prussian demand, and diplomatic relations were broken off.

The Prussian Cabinet determined to await the vote of the Germanic Diet (which was to summon the Elector to restore the Constitution of 1831 and the Electoral Law of 1849) before taking further action in the Hessian affair. The fears at first entertained of an isolated action by Prussia subsided, and my German colleagues were of opinion that the question at issue with the Elector would be finally adjusted by the Diet. Count Bernstorff stated that the Prussian Government were desirous that the difference with Hesse should be arranged in a " regular manner " (implying thereby by means of the Diet) if it were possible, and that if the Prussian demand should be carried out they would be satisfied; but he added that a change of the Electoral Ministry was the important necessity, as it was perfectly impossible to continue to treat with a Government which had acted as the present advisers of the Elector had done.

Although the Elector had accepted the decision of the Diet, and had appointed a new Ministry, it had neither been officially gazetted, nor had the Elector given his approval of the programme of the new Ministry. Neither had any reply been received by the Prussian Government to a notification indirectly conveyed to the Elector on the 18th June. An order was consequently given by the King for the concentration of the 4th and 7th Corps d'Armée on the Hessian frontier preparatory to their entry into the Electorate. This brought the recalcitrant Elector to his senses. The new Ministry was officially installed, the constitution of 1831 re-established, with the Electoral Law of 1849; and thus the dangers which this disagreeable episode had called forth, and which had caused so much alarm, were for the moment allayed.

The differences between the Second Chamber of the Prussian Parliament and the Lower House on the army re-organisation continued unabated. On an adverse vote the Schwerin Ministry resigned and the Parliament was dissolved. A new Ministry of a bureaucratic character was formed under the presidency of Prince Hohenlohe Ingelfingen. The result of the new elections was almost universally in favour of the Liberal Party. Count Bernstorff said that they were "*très mauvaises—même rouges.*"

M. de Bismarck had been re-called from St. Petersburg and had lately arrived at Berlin. Count Bernstorff told me that he was appointed Prussian Envoy at Paris. He observed, "*Vous voulez l'avoir chez vous, et la France également.*" I asked if the French

Government had expressed a wish for his appointment to Paris. He said, "Not precisely, but they would be glad to have him." There was an idea of his taking the place of Auerswald as Minister without a *portefeuille*, but that would not have suited him. The only place he would have accepted in the Ministry was that of Minister President and for Foreign Affairs.

I had a conversation with the President of the Council, Prince Hohenlohe Ingelfingen, and I asked him how matters were going as regarded internal affairs. He said, "badly," and he cited as a proof of the dangerous extremities to which the Democratic Party as he called them were advancing, that in Prussian Saxony, and even here, they had reminded the people that in England Charles I. had been decapitated. I was rather taken aback, but as I saw that he expected an answer I said, "Well, if they look into our Book of Common Prayer they will find a Divine service for King Charles the Martyr, and if they turn over the page they will find a form of thanksgiving for the restoration of the Royal Family."

Baron Budberg, the Russian Minister, who had been on leave at St. Petersburg previous to the departure of M. de Bismarck from that capital, and who was now sent on a special mission to Paris to conduct the affairs of the Embassy there during the temporary absence of the Ambassador, returned to Berlin on the 23rd of May, and left the same evening for Paris. The only visits he paid were to Count Bernstorff and Prince La Tour-d'Auvergne, the French Minister.

It was somewhat remarkable that Baron Budberg's visit to St. Petersburg took place just previously to the departure of M. de Bismarck, and that he was thus enabled to confer with him and Prince Gortchacoff; that shortly after M. de Bismarck's return to Berlin he was appointed Prussian Minister at Paris; that he left Berlin suddenly for Paris; and lastly, that these two diplomatists by some fortuitous accident, if not by some preconcerted arrangement, should both arrive simultaneously at Paris.

Negotiations had taken place with M. de Bismarck for his entry into the Ministry. He was not anxious to join the Cabinet, and he told me that he had expressed a wish to the King to go to London for a short time, as he said "*pour achever son éducation politique.*" But this did not suit Count Bernstorff, who wished to keep the post open for himself. M. de Bismarck's appointment to Paris was with a view to prepare his entry into the Ministry at Berlin, and should his mission to Paris be successful his aim was to replace Count Bernstorff as Minister President and for Foreign Affairs.

There is no doubt, as I have previously mentioned, that the King had at one time scruples in regard to appointing him either to the Foreign Office or as Minister to Paris, on account of his well-known political leaning towards France and Russia, and his acknowledged hatred to Austria. I had reason to believe that M. de Bismarck was unwilling to go to Paris unless his programme should be accepted. His nomination to

Paris, therefore, clearly indicated a change in the opinion of the King, brought about, no doubt, by the altered circumstances of the position of Prussia, both externally and internally, and that the counsels of M. de Bismarck had then assumed the ascendancy.

The support of the Liberal Party in Prussia and in Germany could alone be acquired by the adoption by Prussia of a firm and energetic policy in conformity with the aspirations of the German nation. The King was not personally hostile to Austria, but his eyes had been opened to the fact that the two great Powers could not live harmoniously together on unequal terms in the same " Frankfort" House, and there were evidently no possible means of a solution except by cutting the Gordian knot with the sword.

The programme of M. de Bismarck was to achieve this object by a war with Austria, with a view, if successful, to exclude Austria from Germany, and to place the leadership of Germany in the hands of Prussia. Austria was supported by Saxony and the Southern States of Germany, as was proved in 1866. But in addition to this formidable force the strategic position of Prussia exposed her to further dangers, which would have alarmed any statesman who had not the iron will and daring courage of M. de Bismarck. There was Russia on the one side and France on the other. From the favours shown by Prussia towards Russia during the Crimean War, it was no difficult task for M. de Bismarck to obtain assurances from Russia of her neutrality in the event of a war with Austria. But this task was far more difficult with France without offering to her some compensation. The King had resolutely refused to cede a village on the Rhine to France. Whatever hopes could be held out to France of indemnity elsewhere were uncertain and illusory. The prospect of a Franco-Russian-Prussian Alliance was the only allurement which could be held out to the Emperor Napoleon in exchange for his neutrality should Prussia be engaged in a war with Austria. It is impossible to know what passed between the Emperor and M. de Bismarck in their confidential conversation, or the nature of the engagements, if any were entered into; but the coëval presence of Baron Budberg and M. de Bismarck at Paris could not fail at this moment to give rise to serious conjectures as to coming events.

Count Bernstorff informed me that all the reports and suspicions attached to M. de Bismarck's nomination to Paris were wholly unfounded, and that he was not charged with any species of negotiations with the French Government. He repudiated any intention or idea of an alliance with France and Russia, and stated decidedly that there was no species of combination or connexity between the mission of M. de Bismarck and Baron Budberg. He could not, however, know how far M. de Bismarck might not launch out on his own hook; and in regard to his denying any intention of an alliance with France and Russia, I could only say, "*Credat Judæus Apella—non ego.*"

M. de Bismarck, I learnt, had not been successful at Paris (I presume with the Government), and he asked for permission to go to Vichy during the Emperor Napoleon's stay there, with a view to gain him over to Prussia. How this was to be achieved without corresponding concessions on the part of Prussia was a question for the fertile brain of Bismarck to solve. In the Berlin *Punch* Bismarck was represented as being under the mesmeric influence of the Emperor, who was the Mephistopheles. The words put into the Emperor's mouth were probably dictated by the phrase said to have been used by Bismarck here before he started for Paris: "*Que l'Empereur était trop vertueux pour lui, qu'il allait à Paris pour le corrompre.*"

Lady Augustus and I had the honour of dining with the Crown Prince and Princess at Potsdam on the 5th of July in celebration of the marriage of Her Royal Highness the Princess Alice with Prince Louis of Hesse. The King and Queen were present, but, otherwise, it was strictly private, and merely included the attendants of their Majesties. The King and Queen expressed their warmest sympathy for Her Majesty the Queen in the afflicting reminiscences which on this occasion could not fail to overcloud an event which otherwise would have filled the heart of the Queen with joyful happiness. The King gave the health of the royal bride and bridegroom.

The King did not open on any political subject with me. The only observation he made was with respect to the appointment of the Grand Duke Constantine as Viceroy of Poland, of which he said he highly disapproved: "a member of the Imperial Family, after the attempt on General Luders' life, ought not to have been placed in such a position."

Since then the judgment of the Emperor was unfortunately confirmed by the intelligence received that the Grand Duke was fired at on leaving the theatre and slightly wounded.

I had a letter from Mr. White, attached to the Consul-General at Warsaw (afterwards Sir William White, Ambassador at Constantinople), in which he said :* " The Grand Duke Constantine's appointment is certainly an event of great importance, and is viewed as such throughout Russia. The Poles have been taken so much by surprise that they hardly realise as yet its future possible bearing. I do not wonder, however, at the alarm of the two great German Powers. At present it has no aggressive significance, as the military importance of Warsaw is to be diminished by the removal of the staff of the First Army, but it is pregnant with importance for the future. An ambitious Prince like the Grand Duke Constantine does not transfer his energies to a new field, and take a man like Wielopolski for his guide, unless he has some object in view. The first moves on the board will be worth watching."

A Japanese Embassy arrived at Berlin, and I dined with Count Bernstorff to meet them. They were twelve in number at dinner. Mr. Benson, President of Liberia,

* Sir William White was a remarkable man. He was a clerk to the Consul-Generalship at Warsaw. I recognised his worth, and aided in his appointment by Lord Clarendon to the Consulate at Dantzic. He had a great knowledge of Eastern affairs and of Oriental languages, and was a most able and conscientious public servant.

(a man of colour), dined also—a very unpretentious, amiable gentleman, speaking English perfectly. The Japanese, who live mostly on fish, have a peculiar sauce —something like our "Soy"—which for a Japanese is not a luxury, but a necessity. Countess Bernstorff accordingly procured a bottle from one of their suite, at the sight of which the Ambassador expressed great delight.

The visit of the President of Liberia referred to commercial matters, with a view to bring about a Treaty of Commerce between Liberia and the Zollverein.

The question of the recognition of the King of Italy, urgently recommended by M. de Bismarck and by a resolution of the Lower House, was now seriously under consideration by the Prussian Cabinet. I inquired of Count Bernstorff whether he had received any communication from St. Petersburg on this subject. It appears that a species of "quasi engagement" had been taken between the Russian and Prussian Governments that no step should be taken by either in regard to this question without previous concert, in order that it might be simultaneously adopted by both. Various causes had produced delays, and in consequence thereof the consideration of this question had been momentarily laid aside.

Matters were in this "somnolent" state when quite suddenly the question was taken up by Russia at the instigation of France, and Count Bernstorff was surprised at receiving from Count Gultz, the Prussian Minister at St. Petersburg, a telegram stating, on the authority of Prince Gortchacoff (who till then had been very reserved on the question), that the Imperial Government had decided to recognise the King of Italy. Prince Gortchacoff had stated that having, through the medium of the French Government, submitted to the Cabinet of Turin certain assurances or guarantees required by Russia as the conditions on which Russia would recognise the new kingdom and resume diplomatic relations with King Victor Emanuel, and these requirements having been satisfactorily responded to through the same organ, the Imperial Government, with a view to strengthen the Monarchical principle upheld by the Italian Government, had agreed to recognise the new order of things. No previous intimation of these guarantees had been made to the Prussian Government, nor had they been consulted thereon, nor had they then any precise knowledge of the guarantees required. A courier would leave St. Petersburg in a few days with the official instructions on the subject, with which the Prussian Government would be made acquainted, and a hope was expressed that, if approved, the Prussian Government would also decide within the period of the stay of the Russian courier—viz., twenty-four hours—and would agree to act simultaneously with Russia in making a similar notification to the Cabinet of Turin.

This was too much for Count Bernstorff to bear. He considered it a cavalier mode of proceeding on the part of the Russian Government. He was not willing that Prince Gortchacoff should take the wind out of his sails, nor that Prussia should follow in the wake of Russia on a question of this nature, thus giving to

France the exultation of having effected the recognition of Italy by the two Northern Powers.

The Russian courier could not arrive for some days. Count Bernstorff decided to take his own line independently of Russia. He drew up a despatch to the Prussian Minister at Turin, which received the approval of the King. It was an able despatch. It reverted to the application repeatedly made to the Government by the Minister of King Victor Emanuel. It enumerated the difficulties which had hitherto retarded the measure —viz., the susceptibility of the German Confederation, and the feelings of a large portion of her Catholic population. It stated that the Prussian Government were satisfied to accept the assurance given by the Cabinet of Turin that it desired peace and order; that its policy would be of a pacific nature, externally and internally; and that it would leave the questions of Venetia and Rome to be solved by time and peaceful negotiation. It concluded by stating that the King of Prussia was willing to recognise the Kingdom of Italy if the Cabinet of Turin would renew the assurances of their desire and their intention to continue to maintain order and to pursue a policy of peaceful relations with their neighbours.

The despatch was addressed to Count Brassier de St. Simon, the Prussian representative to the King of Sardinia, for communication to the Cabinet of Turin, and was despatched by a special messenger before the arrival here of the Russian courier; consequently, the recognition of the Kingdom of Italy preceded the

Russian recognition, which was forwarded through the medium of the French Government.

After the despatch had left, the Reactionary Party at Court made attempts to have it revoked, and to suspend the notification till the Russian courier arrived, but Count Bernstorff said it was too late.

The reply of the Italian Government in regard to the recognition of the Kingdom of Italy was received here on the 16th of July, and was accepted by the King as satisfactory and as fulfilling the conditions required by His Majesty. The Italian Minister, Count Launay, was received by the King to present a letter from his Sovereign announcing his assumption of the title of "King of Italy" in virtue of a decree of the representative of the Italian nation.

Count Bernstorff did not attach much importance to the pretended alliance between Russia and France, and categorically denied the truth of any alliance between Prussia and France. He said that the relations of Prussia and France were very good, and that the French Government were amicably disposed towards Prussia. Prussia was also on good terms with Russia, but there was no question of an alliance.

The struggle between the Government and the Chamber on the Army Reorganisation Bill continued without any probability of a solution. The King, I was told, had said, "I have given a promise to carry through the military reorganisation. I am bound, and cannot recede from my word. I must carry it through, or I must abdicate."

I was told that Baron Budberg, the Russian Minister at Berlin, on taking leave of M. de Thouvenel at Paris, was asked by the latter what was doing, or to be done, in regard to the Danish Duchies question.

Baron Budberg replied that he partook entirely of the opinions of Baron Brünnow. On which M. de Thouvenel asked what were the opinions of Baron Brünnow. To this Baron Budberg replied, "*Qu'il fallait les laisser cuire dans leur propre jus.*" M. de Thouvenel entirely concurred in this opinion.

Count Bernstorff told me that, on the occasion of the recognition of the Kingdom of Italy, he had made an appeal to the Italian Government that the misfortunes of the ex-Royal family of Naples might be alleviated by the restoration to them of their private property, and he observed that this appeal was founded on the intimate relations which had existed for so many years between the Courts of Prussia and Naples.

He said that the Cabinet of Turin evinced every disposition to accede to his request, but observed that it could not be expected to place at the disposal of King Francis II. the means of encouraging open hostility to the Italian Government.

Count Bernstorff remarked that it could be hardly expected that a renunciation of his rights should be imposed on King Francis II. as a condition of the restitution of his private property, for it was a condition he could never agree to. He thought, however, that if the ex-King of Naples should retire from Rome and Italy the exigencies of the Italian Government would be fulfilled, and that the difficulties with respect to the restoration of the private property of the exiled family would be removed.

The Crown Princess of Prussia was safely delivered of a Prince on the 14th of August at the New Palace, Potsdam. I had been staying for some days at Potsdam awaiting this event, and signed, with Count Schleinitz, the Minister of the Royal House, the usual protocol recording the event.

CHAPTER IX.

Baron Ricasoli's Visit to Berlin—Prussian Sympathy for Italy—Servia—Disturbances at Belgrade—Conference at Constantinople—Montenegro—Collision with the Turks—Commercial Treaty between Prussia and France signed August 2—Opposed by Southern States—Proposed Treaty of Commerce between Great Britain and Zollverein—Austrian Proposal to enter Zollverein rejected—Dinner at Baron Budberg's—Conversation with him—His Language very conciliatory—Continued Conflict between the Government and the Chamber—Changes in the Ministry—Count Bernstorff succeeded by M. de Bismarck—The Queen's Visit to Germany—My Interview with Lord Russell at Gotha—His Proposals on Danish Question approved by Austria and Prussia—Fatal Effects of their Rejection by Denmark—Missions to Berlin and London raised to Embassies—My Appointment to Munich—The Order of K.C.B. conferred on me by the Queen—Relations between Austria and Prussia—Count Bernstorff's Explanation of his Resignation—His Appointment as Ambassador to England—Rejection by the Chamber of the Naval Budget—Christening of infant Prince.

BARON RICASOLI, the Italian Minister President and Minister for Foreign Affairs, arrived at Berlin early in June. As his visit was not connected with any political object and was restricted to forty-eight hours' duration, he did not ask for a presentation to the King, but he called on Count Bernstorff to thank him for the friendly disposition he had always evinced towards his country and himself.

He was good enough to call on me, and I was thus enabled to become personally acquainted with a statesman for whose high reputation and patriotism I had a great admiration.

The opinions expressed to me by Baron Ricasoli on

the present state and on the future of Italy, more especially as regarded the solution of the Roman Question, were marked by a calmness and nobleness of feeling worthy of his high character. He had all the patriotism and firmness of Count Cavour, without his passion and susceptibility. He was always prepared to await, and profit by, events; Count Cavour was always restless to provoke them. Both were ardent patriots, deeply imbued with the anxious wish to liberate their country.

Baron Ricasoli, in the course of our conversation, laid particular stress on the good sense and moderation which had distinguished the Italian people during their long and arduous struggle. He expressed the greatest confidence that they would continue to evince the same high qualities, and await patiently the development which time would effect in the solution of the Roman Question. He admitted the great difficulties in which the Emperor Napoleon was placed, but he considered that a moment would come, and was not far distant, when the withdrawal of the French Protectorate would force the Pope to yield to necessity, and to accept a position which, with a sacrifice of temporal power, would leave him unfettered in his spiritual jurisdiction. Count Bernstorff stated to me that he had been favourably impressed with the prudent, calm, and moderate language of Baron Ricasoli.

The recognition of Italy by Prussia was hailed by the extreme Liberal Party with great satisfaction. They had for some time past regarded this recognition as a measure of indispensable necessity, and of the greatest importance to the political interests of Prussia, as it subsequently proved in 1866.

The never-ceasing rivalry of Austria and Prussia for preponderance and influence in Germany, and the incidents which had lately occurred to embitter the relations between those States, contributed in no small degree to arouse in the Prussian nation a strong sympathy for Italy. It was felt that in the event of serious complications in Germany (such, for instance, as would have been caused if a Prussian intervention had taken place in Electoral Hesse independently of the Diet) the alliance of Italy would offer a most efficient aid to Prussia, by obliging Austria to concentrate large forces on her Italian frontier, thus paralysing her action in Germany.

Independently of the foregoing considerations there were other motives which led the public opinion in Prussia to view with satisfaction the recognition of the Kingdom of Italy.

A feeling of sympathy with the Italian nation in their struggle for unity pervaded all classes in Germany. A common national feeling and common aspirations formed a strong link between the two nations. Nor could it be supposed that the successful precedent established by Italy could fail to stimulate the ambitious hopes of Germany, more especially when the realisation of these hopes was so intimately blended with the full acquirement of constitutional liberty. It was not surprising, therefore, that there existed in Prussia and with the Liberal Party a wish to aid in consolidating the Kingdom of Italy as a means of rendering it more independent of France. It was foreseen that a nation of twenty-two millions would play an important part in the political affairs of Europe, and that consequently every opportunity should be taken to place the relations between Prussia and Italy on the most favourable footing. A strong, united, and independent Italy would offer to Germany an alliance of great importance, but a weak, divided Italy would necessarily have to lean on France.

Although at that time the relations between Prussia and France were of the most friendly character, and although the feelings of former animosity had greatly diminished, there was still a large portion of the bourgeoisie and of the army who entertained a reluctance towards any intimate alliance with France. It was thought that even if such an alliance could have been beneficial in promoting the ambitious views of Prussia, it could only have been purchased at a price which would be humiliating to Prussia and distasteful to Germany.

Servian affairs now occupied public attention. Dissensions had broken out between the Servian and the Turkish troops in the fortress of Belgrad. It was an absurd anomaly that, although no Turkish troops were allowed to be quartered in Servia, the fortress of Belgrad, commanding the town, was garrisoned by a Turkish force. It was impossible for these two races to live in harmony. Historical antecedents inflamed the minds of the Servians against the Mussulman yoke. The Turkish flag floating at the fortress as a symbol of their subjection to Turkish rule was daily becoming intolerable to a Christian population, and filled their minds with a spirit of hatred and vengeance. A collision had taken place between the Servians and the Turks, and many lives were lost. The Turks retired to the fortress and commenced to bombard the town. The foreign Consuls appealed to their Governments, and telegrams were sent by the several Governments to Constantinople urging the Porte to order the immediate cessation of the bombardment, and to remind the Porte of the 29th Article of the Treaty of Paris.

The question was then referred to the representatives of the Powers at Constantinople, urging the Porte to bring about a satisfactory settlement. A conference of the Powers' was held at Constantinople, and after a long delay the Servian affairs were finally adjusted.

The question in itself was not one of grave importance, except in as far as the dangers which might result to the Porte and to the neighbouring Powers should the spark of insurrection spread, and produce a revolution in the northern provinces of Turkey. Political emissaries had been lately sowing the seeds of revolt among the Christian populations of those provinces. So long as there existed unanimity among the Great Powers, especially France and Russia, these dangers were minimised, and this was happily the case on this occasion.

The Porte, aware of the danger of delay, acted with unusual promptitude. Orders were sent from Constantinople to cease the bombardment. The Governor of the fortress was instantly recalled, and was replaced by another functionary; and Achmet Pacha, with a Civil Commissary, was sent to make full inquiry into the causes of the conflict.

Not long afterwards the fortress of Belgrad was given up by the Porte, and thus any future recurrence of similar disorders was obviated.

Another small volcano had burst forth between the Porte and Montenegro, which, from the protection given to Montenegro by Russia, might equally have led to serious consequences.

The hatred of the Montenegrins (who were also of the Servian race, a warlike people) to the Turks knew no bounds, and they were constantly making raids into Turkish territory, and therefore brought into collision with the Turks. It appears that in an encounter with them on Turkish soil the Montenegrins had made a number of Turkish prisoners. The Porte sent large reinforcements under Omar Pasha to punish the Montenegrins and to liberate the prisoners. Certain proposals made by Prince Gortchacoff for an amicable settlement and supported by France were submitted to Count Bernstorff for his adhesion. Count Bernstorff did not think that they would be accepted by the Porte. He remarked to me that the apparent object of Russia and France was to acquire a seaport on the Adriatic for Montenegro or, perhaps it may be said, more especially for Russia, and it was said the port of Spizza was the one coveted.

The Turkish Minister at Berlin also submitted a basis for an amicable settlement, which consisted of the following points :—1. Withdrawal of the Montenegrins within their frontier and the liberation of the prisoners. 2. Acknowledgment of the suzerainty of the Porte, and the grant thereupon by the Porte of certain arable lands adjacent to Montenegro. 3. Acknowledgment by the Porte of the autonomy of Montenegro under the guarantee of the Great Powers. 4. Free transit through the Albanian territory of articles of primary necessity to Montenegro (except arms and ammunition).

Count Bernstorff considered the foregoing as a fair and honourable arrangement to both parties. I said to Count Bernstorff that in my opinion the demand for the acknowledgment of the suzerainty of the Porte was injudicious, for it was unattainable. Neither Russia nor France had recognised Montenegro as a Turkish province. Why, then, needlessly raise a question which, instead of aiding a settlement, would be sure to obstruct it, and probably give rise to further difficulties?

An engagement took place between the Turks and Montenegrins of a sanguinary nature, in which the latter were repulsed with great losses on both sides. Atrocities were committed by the mountaineers revolting to humanity and degrading to a Christian community. The Turks were likewise accused of similar atrocities. In a conversation with Count Bernstorff he told me that he had counselled the Porte to accept an armistice. I said that the Porte had exhibited the greatest forbearance towards the Prince of Montenegro, and that it was only when all means of conciliation had failed that the Turkish Government had resorted to coercive measures in order to put an end to a state of things which was intolerable. Everyone must deeply deplore the loss of human life, but the blame and responsibility rested with the Montenegrin chief, who had refused the offer of a pacific arrangement when proposed by Omar Pasha.

Count Bernstorff was of opinion that the endeavours to subdue Montenegro would be attended with great difficulties to the Porte, and that it could not be effected without still greater loss of human life, and that it would be politic for the Porte to accept an armistice. The Porte could more easily do so at the present moment, having given proof of her power; but if later the Sultan's troops should meet with reverses, and should fail in effecting the object they had in view, the hopes and pretensions of the Montenegrins would be raised, and it would be more difficult to bring them to terms.

I stated my opinion to Lord Russell that in view of the difficulties to be surmounted in the subjection of Montenegro; in view of the obstacles which would undoubtedly be raised by Russia and France to prevent the Porte from reaping the fruits of her victory; and in the uncertainty as to whether the Turkish forces would be able to hold the country if conquered, it was in the interest of the Porte, as well as in the interests of humanity, that she should accept any fair and honourable proposal for putting an end to this sanguinary and costly struggle. It was of vital importance to Turkey to bring this warfare to an end, as, in the state of Servia and the adjacent provinces, it was to be feared that, if not speedily quenched, fresh fuel might be added to this burning crater, which might then require more than the resources of the Empire could afford to extinguish.

An armistice was finally agreed to and a Conference of the Great Powers was held at Constantinople to arrange the differences between the contending parties.

For some months dating from the early part of 1862 negotiations had been carried on for a Commercial Treaty between Prussia, in the name of the Zollverein States, and France. These negotiations met with many difficulties and delay, but finally they were brought to a satisfactory conclusion, both parties having mutually agreed to concessions.

The treaty was not favourably received by the Southern States, especially by Bavaria and Würtemberg. It was also viewed with jealousy and disapproval at Vienna, and to this circumstance may be in some measure due the opposition to it on the part of the Southern States. I was, however, assured that although Austrian influence might impede the successful issue of the treaty for six months, or even a year, the force of public opinion would oblige the Governments of those States to yield to the material necessities of the Southern States. It was evident that the nearest seaport for the export and import trade of Southern Germany was Trieste, whereas that of Northern Germany and the Northern and Central States of the Zollverein was Hamburg;

but nothwithstanding there were other potent circumstances which acted on the Southern States, and would prevent their withdrawal from the Zollverein in 1866, when the Zollverein Treaties expired.

I was also informed that on the expiration of the then existing Austrian intermediate tariff there would be no renewal of it. This was expressly stated to Mr. Mallet and myself.* This intermediate tariff acted very unjustly as regarded Great Britain, giving separate and exceptional advantages to Austria. It did not merely apply to the German Provinces of Austria but comprised the whole of her non-German provinces, and consequently some thirty millions of population to whom commercial advantages were granted which were denied to other countries.

The Treaty of Commerce was signed by Prussia and France on the 2nd of August, with a protocol providing for the subsequent accession thereto of the States of the Zollverein.

I inquired of Count Bernstorff when the draft of the treaty I had submitted to him on the part of Her Majesty's Government would be agreed to and ready for signature, as Her Majesty's Government had been led to expect that it would be signed contemporaneously with that with France. He replied that a project of law would be immediately submitted to the Prussian Chambers, authorising the Government to apply the new tariff of the French Treaty, whenever it should

---

* Mr. Mallet had been sent to Berlin to assist me in negotiating a Treaty of Commerce between Prussia and the Zollverein.

come into operation, to those foreign States (including Great Britain) with whom reciprocity should be established. Under any circumstances the treaty could not come into operation before the expiration of the Zollverein Treaties.

I stated to Count Bernstorff that it was important to our interests that, whenever the new tariff granted to France should come into operation, it should be simultaneously applied to Great Britain, in order that we might start on fair and equal terms with France, and I reminded him of the formal promises and assurances which he had given to Mr. Mallet and myself.

He replied that this was the wish of the Prussian Government, and to secure this object the project of law above mentioned would be submitted to the Chamber. But the "most favoured nation" clause in the existing treaty between Great Britain and the Zollverein would entitle us to whatever advantages were granted to France in the new treaty.

The Austrian Cabinet at this time addressed a proposal to the Prussian Government to enter the Zollverein with all her non-German provinces. Count Bernstorff replied to these claims, urged by Count Rechberg as being derived from the treaty between Austria and Prussia in 1853, that he could not admit the right of Austria, after the expiration of the time mentioned in the treaty, to demand its execution at any period which might be suitable to her. He gave it to be understood that the commercial negotiations with Austria could only be entered on when the Prussian-

French treaty had received the assent of all the States of the Zollverein, and that, until that period, no negotiations could offer any prospect of a satisfactory result. Thus a fresh schism arose to widen the breach of discord already existing between the two States.

I dined with Baron Budberg, the Russian Minister, on the 29th of August, who had just returned to Berlin, and was on his passage to Switzerland previous to going to Paris. He spoke in great praise of Prince Alfred (Duke of Edinburgh). His language was friendly to us. He said that the conciliatory language Lord Russell had held to Baron Brünnow and Count Flahaut had produced the best impression at St. Petersburg, and gave hopes of an understanding being effected at Constantinople on the Servian and Montenegrin difficulties. In speaking of Turkey, he said that it was the wish of Russia to maintain the Ottoman Empire, but that, in his opinion, the only means of doing so would be by severing completely the Christian provinces and granting to them entire independence. Turkey, he observed, could have no vitality until she had divested herself of them. I asked him whether there was not a danger that, if emancipated, these provinces would fall into anarchy, and become a hotbed of revolutionary parties. In that case they would become a danger to Russia and the neighbouring States. Under the name of a Confederation they would be the focus of republicanism and anarchy. By encouraging such aspirations there would be danger for Russia. Poland was contiguous to those provinces, and the populations, with the exception of

Wallachia and Moldavia, were, equally with the Poles, of Slavonic origin. Those, therefore, who fostered such projects must be prepared to reap their dangers.

Baron Budberg admitted this danger, but said that it would be equally great if they remained under Turkey. He was the most able of the Russian diplomatists. He was genial and agreeable in conversation and social intercourse, with some humour and a certain vein of sarcasm. He was brought up in the school of Count Nesselrode, and was of German extraction—a native of the Baltic province, having property in Lithuania. He belonged to the so-called German party, which, under the Emperor Nicolas, was much favoured, but, under the present *régime*, had no longer the predominant influence it formerly exercised. In conversation with Baron Budberg, I casually alluded to the report of a protocol having been lately signed by him at Paris. He said it was a mere fabrication of the *Indépendance Belge*, and he denied its existence.

Notwithstanding several attempts to bring about an understanding between the Ministry and the several Liberal fractions of the Lower House, no successful result was obtained. The Liberal party stood out first for a reorganisation of the army by a legal and constitutional measure—viz., a law submitted to the Chamber ; and secondly, for a reduction of the military budget, maintaining that, in full peace, the annual addition of nine millions of dollars would weigh too heavily on the taxation of the country, and was in excess of the amount required. They were willing to agree to the new reorganisation provided that the additional expenses could be alleviated by reducing the term of service from three to two years, which they considered sufficient to make a soldier acquainted with his duties.

The Ministry (or perhaps it may be said with more reason, the King and his Military Cabinet) were entirely opposed to any reduction in the term of service or to any concession in regard to the military budget. Thus matters continued at a deadlock, and the Government continued to govern without a legally voted Budget.

In this dilemma the King decided to make a change in the Ministry, and to place the direction of affairs in the hands of M. de Bismarck, who had been lately appointed Minister at Paris.

In September the Queen visited the Duchy of Coburg, and resided at Rosenau, which had been placed at Her Majesty's disposal by the Duke of Saxe-Coburg. It was endeared to Her Majesty as having been the birthplace of the Prince Consort and the residence of his early youth. There were consequently many tender reminiscences connected with it, and though of a sorrowful nature, they were conducive to afford some solace to Her Majesty's afflicted heart. It was a lovely secluded spot, where Her Majesty could also enjoy the calm repose so necessary for her health.

The Queen was attended by Lord Russell, who took up his quarters at Gotha. I was anxious to see him, and he wrote me a line to say that there was no chance of our meeting unless I could be at Gotha on the 16th of September.

Previous to my visit to Gotha, Count Bernstorff charged me to deliver a letter from him to Lord Russell, the object of which was, with the King's sanction, to propose to raise the Mission of England at Berlin and that of Prussia in London to the rank of Embassies.

Count Bernstorff said that when he was at Paris M. de Thouvenel had told him that it was the wish of the Emperor Napoleon to accredit an Ambassador to the Court of Berlin, and that whenever it would be agreeable to the King of Prussia, Prince La Tour-d'Auvergne would receive his credentials as Ambassador. Since then the question had been in abeyance, but lately M. de Bismarck had addressed a report from Paris, in which he referred in very forcible terms to the great disadvantage of the Prussian representative having only the rank of an Envoy; it was a secondary position not becoming to Prussia when the representatives of Spain and Turkey took precedence of him. It had also its political disadvantages. It was important at times that he should be able to see the Emperor on great political questions.

The King thereupon decided to raise his Envoy at Paris to the rank of an Ambassador, and to receive a French Ambassador at Berlin.

Count Bernstorff wished to inform Lord Russell of the motives which had led to this change, in the hope that Her Majesty's Government would agree to place their diplomatic relations with Prussia on a similar footing.

I delivered Count Bernstorff's letter to Lord Russell on my arrival at Gotha, observing that I had been already "uprooted" at Vienna by the creation of an Embassy, and that a similar fate pursued me to Berlin. Lord Russell merely replied that it would make no difference to me. I naturally concluded that it was Lord Russell's intention to confer on me the new Embassy, and other circumstances tended to confirm this impression. But on his return to London a cloud came over these good intentions, and political influences effected a change in them.

I took leave of Lord Russell at Gotha, and soon after my return to Berlin I received the following letter from him:—

Pembroke Lodge, October 15*th,* 1862.

MY DEAR LORD AUGUSTUS,—Since the time when the Prussian Government proposed that our respective Missions should be raised to Embassies, it has been my duty to consider how the Embassy to Berlin should be filled.

On looking over the list of those who had been appointed Envoys, I found twelve or thirteen whose appointment preceded yours in point of time. Among these were two or three well qualified to be Ambassador, and especially Sir John Milbanke, who has been nineteen years Minister at Munich, and knows Germany well. I have therefore recommended to the Queen that Sir John Milbanke should be named Ambassador to Berlin.

I have at the same time proposed that Bavaria should be raised to a first class Mission, and I have to offer it to you as such. You will thus not lose the claims for pension you have acquired at Berlin.

I am aware that this change must be disagreeable to you. Had the Prussian Government been content with a Minister at

Berlin I should have been perfectly satisfied with your continuance there in that character.

But as it is not so, I feel that I might subject myself to a charge of injustice if I were to advise the Queen to raise you to the rank of Ambassador regardless of the claims of others.

I remain,

Yours very truly,

(Signed) RUSSELL.

I replied to Lord Russell as follows :—

Berlin, October 18*th*, 1862.

MY DEAR LORD,—It is my misfortune to be the victim of Embassies, which spring up under my feet apparently for the purpose of uprooting me. I cannot, however, but recognise in your decision that kind consideration for others and that spirit of justice for which your character is so highly distinguished.

My sense of public duty will always lead me to accept any service for which it may please Her Majesty and Her Majesty's Government to employ me, and it will be my constant endeavour as heretofore to perform whatever duties may be appointed to me conscientiously, with zeal and fidelity.

I therefore accept Your Lordship's offer of the Mission at Munich, and beg to thank you for having so considerately placed it on the same rank as the Mission I now hold.

During my visit to Lord Russell at Gotha I had a long conversation with him on the differences between Germany and Denmark. The moment was propitious for a settlement of this question, and was probably the last chance of averting war. I suggested to Lord Russell that he should lay before both parties a basis of settlement on fair and reasonable terms. Before leaving

Berlin for Gotha, I had confidentially ascertained from Count Bernstorff the terms on which an amicable arrangement could be arrived at, and which would be acceptable to Germany.

I drew up a memorandum of my conversation with Count Bernstorff, which recorded the opinions he had expressed in regard to a settlement of the Duchies question, and I submitted it to him in a private form for any alterations or corrections, in order that there should be no possible misunderstanding hereafter as to the correctness of my version of his opinions. I forwarded this to Lord Russell, and he based thereon the proposals which were officially notified to Count Bernstorff in a despatch, addressed, in my absence, to Mr. Lowther, of the 24th of September, subsequent to my interview with him at Gotha.

Count Bernstorff informed me on my return to Berlin that this despatch had given him much pleasure, and that it contained some valuable matter. There were one or two points which required elucidation, but they were only matters of detail. He expressed himself favourably on the proposals, but said that, being on the eve of giving up the direction of the Ministry, he was unwilling to express any decided opinion.

I will not inflict on my readers the details of Lord Russell's proposals. They were declared by the two German Powers acceptable on condition that they received the adhesion of the Germanic Diet.

It was, in my opinion, of great value to know, before their submission to the Danish Government, that they had been declared acceptable by the two German Powers, and were regarded as fair and reasonable. It was, therefore, in the power of the Danish Government by their adhesion to close at once this long-pending dispute with Germany, and thus to avert all the risks and losses occasioned by war.

The Danish Cabinet, under the influence of the Radical Party, rejected the proposals of Lord Russell, and by their refusal subjected the country to war and the loss of the Duchies altogether—the Duchies of Lauenburg, Holstein, and Schleswig being handed over, at the peace of Vienna in 1864, to Austria and Prussia.

If the Danish Government had been rigidly informed that the rejection of these proposals would prevent any further intervention on the part of England, either diplomatically or materially, in her behalf, it cannot be supposed that they would have acted so ill-advisedly and so fatally to the interests of their country by rejecting them; but, unfortunately, after their rejection both in Parliament and out of Parliament, discussions on the interminable question of Schleswig-Holstein continued, and imbued the Danes with delusive hopes that in the event of war " Denmark would not be alone."

Before going to Gotha I had a long conversation with Count Bernstorff on the various political questions in Europe then occupying general attention, of which I drew up a memorandum and placed it in Lord Russell's hands. Among other subjects we spoke of the relations between Austria and Prussia, which apparently were

becoming very embittered. I observed to him that
"It was very regrettable that the two great German
Powers should be so embittered against each other.
The estrangement in ordinary times might not have
been productive of serious consequences, but at this
moment it was pregnant with danger to the peace of
Germany, and possibly of Europe. Each party had
taken up an advanced position from which it would
become later difficult to recede, and circumstances might
at any moment arise which might provoke a collision
between them."

Count Bernstorff expressed his regrets that it was
so, but he exonerated Prussia and himself from being
the cause of it. "We," said the Count, "are not the
aggressors; ours is merely a defensive policy. My
despatch of December last was merely an answer to a
programme proposed to us and which we could not
accept. In that programme for Federal Reform, originally drawn up by Baron Beust, Austria would not even
agree to the *alternat* of the Presidency of the Diet,
although proposed by Baron Beust. This programme
was based on the formation of a 'Third' Power in
Germany called the 'Trias'—viz., Saxony, Bavaria, and
Würtemburg, and the smaller States—to which Prussia
could never agree."

"I may tell you confidentially," said Count Bernstorff, "that at the same time I replied to the Identic
Notes I addressed a confidential despatch to Vienna
expressing a readiness on the part of Prussia to come to
an understanding *direct* with Austria. To this Count

Rechberg never vouchsafed a reply, but immediately after convoked a conference of the minor States to draw up a plan of federal reform.

"Then again," observed Count Bernstorff, "Austria has been the prime instigator of the opposition of the South German States to our Commercial Treaty with France, and has formed a coalition of the minor States directed against Prussia. At this moment," said Count Bernstorff, "Austria is trying to allure the minor States into a promise to vote systematically against every proposal at the Diet submitted by Prussia. We are, therefore, not the aggressors; but we are solely on the defensive. We are determined not to give up our position at whatever price. If it should be war, we will accept it."

I replied that it did not appertain to me to be a judge between the two parties, but that with a wish to serve both for their mutual good, and bearing in mind the important interests of Germany and of Europe, which would be gravely compromised if any open breach should unhappily arise between the two great German Powers, I was anxious to ask him whether there was any possibility, through a third party, of removing the differences existing between them, and of bringing the two parties to a friendly understanding.

Count Bernstorff replied that, "If Austria will abandon all further opposition to our Commercial Treaty with France, and if Austria will *agree to treat directly with Prussia*—that is, *for herself without the co-operation of the minor States, on the basis of a perfect equality in all respects*—then," he said, "*je lui tendrai la main.* I authorise you," continued Count Bernstorff, "to state this to Lord Russell, but at the same time you must be cautious as to the use which is made of this confidential communication, for if it were supposed at Vienna that it came from me, the sense and object of it would be misinterpreted, and in lieu of doing good it would magnify the evil."

I then referred to the internal state of affairs, and asked him what he thought would be the result of the debate on the Military Budget. Count Bernstorff replied that he was convinced that the report of the Committee (for striking out the whole of the extraordinary estimates, amounting to above six million of dollars—about a million sterling) would be accepted by the Chamber, although some of his colleagues were more sanguine. He was of opinion that a compromise should be effected at any price, for the internal discord of parties weakened the position of Prussia externally. He seemed of opinion that the concession of two years' service instead of three might offer practical means for an arrangement, and thus enable all parties to escape from the deadlock in which matters now were; but it was evident to me that this was his personal opinion, and was neither partaken of by his colleagues nor the Military Cabinet.

Early in October Count Bernstorff was relieved of his duties as Minister for Foreign Affairs, and was appointed Prussian Ambassador at the court of Her Majesty the Queen. At the same time, M. de Bismarck-Schönhausen was appointed by His Majesty President of the Ministry and Minister for Foreign Affairs. Other changes in the Ministry took place, the most important of which was the retirement of M. Von der Heydt from the Ministry of Commerce.

Count Bernstorff gave me the following explanation of the circumstances which had brought about the Ministerial crisis, and induced him to retire from the Cabinet :—

"He said that he had for some time seen the necessity of an understanding between the Government and the Lower Chamber on the question of the Budget, and that he had always supported this view.

"By continuing the present course, he felt that the King would at last find himself in a position from which he could only extricate himself by abdication, or by having recourse to extra constitutional means. The first he considered would be a most unfortunate step, placing the Crown Prince in a very painful and difficult position, both as regarded the country and the army ; the latter alternative, he felt convinced, the King would never adopt, for he would never consent to forfeit his word by a violation of the Constitution. Therefore," observed Count Bernstorff, "there remained no other course to pursue than that of a compromise between the Government and the Chamber. Count Bernstorff observed that he had seen with regret that his opinions and conduct had been wrongly interpreted by the English Press, and specially by the *Times*, which represented his retirement from the Cabinet to motives of a retrograde and reactionary nature. This," he said, "was not only not true, but was the reverse of the truth.

"After the rejection of the Budget he had expressed at a council of Ministers his opinion as to the course to be pursued. He was not supported by some of his colleagues, whilst from others he encountered direct opposition. He stated that neither he nor M. Von der Heydt were prepared to govern without a Budget, which would have been a virtual departure from the Constitution. He further stated that he could not assume the grave responsibility of a Cabinet Minister without knowing to what aim the policy of the Cabinet was leading, and to what extreme measures it might have recourse. For his part, he could never have agreed to any measures which would exceed the limits of the Constitution."

From what I could gather, the immediate course which led M. Von der Heydt and himself to tender their resignation was the retractation by the Minister of War of the concession of two years' military service which he had publicly made to the Chamber. He said that General Von Roon had made this concession on his own responsibility and without any previous concert with his colleagues, but having made it, he considered that it should not have been retracted.

Count Bernstorff confined his observations to a mere explanation of his own conduct, without entering into any matters referring to the policy of the country; but he repeatedly remarked that it was his firm conviction that the King would never consent to any measures of the nature of a coup d'état or in violation of the Constitution.

The Ministerial proposals for the Prussian navy met with the same fate as the Military Budget. Out of a sum of 1,400,000 dollars submitted to the sanction of the Chamber, a sum of only 200,000 dollars was granted for the acquirement of training ships!

The christening of the infant prince, son of their Royal Highnesses the Crown Prince and Princess, took place at the New Palace, Potsdam, on the 13th of September, in the presence of the King, the Queen Dowager, and all the members of the Royal Family.

The infant Prince was held at the font by the King, receiving the name of Albert William Henry, and he was blessed with innumerable sponsors to look after his future spiritual welfare. They were their Prussian Majesties, the King of Portugal, the Duke and Duchess of Brabant, the Princess of Hesse, the Princess Helena of Great Britain, the Princess Mary of Cambridge, the Prince of Hohenzollern Sigmaringen and the Hereditary Prince of Augustenburg.

After the ceremony a "defile" Court was held by the Crown Princess, at which all those who had been honoured with an invitation, including the great officers of State, the Ministers, the Representatives of Portugal, Belgium, Saxe Coburg, and all the members of Her Majesty's Legation, offered their felicitations to Her Royal Highness on this happy occasion.

The Court was followed by a gala banquet of 230 *couverts* in the Marble Hall of the Palace. During the banquet His Majesty rose and gave the health of the infant Prince.

The New Palace at Potsdam—the summer residence of the Crown Prince and Princess—is an imposing and handsome building, constructed of red brick faced with white stone. It was built by Frederick II. (the Great) at the close of the Seven Years' War to prove that his finances were not exhausted. It is prettily situated in the grounds which skirt the beautiful gardens of Sans Souci. It had been rather neglected previous to the Crown Prince making it his residence. It was much improved by him, and the garden was laid out with great taste by the Crown Princess, who took great interest in the model farm created at Bornstadt in its immediate neighbourhood, where she established a school, built a church, and greatly aided in other philanthropic institutions.

Potsdam is a town of palaces and barracks. It is prettily situated, and the "Havel," which is beautifully wooded, is most picturesque. The villas of the King and of Prince Charles are quite lovely, and the grounds are beautifully kept. They were both created at enormous expense out of a sandy desert. I have enjoyed many a pleasant day in summer in the fresh air of Potsdam with its luxuriant verdure, escaping from the intolerable heat and dust of Berlin, and the Berliners ought to be thankful to have so enjoyable a spot to resort to. Besides the New Palace, there is Sans Souci with the reminiscences of Frederick the Great, who died there, as did also Frederick William IV. The Marmor

Palais on the "Havel"—in front of which is moored the English frigate presented to Frederick William III. by the Prince Regent in 1815 at a naval review at Portsmouth, when His Majesty observed to the Sovereigns and Princes around him that he "hoped they would not be jealous of his navy." There is also the town Palace, a very comfortable house, where the suite of the Queen were lodged when Her Majesty visited the Prince and Princess of Prussia (afterwards King and Emperor) in 1858 at Babelsberg.

The late Emperor was devoted to Babelsberg. In driving one day with His Majesty after dinner in the grounds, he told me that Babelsberg was entirely his own creation—his child—and he knew every tree that he had planted, regretting that at his advanced age he could not hope to see them reach perfection.

> Linquenda tellus, et domus, et placens
> Uxor ; neque harum, quas colis, arborum
> Te, præter invisas cupressos
> Ulla, brevem dominum sequetur.*

But this great and beloved Sovereign lived for many years afterwards. Having gone through two formidable wars, and successfully fulfilled the highest aspirations of the German nation by the restoration in his person of the German Empire, he peacefully passed away in his ninetieth year.

* Hor., Ode D. 14.

CHAPTER X.

Recall of Prince La Tour-d'Auvergne, French Minister at Berlin: his Appointment to Rome—Ministerial Change at Paris—Importance attached to the Appointment of Drouyn de L'Huys as Minister for Foreign Affairs—Close of the Prussian Session—No Compromise on Internal Questions—Conflict between the two Houses—Conversation with Bismarck; his Departure for Paris to present Letters of Recall—On Russo-Prussian-French Alliance—Appointment of Sir A. Buchanan as British Ambassador at Berlin—My Audience of their Majesties to present Letters—Visit of the King to Lady Augustus Loftus, and to present to me a Magnificent Vase with His Majesty's Portrait—Character of the King—Bismarck—Moltke—Roon—Appointed Envoy to the King of Bavaria—Departure for Munich.

THE French Ambassador at Berlin, Prince La Tour-d'Auvergne, was recalled and appointed Ambassador at Rome. He was succeeded at Berlin as Envoy by Baron Talleyrand, late Minister at Turin. He was a zealous Catholic, of an ancient and historic family, and an ardent defender of the Pope. I had learnt when at Baden on good authority that it was the intention of the Emperor Napoleon to appoint him to Rome. On the offer being made to him, he made certain conditions favourable to the Pope and the Catholic Church, on which his acceptance of the offer depended; and my informant, who was also a strong Ultramontane, observed that Prince La Tour-d'Auvergne's acceptance would give a clue to the future policy of the Emperor in respect to Rome.

Prince La Tour-d'Auvergne's language to me was very

moderate, very conservative, very pacific, and this, he said, was the policy of M. Drouyn de L'Huys. In regard to the Roman question, he remarked that Thouvenel had gone too fast and too far, and that he had often cautioned him against the line he was taking. He personally considered that Thouvenel had placed the Roman question on a wrong basis in making it a political question. The French Government, as he pretended, occupied Rome with the assent of the Catholic Powers, and as their " mandataire ; " consequently they had no right to withdraw from Rome but with the consent of the Catholic Powers. He was of opinion that the *status quo* should for the present be maintained.

Prince La Tour-d'Auvergne, who was subsequently transferred to London, was a very able and distinguished diplomatist, of a mild and conciliatory character, and with very attractive manners. I was intimate with him and much enjoyed his society. He was French Ambassador in London during the Danish Conference. Meeting him at dinner one day, I asked him what he thought would be the result of the Conference. He replied, " *Que le Danemark perdrait quelques-unes de ses plumes* "—meaning the Duchies.

A change, however, of a more important character took place at Paris by the appointment of M. Drouyn de L'Huys as Minister for Foreign Affairs in the place of M. de Thouvenel.

M. Drouyn de L'Huys was known to have strong sympathies for Austria, and his appointment was hailed with joy by the South German States.

It was reported to me privately that on a visit of M. Drouyn de L'Huys to Stuttgardt for the purpose of visiting the Royal Studs (in his capacity of President of an Agricultural Society in France) he had had a conversation with Baron Hügel, the Minister for Foreign Affairs (formerly Würtemburg Minister in London), on the affairs of Germany, and that on this occasion he had declared his certain conviction that France would "never" permit any disruption of the existing Germanic Confederation. This decided opinion of a statesman of such high position, and supposed to enjoy the confidence of his Sovereign, could not fail to be most reassuring to the Würtemberg Minister for Foreign Affairs. The value of this opinion was greatly increased when shortly after M. Drouyn de L'Huys was appointed Minister for Foreign Affairs, which gave great satisfaction to the minor German States, as a proof of which one of my German colleagues observed to me, "*Que les actions de l'Autriche et de ses confédérés avaient beaucoup haussées par l'avènement aux affaires de M. Drouyn de L'Huys.*"

The venerable Prince Metternich once said to me on my using in conversation the word "*jamais*"—"*Mon cher, il ne faut* jamais *dire jamais*"—the truth of which was thus exemplified by the decided opinion expressed by M. Drouyn de L'Huys to Baron Hügel. The Germanic Diet was dissolved four years afterwards without opposition on the part of France, and without even a protest on her part or on that of Europe.

M. de Bismarck, however, who was on the eve of

going to Paris to deliver his letters of recall, was much vexed by this Ministerial change at Paris. It was natural for him to view it in a light favourable to Austria, and possibly also as indicating a future alliance between Austria and France at a time when his hopes were founded on securing the neutrality of France in a future conflict between Austria and Prussia.

The relations at this moment between Austria and Prussia were much strained, and the Ministerial change at Paris was not calculated to improve them. In conversing with M. de Bismarck on this subject, he said that there was to be a meeting of Sovereigns and Princes of Germany at Vienna to take into consideration certain proposals for a federal reform. It would have been more politic, he said, on the part of Austria if she had first requested the presence and co-operation of Prussia, and it would have been more likely to lead to a favourable result if that meeting had been held elsewhere than at Vienna, leaving Prussia no warrantable excuse for not taking part in it.

The Budget as voted by the Lower Chamber, from which the increased expenditure for the reorganisation of the army had been expunged, forming the ordinary Budget as existing in 1859, which had been agreed to by the Lower Chamber, was sent up on the 10th of October to the House of Nobles. The report of the committee proposed, in the form of a resolution, "to send back the Budget as voted by the Second Chamber for reconsideration, expressing disapproval at the Lower

House having expunged the sums demanded by the Ministry."

To this an amendment was moved by Count Arnim Boitzenbourg to the following effect—"That the Upper House reject the Budget as voted by the Lower House, and accept the Budget as primitively submitted to the Lower House by the Ministry."

Previous to the opening of the debate M. de Bismarck made a statement, the purport of which was to inform the House that the Ministry had exhausted all means of coming to an understanding with the Lower House on the Military Budget, and that, consequently, any further reference of the Budget to that Chamber, as proposed in the report of the Committee of the Upper House, would be fruitless. The amendment of Count Arnim was carried by an enormous majority, and the result was to place the two Houses in direct opposition to each other.

The session of Parliament was closed on the 13th of October by Commission. The royal speech was read to the Members of both Houses in the "White Hall" of the Palace by the Minister President, M. de Bismarck.

After the close of the session a certain calm succeeded the fever of political excitement which had previously existed, although it did not betoken any change in the disposition of either of the contending parties, or give hopes that salutary concessions might be expected on the part of the Ministry to the Lower Chamber. The Liberal party felt themselves supported by the great majority of the nation, by the justice and legality of their course, and by a conviction that the principles which actuated their conduct would finally prevail. They were resolved to remain strictly within the limits of the Constitution and of the law, and were fully determined to maintain a firm and passive opposition. The attitude assumed by M. de Bismarck and the vagueness of his political declarations, which, although professing Constitutional doctrines, were strongly tainted with reactionary feelings, did not tend to gain for him the confidence of the Liberal and Constitutional party in the Lower Chamber. The principal organs of the Press, both in the capital and in the provinces, expressed disapproval of the course he had taken, and evinced an open hostility to him—the same journals that four years later lauded him to the skies, and were his abject slaves!

If not premature, it was certainly unjust to judge thus severely the Minister-President (who had only just taken office) before he had had sufficient time to overcome the many difficulties which surrounded his path, and to alter the course which had been hitherto pursued; but M. de Bismarck, who was open to flattery, was callous to criticism, and he was gifted with that iron will which he equally imposed on his friends and foes, and which enabled him to overcome difficulties. It was this iron will, coupled with unexampled daring and aided by consummate skill and foresight, which was the secret of his brilliant success.

M. de Bismarck had been so occupied on his

assuming office that I had been unable to obtain an interview with him, but he obligingly came to see me on his return from Potsdam, on the 17th of October. After some friendly observations on ordinary subjects, the conversation turned to political questions, being opened by a reference to the intelligence received that morning from Paris of the appointment of M. Drouyn de L'Huys as Minister for Foreign Affairs in the place of M. de Thouvenel. The suddenness and cause of this change was a mystery, but it was attributed to the advanced position which M. de Thouvenel had taken in regard to the Roman question.

M. de Bismarck observed that in regard to the Italian question Prussia had taken the same interest with Great Britain in desiring the consolidation of Italian unity, and the maintenance of her independence. In touching on this subject he expressed his opinion that to be strong Italy should neither be dependent on France on the one hand nor on Austria on the other. He expressed, though with some caution and reserve, his doubts that the policy of the Emperor Napoleon was favourable to the independence of Italy, and he seemed of opinion that there was no intention on his part to withdraw his troops from Rome.

M. de Bismarck stated that he had reason to believe that Austria had been for some time looking to an alliance with France, that the question had been broached at Paris, and that Austria was even prepared to accept any arrangement that the Emperor might propose as regarded Italy. I here interposed, "Saving always the question of the Pope and the Papacy;" to which M. de Bismarck replied, "Without any reserve as regarded the Pope, whom," he added, "Austria would sacrifice to-morrow if it suited her interests, or if she could gain her ends by the sacrifice."

M. de Bismarck then reverted to the Ministerial change which had taken place at Paris, stating his opinion that the entry into the Ministry of M. Drouyn de L'Huys portended a complete change in the direction of the French policy, and an understanding between France and Austria on Italian affairs. He was evidently disturbed in mind at the prospects of an Austro-French alliance. He remarked that it was not to be wondered at, however, as Austria had been for some time back soliciting a French alliance *à genoux*, whereas Prussia had continually rejected all the advances made to her by France.

At his first interview with the Emperor Napoleon, His Majesty had expressed himself strongly in favour of a Conservative and Prussian policy, and of his desire to maintain peace and the *status quo* in Europe. The Emperor Napoleon, observed M. de Bismarck, required alliances with dynasties which could in return render him services.

Prussia having continually rejected the advances of the Emperor Napoleon, he had felt it impossible to respond to the Emperor, having no authority from the King, his Sovereign, to do so. Without directly stating it, M. de Bismarck gave me to understand that there was no alliance possible between France and Prussia, unless Prussia could offer some compensatory price, and that finally the Emperor Napoleon would be necessarily led to an alliance with Austria, who would be less scrupulous in meeting his objects and demands.

M. de Bismarck said that he had had no opportunity of conversing lately with the Emperor Napoleon, and he added, somewhat significantly, that he had left Biarritz on the very day before the arrival there of the Emperor, giving me to understand that if the Emperor had wished to see him he would have communicated his wishes to him.

Passing from this topic, M. de Bismarck spoke of the much-rumoured alliance between France and Russia, and the Protocol reported to have been recently signed by them at Paris. He said that undue importance had been attached to this rumour, and that this had been the object of Prince Gortchacoff, whose great desire since the close of the Russian war had been, and continued to be, to break up the alliance between England and France (which he always termed "L'Alliance Occidentale") by sowing jealousy between those Powers. He thought, also, that in the then feeble and paralysed state of Russia, Prince Gortchacoff was pleased to give an appearance of Russian activity on the theatre of European affairs, which intrinsically she was unable to exercise.

M. de Bismarck admitted that a Protocol existed, but he was convinced that it referred merely to the affairs of Servia and Montenegro, and other questions affecting the Northern Provinces of Turkey. He did not believe that its nature and objects exceeded those limits, the importance of which had faded away since those questions had been satisfactorily arranged.

M. de Bismarck then spoke of the relations between Austria and Prussia. He observed that Austria aimed at the first place in Germany, and at placing Prussia in the second rank, considering Prussia as subservient to her. This, M. de Bismarck said, could never be. It was a position which Prussia could never accept. No understanding could be brought about between the two great German Powers (the desirableness of which M. de Bismarck fully admitted both in a German and European sense) except on the basis of a perfect equality. In this sense Austria had hitherto persistently refused her co-operation. M. de Schmerling was bidding to outstrip Prussia in regard to Liberalism in Germany, but if he continued in this course he would find it a losing game which would end in his complete discomfiture.

M. de Bismarck then said that he was very anxious that I should correct the false impression which had been circulated by the Press in regard to certain speeches he had made before a Committee of the Lower Chamber, and which, as he believed, had been designedly falsified. He observed that these speeches had not been made to a public assembly, but to a Private Committee of the Lower Chamber, and consequently they ought never to have been published. He had been for four hours before this Committee, replying to interpellations from its members. He referred especially to the expression so much commented on by the European Press, *Sang et Fer* (*Blut und Eisen*). What he had intended to convey was that, in view of the state of Europe and the necessity for Prussia to be prepared for any emergencies, it was necessary that Prussia should have an army so organised as to be enabled to support, if necessary, the policy of the King's Government. The "Blood and Iron" was used in a figurative and not in a material sense. It did not refer, therefore, to anything of a sanguinary nature, but to the necessity of Prussia having an organised army ready to take the field. Other expressions of his had, he observed, been likewise falsely given and misinterpreted. There had been in the committee room a shorthand writer of whose presence he had been unaware, who, either from a deficiency in the art of reporting or from other causes, had given a false report of his language.

M. de Bismarck observed that he was better than his reputation, and he trusted that Her Majesty's Government would judge him by his acts, and not by the malevolent reports which were industriously spread about against him.

I referred to the question of the Danish Duchies. M. de Bismarck assured me that he was no fanatic on this question, and that he had been much gratified by the last proposals of Lord Russell, which he considered an acceptable basis for an arrangement. He could give no decided answer on the subject till he had submitted them to the King and had taken His Majesty's orders. He said that public opinion both in Prussia and in

Germany was very much excited on this question, viewing it as one of nationality, and that Prussia must take that into account in any arrangements proposed; but M. de Bismarck added that he personally would gladly seize any fair and reasonable means of bringing the question to an amicable adjustment.

M. de Bismarck was very hurried, and our conversation was of a very rambling nature. What struck me most was that his mind was evidently preoccupied with the Ministerial change at Paris, and that he was apprehensive of some secret understanding between France and Austria, or that the change indicated would lead to one, which would be most detrimental to his long-formed plans and to the interests of Prussia.

He said that he should go to Paris in a few days to present his letters of recall, when he should have the opportunity of conversing with the Emperor, and that it would be his object to solve what he termed the "secret of this mystery."

The flitting of Budberg to and fro to Berlin and St. Petersburg, his repeated interviews with M. de Bismarck, and the apparent connexity existing between M. de Bismarck's oft-deferred departure for Paris and the arrival at Berlin of Baron Budberg naturally gave rise to comments and conjectures which suggested the possible negotiation of a Russo-Prussian-French Alliance, which had been the long-cherished dream of M. de Bismarck.

Without attaching undue importance to these rumours, and without in any degree accepting their authenticity, I may mention that the reported basis of this Triple Alliance was as follows:—

France to have freedom of action as regarded Switzerland, Belgium, and Holland; Prussia to be allowed to obtain the supremacy of Germany; and both to support Russian policy in the East.

But whatever hopes M. de Bismarck may have entertained of carrying out his long-cherished dream of a Triple Alliance of Russia, Prussia, and France, which he had so openly avowed, he met with no support or approval from the King, and he received no authority or commission from His Majesty to enter into any negotiations with France in regard to a French alliance. The utmost he was charged with was to express the wish of the King to maintain the most friendly and cordial relations with the Emperor of the French.

But M. de Bismarck, by his diplomatic skill, by the influence of his strong mind, and by the force of his persuasive eloquence and arguments on the mind of the Emperor Napoleon, obtained a result which calmed all his fears and encouraged all his hopes. He obtained the assurance of French neutrality in the event of a war with Austria.

So satisfied was M. de Bismarck that he could count on the neutrality of France, that, when the war with Austria broke out in 1866, no defensive military measures were taken on the Rhine and Western Frontier. He had no fears of Russia on the Eastern Frontier, and he was therefore able to concentrate the military forces of Prussia against Austria and her South German Allies. He was bent on placing Prussia at the head of Germany. He had with him the aspirations of the majority of the German nation, a magnificent army in the highest state of preparation and perfection, and he sought his further support at Paris and St. Petersburg. None of his calculations failed him, and his foresight and skill were crowned with success.

The internal state of Prussia and the complicated questions then at issue in Germany both as regarded her political and material interests—for the two were inseparable—were matters of grave importance not alone for Germany but for Europe. A strong, united, and powerful Germany would offer the best security for the peace of Europe; a divided, and consequently powerless Germany would be a constant source of danger both to itself and to Europe.

On the 8th of November I officially informed M. de Bismarck that Her Majesty the Queen had appointed Sir Andrew Buchanan, then Minister at the Hague, to be Her Majesty's Ambassador at Berlin.

On the 27th of November I had an audience of the King and Queen of Prussia to present my letters of recall. Their Majesties were pleased to receive me most graciously and kindly, reminding me that it was just twenty-five years since I had been presented to them, and they expressed their sincere regret at my leaving the Court of Berlin, assuring me of the continuance of their high esteem and regard.

The kind and gracious interest evinced by their

Majesties towards Lady Augustus and myself was most gratifying to us both. Their Majesties were pleased to invite us to an evening party on the 29th, at which we were permitted to take final leave of their Majesties.

The day before my departure the King was graciously pleased to send me a magnificent porcelain vase, with his portrait and a view of his palace at Berlin, as a mark of his esteem on my leaving his Court, which I was permitted by Her Majesty the Queen to accept. His Majesty was further pleased to honour Lady Augustus and myself with a visit at the Legation to bid us adieu, an honour rarely conferred on a Foreign Minister on the eve of his departure.

This was my third departure from official service at Berlin. I left first as paid Attaché in 1842, again as Secretary of Legation in 1858, and as Minister in 1862. I was destined to return as Ambassador in 1866 till 1871, when I was transferred to the Embassy at St. Petersburg. Thus I witnessed, during thirty-four years, the various progressive stages through which Prussia had passed, until finally, in 1871, when in the palace of Versailles, with the unanimous consent of the German Sovereigns and Princes, the German Empire was proclaimed, and King William I. of Prussia was invested with the hereditary title in the royal house of Prussia of "German Emperor."

King William commenced his eventful reign at an age when other great Sovereigns of past history had already completed the era of their renown—when

Frederick the Great had long before achieved his victorious campaigns.

No one could have foreseen, or even imagined, the great transformation which Prussia and Germany would undergo under King William, or the great changes which his reign would produce. The King was never held to be a great statesman nor considered to be a great politician, but he was possessed of other valuable qualities. He was gifted with great shrewdness and sagacity; he was deeply impressed with a sense of duty; he allowed of no backstairs influence or intrigue; he was frank, straightforward, and honest in all his thoughts and deeds; he was gifted with great firmness of character, and when, after mature consideration, his decision was taken it was irrevocable; he was of a noble, chivalrous character, genial and courteous to all, and in conversation was ever ready with a smile and a joke to please and captivate.

It must be always remembered that the King from his earliest youth was a soldier. He had taken part in the march of the allied troops to Paris in 1814, and distinguished himself in an engagement with the French at Arcis-sur-Aube, for which he received the Cross of St. George from the Emperor Alexander I. of Russia.*

The King had been brought up in the school of militarism and absolutism. He had witnessed the sad

---

* The Emperor William, after the campaign of 1866, received from the Emperor Alexander II. the Grand Cross of St. George, the only Grand Cross, I believe, then existing.

misfortunes which had befallen his country in the earlier part of the century, and the severe trials which his mother, Queen Louisa, had undergone. He had witnessed the ravages caused by the French invasion, and the effect of the Revolution of 1792–93 and its demoralising doctrines. It is not surprising, therefore, that he, being no politician, looked to the army as the pillar of support for the monarchy and for the defence of the country externally and internally. He took the oath prescribed to the Constitution on his installation as. Regent, and nothing would have induced him to violate that oath by any unconstitutional act. He would have abdicated in favour of his son (which during the opposition of the Lower Chamber to the Army Reorganisation Bill in 1862 he threatened to do), but nothing could have induced him to take any step in violation of the Constitution.

The King was a thorough patriot, and had the love of his country at heart. There were three great actors who served the King with zeal and fidelity, and enabled him to carry out the great work of the regeneration of Germany. They were M. de Bismarck (afterwards Prince Bismarck), General Moltke (afterwards Field-Marshal Count Moltke), and General Von Roon, Minister of War (afterwards Field-Marshal Von Roon). These names will be handed down to future generations as the noblest of Prussian patriots, and as the regenerators of Germany.

Of M. de Bismarck I have already spoken in these memoirs. I have now only to say that his acts and the brilliant success which attended them will form the brightest page of Prussian history.

Field-Marshal Von Moltke was universally recognised as the first strategist in Europe. I knew him personally for fifty years, having made his acquaintance on his return from Turkey, where he had been employed to reform and instruct the Turkish Army. He was the most simple, unassuming, and kindhearted man I ever met, even when he was at the summit of his glorious career. His calmness and composure never forsook him, and his powers of organisation were marvellous. He was never put out, never uttered a hasty word. When Prussia was on the brink of war with Austria, and his aide-de-camp came to announce some important intelligence, he found General Moltke reading an English novel.

He had married an English lady, to whom he was devotedly attached. He was a good linguist, or, as was said, "he was silent in five languages," for he was by nature taciturn and reserved in conversation; but his observations were always remarkable for their lucidity, moderation, and consummate good sense. He was a very religious man, and his actions were always governed by the highest principles of justice and duty. He was very humane, and during the war in France often counteracted the stern severity of Count Bismarck. I remember when Count Bismarck threatened to shoot all captives from balloons, General Moltke interposed, as such orders could only emanate from the Chief of the Staff.

A case of this kind occurred when I was Ambassador at Berlin in 1870.

M. Worth, the great modiste, or a member of his firm bearing that name, was made prisoner by the Prussians out of a balloon from Paris. His brother, or a relation of his, arrived at Berlin in great haste and trepidation, fearing that the captive, who had been sent to Cologne, would be summarily disposed of as threatened by Count Bismarck. This gentleman rushed into my room at ten o'clock at night, and in an agitated tone of voice claimed his captured relation. I first informed him that the captive was not in the possession of Her Majesty's Embassy, and I next calmed his fears as to his future fate. I told him that I had already taken official steps for his release, and I had no doubt that in a few days he would be restored safe and sound to the bosom of his family. I observed that it was regrettable that he should have been inconvenienced and his family alarmed by the untoward incident, but that in time of war, if gentlemen sought to escape from a besieged city in a balloon, which did not, unfortunately, land them at the destination they wished, but reached *terra firma* in the centre of the besieging army, they could not be surprised at their being looked upon as involuntary spies, and consequently kept in detention while inquiries were taking place as to their personality. I added that his family need be under no alarm as to his early liberation. The over-excitement and agitation of my visitor may have been excusable, but it was in reality rather comical.

The third coadjutor with Bismarck and Moltke in enabling the King to carry out the reorganisation of the army so successfully as I have referred to was General Von Roon, Minister of War. He was a man of considerable administrative ability, and possessed of a strong will. He was not an admirer of constitutional government, nor of a Representative Chamber, although he was a remarkably able and eloquent speaker, and might justly have been proud of his success in that respect. He had admirably carried out, under the King's personal direction, the new organisation of the Prussian army, which, through his administrative talents, reached the highest state of perfection.

No Sovereign ever possessed more able, more zealous or more devoted public servants than Bismarck, Moltke, and Roon, and the brilliant successes of two wars fully proved the value of their services to their Sovereign and their country.

I cannot close this volume without bearing testimony to the valuable assistance I received during 1861-62 from Mr. Morier (now Sir Robert Morier, Her Majesty's Ambassador at St. Petersburg), who was then senior Second Secretary at Her Majesty's Legation at Berlin. His perfect knowledge of the German language, and of German affairs, which at that period were greatly complicated, was of the greatest service to me, and he rendered this service with zeal and efficiency. I then foresaw the tokens of that diplomatic ability which has since raised him to the highest rank in his profession, and no one has been more gratified than myself by the reward of his deserved merits.

Nor can I fail to mention two other fellow-labourers in my vineyard, who performed their duties with exemplary zeal and assiduity, viz., the Hon. Nassau Jocelyn, who is now Her Majesty's Chargé d'Affaires at Darmstadt, and the late Hon. T. Grosvenor, whose early death has deprived the diplomatic service of a most promising and zealous public servant.

"Vitæ summa brevis spem nos vetat inchoare longam."

They were both cheery and agreeable companions, and their genial society greatly tended to mitigate the gloom with which my late severe affliction had then overshadowed my mind.

In presenting to an indulgent public these volumes —as forming the first series of my diplomatic reminiscences—I must claim their lenient judgment of a work the sole aim of which is a faithful historical account of events which had come under my personal notice, and in some of which I had been an actor. Among the most interesting of these are the origin of the Austro-Italian War, the startling preliminaries of peace resulting from a meeting of the two Emperors at Villa Franca, and the constitution of an united Italy under King Victor Emanuel.

In delineating the characters of many of the distinguished men referred to, who were personally known to me, I have been guided by feelings of truth and justice, and by the anxious wish to avoid any expression of opinion which could in the smallest degree give pain or offence.

I appeal to my readers to excuse and pardon the many shortcomings and omissions to be found in these volumes, arising chiefly from my wish to condense my narrative as far as possible, and not to weary them with details, but simply to record the events as they occurred as clearly and cursorily as I could, leaving them to form their own judgment and opinion of them; and finally, this being my first attempt at authorship, I beg them to be

> " To my faults a little blind,
> And to my labours somewhat kind."

APPENDIX.

Lord A. Loftus to the Earl of Malmesbury.—(Rec. Mar. 28.)
(Extract.)   *Vienna, March* 19, 1859.

I had the honour to receive, late on the evening of the 18th instant, Your Lordship's telegram of that date, informing me of the proposal of the French Emperor and Government for a Congress of the five Powers, to be held in a neutral town, and desiring to be informed whether the Austrian Cabinet would accept this proposal on the following conditions, viz., that no allusion should be made to her territory; that the subjects to be treated by the Congress should be confined to the evacuation of the Roman States by the foreign armies; to the reforms to be proposed to the Roman and other Italian Governments; and, lastly, to the question of agreeing upon some substitution for the Treaties between Austria and the Italian Duchies.

In order to meet Your Lordship's desire to receive, if possible, a reply on the following day, previous to the meeting of the Cabinet at 3 o'clock, I lost no time in requesting an interview with Count Buol, and His Excellency was good enough to receive me at a late hour on the same night.

On my communicating to His Excellency the substance of my instructions, he did not appear unprepared for such a communication, for he at once stated to me that he had learnt that a proposal of this nature had emanated from Russia, and had been accepted by France.

APPENDIX.

In referring to the subjects laid down in Your Lordship's telegram, to be brought before the Congress (and with reference more especially to reforms to be proposed to Italian States), Count Buol called my attention to the Protocol attached to the Treaty of Aix-la-Chapelle of 1818, in which the contracting parties agreed, that "meetings or Congresses on affairs specially connected with other of the European States could only take place on a formal invitation on the part of those States to whom these affairs related, and on the express reserve of their right to participate therein, directly or indirectly, by their Plenipotentiaries."

I replied to His Excellency that no one would for a moment contest the validity of this Protocol, but that many, if not all, would, under present circumstances, consider its application inappropriate and inapplicable. Vital interests were now at stake. The question at issue was that of peace or war. The Great Powers, ever watchful for the common interest of Europe, were ardently desirous of maintaining the former, and of averting from mankind the miseries of the latter.

It was, therefore, paradoxical to raise from the dust, after the lapse of forty years, an Article from a Protocol, the very object of which, when agreed to, was for the purpose of consolidating good amity and friendship between all States, and to use it now as an element of obstruction to the laudable efforts of those who were labouring in the cause of peace. I reminded him that very large holes had been made in the Treaties of 1815, without rendering those Treaties less efficacious as a whole; and that Austria was not free from this charge.

"How so?" said His Excellency. I replied that the incorporation of Cracow was of too much importance, and of too modern a date, to have escaped my memory. This allusion, made in the form of earnest reasoning rather than in an invective tone, was received by His Excellency in the spirit in which it was offered, and seemed to produce its effect.

I expressed to His Excellency my anxious hope that the Austrian Government would not reject the proposals for a

Congress, as the most serious and prejudicial effect would be produced if Austria should be the only one of the Great Powers adverse to it.

I further observed to His Excellency that a Congress was not a tribunal, and that Austria, by accepting a Congress, did not undertake any binding engagement; on the contrary, by acceding to the general wish of the Great Powers cordially and with good grace, Austria would afford to Europe the strongest proof of her desire for peace, and would thereby gain for herself the respect and esteem which is universally accorded to a Power whose policy is actuated by principles of right, and not of might.

Count Buol said he had seen Lord Cowley with great pleasure. "But he should have gone to Turin; it is at Turin that you can render eminent service to the cause of peace; it is there that you ought to urge your peaceful efforts. It is Piedmont that is agitating and preparing for war. We are not aggressive. We have positively assured you that we shall not attack Sardinia, nor anybody else. Have you received the same pacific assurance from Turin?"

I replied to Count Buol that Earl Cowley's mission had been one of confidential and friendly interest for Austria, but that we had not confined our peaceful efforts to Vienna. Her Majesty's Government had been equally and energetically active in the cause of peace at Turin.

His Excellency informed me that he would, on the following morning, submit to the Emperor the communication which I had been instructed to make, and would inform me of His Imperial Majesty's decision at the earliest moment on the following morning.

On taking leave of His Excellency, I could plainly perceive that the Austrian Government would, under conditions, and with reserves, accept the proposals offered by Her Majesty's Government for a pacific solution of the Italian complications.

Lord A. Loftus to the Earl of Malmesbury.—(Rec. Mar. 28.)

(Extract.)   Vienna, March 21, 1859.

I waited by invitation on Count Buol on the 20th instant, at 10 a.m.,* when His Excellency informed me that he had just left the Emperor, and that His Majesty had charged him to acquaint me with the following decision he had taken on the subject of the proposals for a Congress :—

Austria will agree to enter at once, conjointly with the other Great Powers, into negotiations with the Papal Government at Rome, through the ordinary diplomatic channel, on the subject of the evacuation of the Roman States by the foreign armies, and on the reforms which it may be deemed advisable to recommend to the Pope. The Austrian Government will be ready to take the project drawn up in 1831 as the basis, or starting point, for their deliberations.

Count Buol considers that these two questions are not of a nature which can be discussed by a European Congress at which the Pope was not represented; and he is confident that His Holiness would not consent to take part in a Congress assembled for the discussion of his internal affairs out of the limits of his States.

The Austrian Government, therefore, propose to separate these two questions, and to eliminate them from the subjects to be discussed by the proposed Congress. The Austrian Cabinet were, however, willing, at the same time, to lend their co-operation for their satisfactory arrangement by ordinary diplomatic negotiations at Rome, in the same manner, and on the basis, in which they were conducted in 1831.

There only then remained the fourth point of Your Lordship's conditions to be submitted to a European Congress, namely, " the substitution for the Treaties which Austria had entered into with the Duchies of Modena and Parma in 1847 ; " and the

* No. 127 is the reply to the telegram on which this despatch is founded

Austrian Government declare themselves ready to agree to the proposed Congress on condition that—

1. There shall be no question of any territorial changes.
2. That, previous to the Congress meeting, Sardinia shall disarm, and shall give an engagement to respect the existing territorial treaties, and also those with her neighbours.
3. Austria will require a strict observance of the terms of the Protocol annexed to the Treaty of Aix-la-Chapelle of 1818, which virtually implies a participation in the Congress on the part of those Italian States whose affairs are to be treated of.

If these conditions are complied with, Austria will not object to an arrangement by which the internal safety of the minor Italian States may be secured, and which will no longer render necessary the maintenance of the Treaties of 1847 with the Duchies.

Count Buol, in communicating to me this reply to Your Lordship's proposals, stated that there was evidently a desire at Paris to make a retreat, and that the Austrian Cabinet were willing to meet that desire in a spirit of conciliation and moderation.

In reference to the Protocol of 1818, Count Buol stated, at an interview I had with him on the following day, that Count Walewski, on a previous occasion, had fully recognised the validity of this Protocol, when some allusion was made to it at Paris (I think) in 1856 or 1857; and His Excellency read me part of a despatch from M. Hübner testifying to the fact.

Basing his argument on this Protocol, Count Buol said that he could not discuss in a Congress the affairs of independent foreign States unless they were therein represented.

I observed to him that if the Duchies were to be represented in the Congress, it was an impossibility to exclude Sardinia.

His Excellency replied that the only two treaties lately referred to were those with the Duchies; consequently, according to the Protocol of the Treaty of Aix-la-Chapelle, they had a right to be represented, but that as no Treaties with Sardinia were to be discussed, she could not claim a participation in the Congress.

I observed to him that this might be logical, but that it was impracticable, and that Sardinia could not be excluded if the others were admitted.

"If," replied Count Buol, "Sardinia were to apply to the European Powers for a Congress to aid her with their advice and counsels to rid herself of the propagandism which had taken possession of the country, I should be the first to accept and to render her every assistance."

His Excellency then cited the Congresses of Laybach and Verona, both of which had been respectively summoned on the express invitation of the Kings of Naples and Spain.

I represented to His Excellency that time and circumstances changed very much the character of political situations, and that what was applicable, and even necessary, at one moment, might become totally different at another.

In the present case political necessity urged on Austria the frank acceptation of a Congress, and that if she raised trivial difficulties to its realisation they would later 'fall on her own head, and she alone would be responsible for the consequences which might result therefrom.

I communicated to Count Buol the substance of Your Lordship's telegram of the 19th. He was, on this occasion, less favourably disposed than he had been on the previous day, and appeared to entertain great suspicions with respect to a Congress, fearing that the Emperor of the French was not sincere, and that his sole object was to gain time.

On leaving His Excellency I was less hopeful than I had been on the previous day that the proposals for a Congress would be accepted on such terms as would meet the end desired, and the approbation of Her Majesty's Government.

The Earl of Malmesbury to Lord A. Loftus.

Foreign Office, March 30, 1859.

My Lord,—I have to express my regret to Your Lordship at what may be called the inevitable misapprehensions arising from a succession of telegraphic despatches; but on this occasion they have been of no consequence. The main features of our communications with Austria should be well understood by the Austrian Cabinet, and I will define them at length to Your Lordship in the present despatch.

When Lord Cowley left Vienna, Her Majesty's Government were induced to believe, from his conversations with Count Buol, that should a mediation be carried out through the friendly offices of Great Britain, four subjects would exhaust the Italian question, and if judiciously treated would restore harmony to the relations between Austria and France. Those four subjects were:—

1. Security for peace between Austria and Sardinia.
2. Evacuation of Roman States.
3. Reform of the Italian States.
4. Substitute which might lead to the abrogation or modification of the Austro-Italian Treaties.

Lord Cowley's mission, having been made with the full concurrence of France, and with an intimate knowledge by His Lordship of the French views upon the Italian question, which rest upon the same objects, increased the hopes that Her Majesty's Government entertained of a pacific solution.

The position was, however, somewhat changed on the return of Lord Cowley to Paris, on the 16th of March, when he found that communications had taken place between France and Russia which would probably result in an offer by the latter to the five Powers to hold a Congress in which the Italian question should be discussed.

Although this was announced by both Lord Cowley and the

Duc de Malakoff, on the 18th instant, the proposal was not made officially to Her Majesty's Government by Baron Brünnow till the 23rd; but Her Majesty's Government had, on the 19th, informed Sir J. Crampton, by telegraph, that they should accept such a proposal provided the Treaties of 1815 and territorial arrangements were not altered. Her Majesty's Government then anticipated the Russian announcement by stating to Baron Brünnow, on the 20th, that this must be the basis of any Congress which might take place in which Her Majesty's Government took a part, and, further, that the subject-matter there discussed must be restricted to the four points which I have enumerated above. Russia at once accepted these conditions, and on the 23rd Baron Brünnow made his official proposal of a Congress, which Her Majesty's Government accepted. Her Majesty's Government see no reason for departing from their opinions as to the subject-matter thus deliberately considered by them as containing, on the one hand, the whole pith of the Italian question, from which, if that question is to be discussed at all, there can be no escape, and, on the other, as containing as much as it would be just and politic to ventilate.

Her Majesty's Government submit earnestly to the Cabinet of Vienna that the first point, namely, the future security against a war between Austria and Sardinia, might immediately, and previously to the Congress, be solved in the following manner:—

Austria should consent to the four points laid down by Her Majesty's Government being discussed in a Congress, and declare that she would withdraw her troops from the Piedmontese frontier on the condition that the four Powers would summon Sardinia to disband her contingents, and withdraw her troops to their usual posts; Sardinia being guaranteed against an attack from Austria by England and France, and Austria declaring that she would not attack her.

The second point, namely, the evacuation of the Roman States, would be treated of in Congress only as far as to declare it an act to be performed within a given time; the details of this military operation being left to Rome, Austria, and France to arrange.

On this point, however, Her Majesty's Government cannot agree with Count Buol that a Congress has no right to interfere.

The continued presence for ten years of foreign troops in the centre of Italy becomes a permanent occupation never contemplated by any school of statesmen or any category of treaties, and is visibly a patent grievance, dangerous to the peace of Europe, because absolutely repulsive to the feelings of the whole Italian Peninsula. It is a fair and proper subject for the deliberation of the Great Powers, and it is a duty which they owe to Europe to examine and advise upon it.

The third point is that of reform; and Her Majesty's Government are of opinion that, upon this question, the Congress, having laid down certain principles consolidated from the propositions discussed in 1831 and 1857, would submit them to be carried out in detail by the States which they concerned. Her Majesty's Government cannot be parties to impose any such reforms upon any independent State; and it would be only with an anxious wish that they might contribute to its security and happiness that they would advise or urge the acceptance of their counsels.

The fourth and last point, namely, a substitute which might tend to abrogate or modify the Austro-Italian Treaties, Her Majesty's Government feel to be one of great delicacy as regards Austria, and would desire to approach it with the deference due to the feelings of that Court. They rejoice that Austria does not advocate its omission in a Congress upon the affairs of Italy, because it is inseparable from the causes of the dissatisfaction and danger which exist in that country. The substitutes which were sketched out as possible in Count Buol's conversations with Lord Cowley lead Her Majesty's Government to hope that if Austria would take the initiative at the Congress upon this subject, a substitute might easily be discovered, which, far from diminishing the dignity of Austria or the security of the

Duchies, would tend to increase both, by removing unpopular and unnecessary obligations.

Her Majesty's Government, while they admit the undoubted right of independent Powers to make offensive and defensive treaties with one another as regards external foes, will not conceal from the Austrian Government that Article III. of those Treaties of Austria with Parma and Modena is repulsive to the ideas of this country. This Article deprives Austria of the right of judging for herself whether the internal discontent which may break out in these Duchies is justifiable or not, and she appears to Her Majesty's Government to be in a deplorable position of being forced, perhaps against her own convictions and feelings, to become the executioner of an unjust decree.

Such, my Lord, are the views of Her Majesty's Government on the subjects which they propose the Congress should consider, and to which they think it should strictly be confined.

It is now my duty to speak of its composition.

Her Majesty's Government feel most strongly that upon this solely Italian question it is impossible, on every principle both of equity and sound policy, to exclude Italy from the scene and court of deliberations which concern so intimately its political existence and social happiness.

In this country, at least, such a course would meet with universal reprobation, and it is one to which Her Majesty's Government could never give their consent.

But Her Majesty's Government see no difficulty in this matter, and regret that some objections appear to influence Count Buol with respect to the proposals of Her Majesty's Government on this point.

Her Majesty's Government are of opinion that all the Italian States should be invited by the Great Powers to attend the Congress by representatives who should, if so required, be heard before it upon the several points of their deliberations which affect these States respectively. Thus, the representative of Rome would be heard on the question of evacuation; those of Rome, Modena, Parma, and Tuscany on the subject of a possible confederation of States, should that idea be mooted, or on recommendations of reforms.

But Her Majesty's Government could not consent to exclude from this invitation either Naples or Sardinia, because the whole of Italy must be interested in the fate of its neighbouring States, and its component parts; and Her Majesty's Government consider they would have a right, even if not called in by the Congress, to be permitted to state their views, and declare whether the changes proposed would bear disadvantageously upon their own interests.

This is the equitable view of the subject, and the political one is not less clear to Her Majesty's Government. They are convinced that nothing would be more unwise than to give any Italian Government the right hereafter of declaring that, having had no share, direct or indirect, at a Congress which discussed the political and social state of Italy, it was entirely free from all liens, and irresponsible for all results.

Her Majesty's Government entreat the Austrian Government not to approach this Congress with distrust and reluctance, but to take the lead in its formation, and, when formed, in its deliberations. It will find in Her Majesty's Government a sincere ally, anxious to relieve it from unfair pressure, and to maintain its rights. At the same time, that same sincerity of friendship obliges Her Majesty's Government to point out to the Court of Vienna that a suspicious repugnance to our propositions, either as regards the subject-matter for the Conference or its composition, which is not founded on substantial proofs of injustice or danger, will result in fatal delays, alienating from Austria that public sympathy which is felt towards her, and inducing the world to believe that she is little anxious for the attainment of those objects by which a lasting peace may yet be secured.

Your Lordship will read this despatch to Count Buol, and if he desires it, give him a copy.

I am, &c.,

MALMESBURY.

Lord A. Loftus to the Earl of Malmesbury.—(Rec. April 11.)

Vienna, *April* 6, 1859.

MY LORD,—I did not fail to bring under Count Buol's notice, at the earliest moment possible after its receipt, Your Lordship's telegram of the 31st ultimo,* and I urged on His Excellency, in conformity with Your Lordship's instructions, the great desirableness for Austria to place herself right in the public opinion of Europe by settling at once the matters under discussion relating to the meeting of the Congress.

His Excellency observed, with respect to the participation of the Italian States, that he had reason to know that none of those States would appear at the Congress in the form and manner which has been proposed, and that both the Pope and the King of Naples had already positively expressed their refusal to do so.

With respect to the proposal for a general disarmament, Count Buol stated that he had never intended that it should bear the character of a preliminary condition, but that it should be taken into consideration on the meeting of the Congress; he considered that its acceptance would afford the best proof of the pacific intentions of the Great Powers, and would give a further guarantee that all their efforts would be directed to secure a lasting peace.

I then alluded to the important point, the fulfilment of which the Austrian Cabinet exacted as a *sine quâ non* condition of their entering the Congress, viz., the previous disarmament and disbanding of the Free Corps by Sardinia; and I represented to His Excellency that the imperative form in which this condition was expressed would not produce an impression in Europe favourable to Austria. His Excellency, I stated, must admit that it was never desirable, in negotiations, that any party should advance and lay down a condition the fulfilment of which might be impossible, and in respect to which no means

* No. 193.

were left for harmonising dissentient opinions. Such a course was neither likely to conciliate opinions, nor to be acceptable to friends.

His Excellency replied that he could give me no hope that the Austrian Cabinet would yield on this point. It was the condition on which the Emperor, his master, had accepted the Congress and the four points submitted by Her Majesty's Government as the basis for deliberation, and His Imperial Majesty would not deviate from it.

I stated to His Excellency that it could be scarcely supposed that a great military Power like Austria should entertain fears of a military attack upon her by a State like Sardinia, although the conditions imposed by Austria would be undoubtedly interpreted in this light, and there could scarcely exist other valid reasons for enforcing such a condition in opposition to the united counsels of Europe. His Excellency replied, "We are not afraid of Sardinia. We have not armed against Sardinia; but we consider Sardinia to be the advanced guard of France. If France will disarm, and thereby give proof of her pacific intentions, we shall no longer insist on the disarmament of Sardinia. What we require to have is security against France. We have no confidence in her Emperor nor in the Government. If," continued His Excellency, "Great Britain and Prussia will sign a defensive Treaty with us, and will secure us against France, we will no longer insist on this condition. But we must know that France is not seeking to gain time by negotiation in order to complete her armaments. If war is to be, we prefer to have it now. We cannot endure this continued suspense, this continued armed peace, which is more prejudicial to the country than war."

I reminded His Excellency that the counsels of Her Majesty's Government were those of friends, who were anxious and most deeply interested for the welfare and security of Austria; but that Her Majesty's Government could not disguise from themselves that, if the conditions now exacted by Austria were insisted on, the failure of the Congress must inevitably result, and that it was evident that the Austrian Cabinet, by such a course, would be playing the game of their adversary. It was patent to all that Count Cavour was anxious that the Congress should not meet, and nothing could facilitate and further his designs more effectively than the refusal of the Austrian Cabinet to enter it. The failure thereof, and the inevitable result, which would be war, would be attributed to Austria. On her would be laid the blame; and this fatal error on her part would, I feared, completely deprive her of the sympathies and moral support which had hitherto been given to her both in England and in Germany.

I entreated, therefore, His Excellency to pause and to reflect before he persisted in a course which would only rejoice his adversaries, and, I feared, alienate his friends.

Count Buol said that he could not change the decision taken. He did not think that either the Parliament or public opinion of England would withdraw their sympathies from Austria on such grounds, for he respected too much the sound reason and impartial judgment of England to entertain these fears. Austria confided in the justice of her cause and in the legality of her sacred rights. If she drew the sword then, it would only be in their defence and for their maintenance.

I have, &c.,

AUGUSTUS LOFTUS.

Lord A. Loftus to the Earl of Malmesbury.—(Rec. April 11.)

Vienna, April 6, 1859.

MY LORD,—I have not the smallest hope that the Austrian Government will agree to any such measure as that of retiring their forces ten leagues from the Piedmontese frontier.

Baron Werther, the new Prussian Minister, has received

a direct negative to this proposal, and is not disposed to revert to the subject again.

I had some conversation with Count Buol late this evening (for I was unable to see him during the day) on the subject of the disarmament of Sardinia. It is not necessary, neither will my time permit me (hurried as I am by the forced departure of the messenger to-morrow), to repeat the arguments I brought forward to urge His Excellency to modify this condition of the Austrian Cabinet.

His Excellency replied, "You know what the Emperor told you; I can only repeat it. I could give up my post, but I could not obtain any change of decision in this respect."

I then brought before His Excellency the substance of the telegram I had received from Earl Cowley, requesting to be informed whether he might say that he had been positively assured at Vienna that when Sardinia had disarmed Austria would do so likewise.

His Excellency said that Earl Cowley was correct in the statement he made; but that when he (Count Buol) made the declaration referred to, matters were in a different position and there was no question of a Congress.

After some argumentative discussion, I got His Excellency to state that if Sardinia would disband the Free Corps, Austria would give the most solemn assurances not to attack her; and that Austria was ready at once, previous to the meeting of the Congress, to come to an agreement for the general disarmament of the Great Powers. If these terms were complied with, Austria would then go into Congress.

"What we require," observed Count Buol, "is security against France. If you and Prussia will give us that security we will equally go into Congress."

With reference to Lord Cowley's proposal, His Excellency observed that Austria, situated as she was towards France, could not disarm merely because Sardinia did so. But, said Count Buol, if the Emperor Louis Napoleon is really sincere, and will openly and straightforwardly state his desire and intentions of bringing the affairs of Italy to a peaceful solution, and that these intentions should be supported by evident proofs of sincerity, then, said Count Buol, we shall most readily meet him, and reciprocate those assurances. All parties might then disarm, and the difficulties of the present situation would be at once removed.

But it is clear that His Excellency does not entertain any hopes of so peaceful a nature. In his opinion it will be the sword, and not the olive branch, which France will hold out.

I have, &c.,
AUGUSTUS LOFTUS.

Count Buol to Count Apponyi.—(Communicated to the Earl of Malmesbury by Count Apponyi, April 23.)

(Translation.) *Vienna, April* 20, 1859.

M. LE COMTE,—Lord A. Loftus has read to me, and given me a copy of, the despatch of Lord Malmesbury, of which I have the honour to transmit to you the text inclosed.

This document is intended as an answer to the note which I addressed to Lord A. Loftus, dated the 31st of last March.

The Earl of Malmesbury declares that he is unable to accept the interpretation given by me to the four bases of discussion proposed by England, or rather, that he cannot undertake the task of confining the discussion on these four points to the limits traced by us.

In his opinion such a restriction would impose unusual restraints on the liberty of judgment of the Plenipotentiaries, and would prejudge their decisions.

This tendency was not sought by us. We have only aimed to prepare the way to the final understanding, by occupying ourselves in defining more exactly that which was vague and indefinite in the four points as they were expressed. To attempt to agree beforehand on the starting-points of a discussion is to obtain one more chance of a definite agreement between the deliberating parties. We see, with regret, that this chance has escaped us; but we believe ourselves none the less to have performed an act of loyalty and frankness in allowing no doubt to exist about the limits which the Imperial Government on its part cannot pass in deliberations, the initiative in which does not belong to them, and to which they have only consented under certain reservations.

As to the fifth point of discussion proposed by us, and relating to the disarmament of the Great Powers, Lord Malmesbury is ready to unite with all the other Powers in its acceptance and in its satisfactory solution. This question, moreover, has entered into a new phase by the telegraphic communications of a more recent date.

As far as concerns the result of the offer of Great Britain to insist, conjointly with France, on the disarmament of Sardinia, Lord Malmesbury declares that, in the intention of the British Government, the exhortation to be addressed to the Cabinet of Turin to obtain the disarmament was to be accompanied by a collective guarantee, which would have been given to it by England and France, against an attack on the part of Austria. The French Government having declined to take part in this guarantee, and the British proposal having consequently remained unexecuted, Lord Malmesbury does not agree with us in the justice of a summons which we should address directly to Sardinia to induce her immediately to adopt the peace establishment.

My despatch of the 12th instant, which Your Excellency has communicated to Lord Malmesbury, having crossed that of the British Cabinet which is the subject of our analysis, we hope that, from the details contained in our despatch, His Lordship will derive the conviction that the right of legitimate defence fully authorises us to obtain, by all the means in our power, the disarmament of a bordering State which has placed itself in a state of open and permanent aggression against us.

You will be so good, M. le Comte, as to read this despatch to Lord Malmesbury, and give him a copy of it if he desires it.

Receive, &c.,

BUOL.

Count Buol to Count Apponyi.—(Communicated to the Earl of Malmesbury by Count Apponyi, April 23.)

(Translation.)   *Vienna, April* 20, 1859.

M. LE COMTE,—By my despatch of the 12th instant, which Your Excellency has communicated to Lord Malmesbury, the British Government has been informed of the motives which suggested to the Emperor, our august master, the resolution of making a final effort to obtain, by means of a direct summons, the placing on the peace footing of the Sardinian army.

In order to carry out this decision, I addressed to Count Cavour the letter of which I have the honour to transmit to Your Excellency a copy enclosed.

While insisting on the immediate disarmament of the Sardinian Government, which has openly assumed an attitude of permanent aggression towards us, we still do not consider as retracted our proposal of proceeding, at the same time, by a joint agreement in the re-establishment of a peace footing on the part of all the Powers who have made extraordinary armaments. It should, however, be well understood that the negotiations for bringing about this latter result can neither arrest nor modify the course which we have marked out for ourselves with regard to Sardinia.

The consent to the execution of the general immediate disarmament would only have, in our eyes, the value of an effective proof of the pacific sentiments of all other Powers, in so far as it is not attached to conditions which it is already known, by our previous and reiterated declarations, we cannot admit.

Of this number would be the admission of Sardinia to the deliberations of the Congress on whatever pretension she might found her claim.

What we have accepted is the invitation to a Congress of the five Powers. On this subject we have referred to the Protocol of Aix-la-Chapelle, to point out that, the Italian Governments having in no way demanded the intervention of the Great Powers in their internal affairs, these Powers would not be authorised to take on this subject decisions obligatory on independent States not represented at the Congress, and having no right to do so.

To invite these States to the Congress would essentially alter the nature of the proposal which has been addressed to us by the Court of St. Petersburg, and to which we have only agreed in the conviction that its basis would not be altered. The Government of Her Britannic Majesty has, from the beginning, shared in our opinion so far as to be unwilling to allow the Italian States to sit in the Congress, although of opinion that they should be invited to send delegates to it in a consultative character.

All that we, on our part, have agreed to, and which we still adhere to, is that the Italian Governments, if they consider it suitable, should send agents in an unofficial character to the seat of the Congress.

For still stronger reasons we could not but reject any combination destined to open to the Cabinet of Turin the access to the Congress, since it is notorious that this Cabinet has, in its last public manifestoes, raised, with incomparable audacity, pretensions entirely incompatible, either with the dignity and sovereign rights of our august master the Emperor, or with those which His Majesty exercises in virtue of European Treaties.

I invite Your Excellency to read this despatch to Lord Malmesbury, and give him a copy of it.

Receive, &c.,

BUOL.

Inclosure.—*Count Buol to Count Cavour.*

(Translation.) *Vienna, April* 19, 1859.

The Imperial Government, as Your Excellency is aware, has hastened to accede to the proposal of the Cabinet of St. Petersburg to assemble a Congress of the five Powers with the view to remove the complications which have arisen in Italy.

Convinced, however, of the impossibility to enter, with any chance of success, upon pacific deliberations in the midst of the noise of arms, and of preparations for war carried on in a neighbouring country, we have demanded the placing on a peace footing of the Sardinian army, and the disbanding of the free corps, or Italian volunteers, previously to the meeting of the Congress.

Her Britannic Majesty's Government find this condition so just, and so consonant with the exigencies of the situation, that it did not hesitate to adopt it, at the same time declaring itself to be ready, in conjunction with France, to insist on the immediate disarmament of Sardinia, and to offer her in return a collective guarantee against any attack on our part, to which, of course, Austria would have done honour.

The Cabinet of Turin seems only to have answered, by a categorical refusal to the invitation to put her army on a peace footing, and to accept the collective guarantee which was offered her. This refusal inspires us with regrets, so much the more deep that, if the Sardinian Government had consented to the testimony of pacific sentiments which was demanded of her, we should have accepted it as a first symptom of her intention to assist, on her side, in bringing about an improvement in the relations between the two countries which have unfortunately been in such a state of tension for some years past. In that case it would have been permitted us to furnish, by the breaking up of the Imperial troops stationed in the Lombardo-Venetian Kingdom, another proof that they were not assembled for the purpose of aggression against Sardinia.

Our hope having been hitherto deceived, the Emperor, my august master, has ordered me to make directly a last effort to cause the Sardinian Government to reconsider the decision which it seems to have resolved on. Such is the object of this letter.

I have the honour to entreat Your Excellency to take its contents into your most serious consideration, and to let me know if the Royal Government consents, yes or no, to put its army on a peace footing without delay, and to disband the Italian volunteers.

The bearer of this letter, to whom, M. le Comte, you will be so good as to give your answer, is ordered to hold himself at your disposition to this effect for three days.

Should he receive no answer at the expiration of this term, or should this answer not be completely satisfactory, the responsibility of the grave events which this refusal would entail would fall entirely on His Sardinian Majesty's Government.

After having exhausted in vain all conciliatory means to procure for these populations the guarantee of peace, on which the Emperor has a right to insist, His Majesty will be obliged, to his great regret, to have recourse to the force of arms to obtain it.

Inclosure.—*Count Cavour to Count Buol.*

(Translation.) *Turin, April* 26, 1859.

M. LE COMTE,—Baron Kellersberg delivered to me on the 23rd instant, at 5.30 p.m., the letter which Your Excellency has done me the honour to address to me, summoning me, in the name of the Imperial Government, to answer by a "yes" or by a "no" the invitation which has been made to us to reduce the army to a peace footing, and to disband the corps formed of Italian volunteers, adding that if, at the end of three days, Your Excellency should receive no answer, or should the answer returned to you not be completely satisfactory, His Majesty the

Emperor of Austria was resolved to have recourse to arms in order to impose upon us by force the measures which form the object of his communication.

The question of the disarmament of Sardinia, which constitutes the basis of the demand which Your Excellency addresses to me, has been the object of numerous negotiations between the Great Powers and the Government of His Majesty. These negotiations have resulted in a proposition, drawn up in due form, by England, to which France, Prussia, and Russia have agreed. Sardinia, in a spirit of conciliation, accepted it without reserve or afterthought. As Your Excellency cannot be ignorant either of the proposition of England, or of the answer of Sardinia, I can add nothing towards making you acquainted with the intention of the Government of the King with regard to the difficulties which were opposed to the assembling of the Congress. The conduct of Sardinia on this occasion has been appreciated by Europe. Whatever may be the consequences that it may produce, the King, my august master, is convinced that the responsibility will devolve upon those who were the first to arm, and who have rejected the propositions formerly drawn up by one Great Power, and recognised as just and reasonable by the others, and who now substitute for it a threatening summons.

I seize, &c.,

C. CAVOUR.

Lord A. Loftus to the Earl of Malmesbury.—(Rec. Apr. 26.)

Vienna, April 22, 1859.

MY LORD,—In conformity with your Lordship's despatch of the 11th instant,* and with the instructions contained in Your Lordship's several telegrams therein referred to, I have been unremitting in my endeavours to dissuade this Cabinet from

* No. 269.

APPENDIX. 313

taking any precipitate resolution.with regard to Sardinia, and in exposing every danger which they would incur in doing so.

Continuing in this course, I have again to-day exhausted all my efforts to induce Count Buol to arrest the execution of the orders sent to General Giulay, stating that he could reasonably do so on the communication made to His Excellency by M. de Banneville yesterday, that Sardinia had agreed to disarm at the instance of England and France, without conditions.

Count Buol replied that he had no knowledge that Sardinia had agreed to disarm without conditions, but that under any circumstances he could not interfere with the Imperial decision, and the orders given; and that no recall or modification of them was possible. "You do not know us," said His Excellency, "if you think that in such matters we retrace our steps. We have borne the weight of indecision and doubt long enough. It is now full time for it to cease."

I reminded His Excellency, however, that the moment for taking this decision would appear in the eyes of Europe most unpropitious, if not unpardonable, and would infallibly alienate from them the sympathy and support of public opinion both in England and elsewhere.

"It may be so," said His Excellency, "and we shall regret it; but you must consider that we also have a public opinion to take account of, and a young and chivalrous Emperor, to whom the dignity and honour of his country is dear. We have been bearded, provoked, and insulted by Sardinia for a long time past. We have borne it with patience, and have evinced the greatest proofs of moderation and of our love of peace. All efforts having failed in procuring that condition which we laid down as indispensable for our entry into Congress, we have taken the matter into our own hands. It is against the 'revolution' that we are acting, and although you may protest against the disbanding of the free corps as a dangerous measure, we consider that the very fact of their embodiment constitutes a danger; and the very argument put forth, of the impracticability of their being disbanded, only proves in our estimation the reality of this danger, and the necessity of removing it."

But, I remarked to His Excellency, there were other dangers as imminent, and of no lesser degree, of which the Austrian Cabinet in their late decision had appeared to take no account. Had they calculated on the consequences of the step they had taken? Had they not acted in a manner to alienate their friends? I could only repeat to His Excellency what I had stated to him on Sunday evening last, previous to the departure of the summons—that such a measure would produce war, isolation to Austria, and probably desolation to Europe. It was, therefore, I said, a grave responsibility, the consequences of which would rest wholly with the Austrian Cabinet.

His Excellency replied that the Austrian Cabinet could not be accused of any precipitation in taking this step. They had previously announced their intention to do so both to Her Majesty's Government and to that of Prussia; months had passed in vacillating proposals and counter-proposals, which only served to evince the bad faith of Sardinia, and her increasing defiance of Austria, till at last the patience and forbearance of Austria were wholly exhausted, and the spirit of the nation could no longer passively endure a position intolerable to them.

In reply to the inquiry as to whether His Excellency had been informed that Sardinia had agreed to disarm before the letter had been dispatched to General Giulay, he stated that he had not been acquainted with that fact on the evening of Tuesday the 19th, when his letter was sent off. It was on the following morning that I communicated to His Excellency this intelligence, which had reached me both from Your Lordship and Earl Cowley, by telegraph, late on the Tuesday night. That letter was forwarded by General Benedech, who, I believe, is the bearer of it to Turin.

I then communicated to His Excellency the substance of Your Lordship's telegram of yesterday, 6.30 p.m.,* which reached me this morning, stating that Her Majesty's Govern-

* No. 366.

ment would protest in the strongest manner against the step taken by Austria in the threatened invasion of Sardinian territory, and that by this untimely measure Austria had forfeited all claim to the support and sympathy of England.

In reply, His Excellency said that, when the whole subject was clearly and truthfully submitted to the impartial judgment of public opinion in England, he could not believe that they would withdraw their sympathies from Austria; but he repeated that the Austrian Cabinet had likewise to consult, and to be guided by, the public opinion of their own country, which had loudly called for energetic action to relieve the country from the weight of doubt and suspense which had for some time past completely paralysed all commercial and industrial undertakings.

With reference to the concluding paragraph of Your Lordship's telegram, expressing a hope that Austria would still be induced to act on the 23rd Protocol of the Treaty of Paris in 1856 by accepting mediation, which proposal had been made to His Excellency on a previous occasion by Baron Werther, I have to remark that Count Buol's opinion rather differed, as regards Sardinia, from the language which Baron Werther had mentioned that he had held to him; for in expressing himself to me on this point, His Excellency was of opinion that Austria might have no objection to a mediation between France and herself, but that he felt convinced that the Emperor Francis Joseph would never accept of any mediation with Sardinia. He said, however, that he would report the substance of Your Lordship's telegram to the Emperor, and take His Majesty's orders thereon.

Although I fervently hope, and do not wholly despair, that my observations, and more especially the strong disapprobation expressed in Your Lordship's telegram above referred to of the step taken by the Austrian Cabinet, may avail in inducing Count Buol to reflect on the gravity of their late decision, and the dangers of the path on which they have entered, my conversation with Count Buol did not lead me to expect that

His Imperial Majesty would deviate from the course which he has laid down.

I have, &c.,

AUGUSTUS LOFTUS.

Lord A. Loftus to the Earl of Malmesbury.—(Rec. April 26.)

Vienna, *April* 23, 1859.

MY LORD,—Late on the evening of the 19th instant I had the honour to receive Your Lordship's telegram,* as also one from Earl Cowley, announcing that Sardinia had accepted the disarmament.

On the following morning I sought an early interview with Count Buol, and on entering his *salon* I greeted His Excellency with the agreeable announcement that I was the bearer of a pacific and satisfactory arrangement. After informing his Excellency of the above-named intelligence I had received by telegraph, Count Buol stated that he had forwarded on the previous evening (Tuesday, the 19th instant) a letter he had addressed by the Emperor's orders to Count Cavour, in which, referring to the difficulties which had arisen concerning the disarmament, and which had given rise to various and divergent proposals, the Austrian Cabinet had finally resolved to address themselves directly to the Sardinian Government, to invite them to disband the free corps, or volunteers, and to place their army on the peace footing.

The officer charged to present this letter at Turin would be instructed to wait there three days for the reply. I am informed, although I have not seen this document, that it terminated by stating that, in the event of a refusal, the Austrian Government, however deeply they would regret it, would, nevertheless, find themselves under the disagreeable

* No. 354.

necessity of resorting to war (*pénible nécessité d'avoir recours à la guerre*).

Count Buol did not state to me that this alternative had been put, but he gave me clearly to understand that such would be the case.

I replied to His Excellency that this step was one of very great gravity and importance, and would produce considerable sensation in England, and, I feared, in a sense very disadvantageous to Austria.

I regretted that His Excellency had not awaited the result of the negotiation now being carried on between the English and French Governments and that of Sardinia on this question of disarmament; for, as I had just informed him, the Sardinian Government had now consented to that measure.

I feared, therefore, that the summons of the Austrian Government would be productive of great mischief, and at the very moment when our unceasing efforts in the cause of peace gave well-founded hopes of success.

I have, &c.,

AUGUSTUS LOFTUS.

Inclosure.—*Lord A. Loftus to Count Buol.*

Vienna, April 26, 1859.

The undersigned, &c., having apprised Her Majesty's Government by the telegraph of the communication made to him by Count Buol, &c., on the 20th instant, that a formal demand had, on the previous day, been sent, through General Giulay, to the Cabinet of Turin requiring that Sardinia should disarm, he has been instructed to address to His Excellency the following observations in reply.

Her Majesty's Government, from the commencement of the painful discussions on the affairs of Italy, in which the Governments of Austria, France, and Sardinia have for some time been engaged, have earnestly endeavoured to promote a good understanding between the respective parties, and, although having themselves no direct interest in the questions at issue, they have spared no pains to avert the consequences of a protracted difference of opinion between Powers with whom Great Britain has long been connected by bonds of amity and alliance.

With this view Her Majesty's Government did not hesitate, in the month of February last, to depute on a confidential mission to the Court of Vienna one of the ablest and most distinguished servants of the British Crown, who, from the position which he occupied as Her Majesty's Ambassador at the Court of France, no less than personal acquaintance with the Minister charged with the conduct of the foreign relations of Austria, appeared to be eminently qualified for the delicate commission with which he was entrusted. This task was to ascertain whether any bases could be established for the settlement of the various points which the existing state of things in Italy invested with peculiar importance.

The undersigned need not remind Count Buol of the details of what passed between His Excellency and Earl Cowley; but it is enough for him to say that Her Majesty's Government were much gratified with the disposition shown by the Cabinet of Vienna to lend itself to an amicable settlement of Italian questions, and were induced to hope that the explanations which Her Majesty's Ambassador, on his return to Paris, would be able to give to the French Government as to the policy of Austria would much facilitate the resumption of cordial and friendly intercourse between the respective Governments.

It would be equally superfluous for the undersigned to explain to Count Buol the process by which any good effects that might have arisen directly from Earl Cowley's intervention were apparently neutralised; but Count Buol could not have failed to recognise in the four points, to which Her Majesty's Government proposed to confine the deliberations of the Congress, which the Great Powers were invited by Russia to hold on the affairs of Italy, the same principles which had been in discussion between His Excellency and Count Buol, and which Her Majesty's Government had every reason to suppose were fully acquiesced in by the Cabinet of Vienna.

The Great Powers of Europe, including Austria, successively accepted the bases propounded by Her Majesty's Government. They agreed, moreover, in the principles that the several States of Italy should be admitted to send representatives to be heard at the Congress, and that a general disarmament should form part of the measures for the settlement of the affairs of Italy.

Count Buol will do Her Majesty's Government the justice to admit that they have shown no indisposition to defer, as far as was compatible with the maintenance of the general principles on which the Congress was convened, to any representations that may have been made by the Austrian Government. It has been only when Austria has insisted upon conditions in respect to the disarmament of Sardinia without any equivalent security, and to the disarmament of the free corps enrolled in that country, which appeared to Her Majesty's Government to be not only unjust in the former case, and in the latter dangerous to the tranquillity of Italy, that Her Majesty's Government expressed themselves decidedly opposed to the demands of Austria, and urged their modification.

The undersigned is not instructed to enter into details as to the various hues which, for some time past, the discussion in regard to disarmament has assumed, and as to the unnecessary delays which have been interposed, to the extreme disappointment of Her Majesty's Government, who were anxious that no impediment should exist to the meeting of the Congress on the appointed day.

But the undersigned is instructed to press upon Count Buol the fact that within the last few days an agreement was arrived at among the Great Powers for a general disarmament, and that on the 19th instant Sardinia expressed her readiness to agree also to disarm, without insisting any longer on the condition that she should be admitted, in common with the Great Powers, to take part in the Congress.

Her Majesty's Government had, however, in the meanwhile, come to the conclusion that some of the difficulties which impeded the meeting of the Congress might be removed if the original understanding as to the position which the Italian States should occupy before the Congress were departed from, and those States should all be invited, as at the Congress of Laybach in 1821, to sit in Congress by their representatives on the same footing with the Great Powers of Europe.

The Governments of France, Prussia, and Russia coincided in this view of the case; but Austria has declined to adhere to the proposition to that effect, which the undersigned, by order of his Government, has communicated to Count Buol.

Under these circumstances, Her Majesty's Government have received, with equal disappointment and surprise, the intimation which Count Buol has given to the undersigned of the peremptory demand which His Excellency appears to have addressed to the Prime Minister of Sardinia for the disarmament of the forces, and for the disbandment of the free corps recently enrolled in that country.

The undersigned is instructed to say that Her Majesty's Government look forward with dismay to the consequences of this precipitate measure on the part of Austria, wholly uncalled for, as it is, by the circumstances of the present time. Sardinia has yielded to the representations made by other Powers, and has agreed to disarm; and this deplorable act on the part of Austria is calculated, by wounding the natural pride of the Sardinian nation, to compel the Cabinet of Turin to retract its consent to a measure which has been insisted upon by its allies as the surest method of averting the impending interruption of the general peace, and of enabling the Powers of Europe to decide in Congress upon the arrangements best calculated to insure the tranquillity of Italy and the happiness of its populations.

It may be, indeed, that when the summons was dispatched to Turin, the Cabinet of Vienna was not aware that Sardinia had consented unconditionally to disarm; and if that be so, Her Majesty's Government would fain hope that that summons would at once be recalled. Otherwise, the reproach will attach to Austria that the armaments of Sardinia were not the only cause of her jealousy and distrust, even to the extent of provoking her to war, but that another feeling urged her to have recourse to the step that she has now taken; that feeling being a determination to resist the appearance at the Congress of a Sardinian Plenipotentiary on an equal footing not only with the Plenipotentiaries of the Great Powers, but with the representatives of the States of the rest of Italy. The Government of Austria has expressed its concurrence in the propriety of inviting the Italian States to send representatives to be present, in some character or other, at the Congress; and Her Majesty's Government can hardly suppose that it would be prepared to encounter the desperate extremity of war rather than allow a Sardinian representative to sit in the Congress on the same footing with the representative of Austria.

Be that as it may, Her Majesty's Government can only now deal with the case as it is presented before them, namely, that Austria has peremptorily summoned Sardinia to disarm under penalty of immediate war; and the undersigned is directed to say that Her Majesty's Government feel it due to themselves, and to the great interests of humanity which they have so earnestly striven to uphold, and also to those who have aided them in their endeavours, solemnly to record their protest against the course that Austria, regardless of the terrible consequences to Europe, and indifferent to the public opinion of the world, has so rashly and, as Her Majesty's Government believe, so unjustly adopted. They assign to Austria, and fix upon her, the last responsibility for all the miseries and calamities inevitably consequent on a conflict which was on the eve of being averted, but which, once begun, will infallibly produce a more than ordinary amount of social suffering and political convulsion.   The Undersigned, &c.,

AUGUSTUS LOFTUS.

Lord A. Loftus to the Earl of Malmesbury.—(Rec. May 2.)

(Extract.) *Vienna, April* 28, 1859.

ON the receipt of Your Lordship's telegram of the 25th instant,* I lost no time in informing Count Buol that Her Majesty's Government had offered their mediation to France.

In reply to my pressing request that, under these circumstances, His Excellency would use his influence to defer the execution of the orders sent to General Giulay, and would arrest the advance of the Austrian troops, His Excellency informed me that he was utterly powerless in this matter, and that the decision in this respect rested solely with the Emperor and the military authorities. His Excellency could further give me no hope that any modification of the original instructions to General Giulay would be assented to.

So strong is the conviction here in the minds of the military, and, indeed, of all parties, that the Emperor of the French is intent on war, and is only seeking to gain time for his military preparations, that the chief and principal aim of the Austrian Government, in the course they have taken, is to forestall the French, and to carry out their object in reducing Sardinia before sufficient aid from France can arrive.

Lord A. Loftus to the Earl of Malmesbury.— (Rec. May 2.)

Vienna, April 28, 1859.

MY LORD,—I have read to Count Buol Your Lordship's despatch of the 22nd instant (of which I had previously com-

* No. 408.

municated to His Excellency the substance received by telegraph), expressing the strong feeling of indignation in London at the summons addressed by the Austrian Government to Sardinia, calling upon her to disarm under penalty of immediate hostilities.

The grounds on which the Austrian Government explain this step are that, for a long time past, the language and bearing of the Sardinian Government have been most provoking and insulting to Austria; and that the time had now arrived when they (the Austrian Government) could no longer remain passive; that having, during several months, evinced the greatest patience and moderation, in the hopes that the Great Powers would be able to bring these matters to a satisfactory and pacific solution, and being now fully convinced that there existed a firm and fixed purpose on the part of Sardinia, aided by France, to have recourse to war in order to obtain their ends, the Imperial Government could no longer delay in bringing matters to an issue.

No impartial Government, it is argued, could expect that, after having given the most striking proofs of their desire for peace, Austria should calmly and passively await the moment when her adversaries should be perfectly prepared for the contest, whilst, during that period of delay, Austria was expending her resources and ruining herself by a costly state of armed preparation.

I have, &c.,

AUGUSTUS LOFTUS.

Lord A. Loftus to the Earl of Malmesbury.—(Rec. May 2.)

Vienna, April 28, 1859.

MY LORD,—I have the honour to forward to Your Lordship a translation of a Manifesto and Declaration of War against Sardinia, which has been addressed by the Emperor Francis Joseph to his people.

I have, &c.,

AUGUSTUS LOFTUS.

Inclosure.—*Manifesto.*

To my People.

(Translation.)

I have ordered my faithful and gallant army to put a stop to the inimicable acts (*Anfeindungen*) which for a series of years have been committed by the neighbouring State of Sardinia against the indisputable rights of my Crown, and against the integrity of the realm placed by God under my care, which acts have lately attained the very highest point. By so doing I have fulfilled the painful but unavoidable duty of a Sovereign. My conscience being at rest, I can look up to an omnipotent God, and patiently await His award. With confidence I leave my decision to the impartial judgment of contemporaneous and future generations. Of the approbation of my faithful subjects I am sure. When more than ten years ago the same enemy, violating international law and the usages of war, and without any cause being given, invaded the Lombardo-Venetian territory with an army with the intention of seizing upon it, although he was twice totally defeated by my gallant army, and at the mercy of the victor, I behaved generously, and held out my hand to a reconciliation. I did not appropriate to myself one inch of his territory; I encroached on no right which belongs to the Crown of Sardinia as one of the members of the European family of nations. I insisted on no guarantees against the recurrence of similar events. The hand of peace which I, in all sincerity, extended, and which was taken, appeared to me to be a sufficient guarantee. The blood which my army shed for the honour and right of Austria I sacrificed on the altar of peace (*dem Frieden brachte Ich das Blut meiner Armee zum Opfer*). The answer to this forbearance, which has hardly had an example in history, was a resumption of hostility, and an agitation carried on by all the expedients of perfidy, increasing from year to year, against the peace and welfare of my Lombardo-Venetian kingdom. Well knowing how much I ought to value the priceless boon of peace for my people and for Europe, I patiently bore with these new hostilities. My patience was not exhausted when the more extensive measures which recently I was forced to take, in consequence of the revolutionary agitation on the frontiers of my Italian provinces, and within the same, were made an excuse for a higher degree of hostility. Willingly accepting the well-meant mediation of friendly Powers for the maintenance of peace, I consented to become a party to a Congress of the five Great Powers. The four points proposed by the Royal Government of Great Britain, as a basis for the deliberations of the Congress, were forwarded to my Government, and I accepted them, with the conditions which alone were calculated to bring about a true, sincere, and durable peace. But in the consciousness that no step on the part of my Government could, even in the most remote degree, lead to a disturbance of the peace, I required at the same time that the Power which was the cause of the complication, and had brought about the danger of war, should, as a preliminary measure, disarm. Being pressed thereto by friendly Powers, I at length accepted the proposal for a general disarmament. The mediation failed in consequence of the inadmissible nature of the conditions on which Sardinia made her consent dependent. Only one means of maintaining peace remained. I addressed myself directly to the Sardinian Government, and summoned it to place its army on a peace footing, and to disband the free corps. Sardinia did not accede to my demand; therefore the moment for deciding the matter by an appeal to arms has arrived.

I have ordered my army to enter Sardinia.

I am aware of the vast importance of the measure, and if ever my duties as a monarch weighed heavily on me it is at this moment. War is the scourge of mankind. I see with emotion that the lives and property of thousands of my subjects are imperilled, and deeply feel what a severe trial war is for my realm, which, being occupied with its internal development, greatly requires the continuance of peace. But the heart of the monarch must be silent at the command of honour and duty.

On the frontiers the enemy stands in arms, in alliance with the revolutionary party, openly announcing his intention to seize upon the possessions of Austria in Italy. To support him the ruler over France, who, under futile pretexts, interferes in the legally established relations of the Italian Pennisula, has set his troops in movement. Detachments of them have already crossed the frontiers of Sardinia. The Crown which I received without spot or blemish from my forefathers has already seen trying times. The glorious history of our country gives evidence that Providence, when the shadows of a revolution, menacing to the highest good of humanity, appear about to spread over this quarter of the world, has frequently used the sword of Austria in order to dispel those shadows with its lightning. We are again on the eve of a period when the world is threatened with an overthrow of everything subsisting, and that not by parties only, but from thrones downwards. If I draw the sword, that sword receives a consecration as a defence for the honour and the good right of Austria, for the rights of all peoples and States, and for all that is held most dear by humanity.

To you, my people, whose devotion to the hereditary reigning family may serve as a model for all the nations of the earth, I now address myself. In the conflict which has commenced, you will stand by me with your oft-proved fidelity, devotion, and self-sacrifice. To your sons, whom I have taken into the ranks of the army, I, their commander, send my martial greeting. With pride you may regard them, for the Eagle of Austria will, with their support, soar high in honour.

Our struggle is a just one, and we begin it with courage and confidence. We hope that we shall not stand alone in it. The soil on which we have to do battle was made fruitful by the blood lost by our German brethren when they won those bulwarks which they have maintained up to the present day. There the crafty enemies of Germany have generally begun their game when they have wished to break her internal power. The feeling that such a danger is now imminent prevails in all parts of Germany, from the hut to the throne, from one frontier to the other. I speak as a Sovereign member of the Germanic Confederation when I call attention to the common danger, and recall to memory the glorious times in which Europe had to thank the general and fervent enthusiasm for its liberation.

For God and Fatherland!

Given at my residence and metropolis of Vienna on this 28th day of April, 1859.

FRANCIS JOSEPH.

Garibaldi's Address of Farewell to his Companions in Arms on leaving Naples for Caprera.

TO MY COMPANIONS IN ARMS!

Arrived at the last stage but one of our regeneration, it is necessary for us to take into consideration the period which is about to finish, and prepare ourselves to terminate splendidly the stupendous conception of the elect of twenty generations, the execution of which has been assigned by Providence to this fortunate generation.

Yes, young men! Italy owes to you an enterprise which merits the applause of the world.

You have conquered—and you will conquer; for you have now and for ever learnt those tactics which decide battles.

You have not degenerated from those who entered into the deep ranks of the Macedonian phalanx, and rent open the breasts of the proud conquerors of Asia.

To this stupendous page in the history of our country shall follow one still more glorious, and the slave will finally show to his free brother a link which belonged to the rings forming his chain.

To arms, all! all! and the oppressors—the all-powerful—shall be swept away like dust.

And you, O women! put away from you all cowards; they

will engender but cowards: and you, daughters of the land of beauty! have need of a brave and generous offspring.

Let the cowardly doctrinarians drag elsewhere their servility and their paltry sentiments.

This people is now its own master. It wishes to be a brother of other peoples, but to look upon the arrogant with an uplifted brow; not fawning and begging its liberty—not towed along by men whose hearts are dirt. No! no! no!

Providence has given Victor Emanuel to Italy. Every Italian should unite himself to him. All should gather close around him. By the side of the "*Ré Galantuomo*" every strife should disappear, every rancour be dissipated. Once again I repeat my cry to you—To arms, all! all! If the month of March, 1861, does not find a million of Italians under arms, oh, then, poor liberty! alas, for Italian existence! Oh, no! away with a thought which I loathe as poison. March, 1861, and February if necessary, will find us all at our post.

Italians of Calatafimi, of Palermo, of the Volturno, of Ancona, of Castelfidardo, and of Isernia, and with us every man of this land who is neither servile nor a coward—all, one and all —gathered closely around the hero of Palestro, we will give the last shock—the last blow, to the crumbling tyranny.

Receive, young volunteers, honourable survivors of ten battles, one farewell word. It parts laden with affection from the depths of my soul. I leave you to-day; but for a short time only. The hour of combat will again see me among you, by the side of the soldiers of Italian liberty.

Let those alone that are called by imperious family duties return to their homes, and those who, by their glorious wounds, have deserved the gratitude of their country. They will still serve her around their hearths, by their counsels and the sight of the noble scars which decorate their manly brows of twenty years. These excepted, let all remain to guard our glorious banner.

We shall soon meet again, to march together towards the redemption of our brethren, still slaves of the stranger. We shall soon meet again, to march together to new victories.

Naples, November 8, 1860.   (Signed)   G. GARIBALDI.

INDEX.

Aberdeen, Lord, Belief in break-up of Ottoman Empire, i. 43; opposed to Crimean War, 189; replaced by Lord Palmerston, 230

Adelaide, Mme., Rumoured secret marriage, i. 7; wisdom and influence, 7, 8

Aix-la-Chapelle, Treaty of, Adduced to exclude Sardinia from the proposed Congress on Italian question, ii. 18; Baron Schleinitz on its applicability to the case of Sardinia, 177

Alexander I., Emperor of Russia, Mystery about his death, i. 68

Allen, Richard, Visit to Berlin, i. 64

Ancillon, M., favours maintenance of Ottoman Empire, i. 43

Appendix—Despatches: Baron Brünnow to Earl of Clarendon, i. 416; Count Buol to Count Apponyi, ii. 306, 308; to Count Cavour, ii. 310; Count Cavour to Count Buol, ii. 311; Earl of Clarendon to Baron Brünnow, i. 420; to Sir G. H. Seymour, i. 401; to Earl of Westmorland, i. 407; Lord Augustus Loftus to Count Buol, ii. 317; to Earl of Malmesbury, i. 425; ii. 291, 294, 302, 304, 312, 316, 322, 323; Earl of Malmesbury to Lord Augustus Loftus, ii. 297; Count Nesselrode to Baron Meyendorff, i. 409. Documents: Russian analysis of Turkey's modifications of Vienna Note, i. 413; treaty of alliance between England, Austria, and France, i. 422; Emperor of Austria's manifesto to his people, ii. 324; Garibaldi's farewell address to his companions-in-arms, ii. 327

Apponyi, Count George, Accepts seat on Imperial Council, ii. 153; and appointment to Reichsrath, 155; his use of the term "the historical rights of Hungary," 153

Arbitration, Necessity of a system of, i. 366

Athens, Description of, i. 154—156

Austria: Attitude on Spanish and Portuguese succession questions, i. 34; a party to quadruple alliance against Mehemet Ali, 49; state of the country in 1848, 133; attitude on the Eastern Question, 174; Austria and France, curious anecdote, 215; ultimatum to Russia, 216; attitude on Neufchâtel Question, 278; distrust of Emperor Napoleon on Italian Question, 331; attempted reconciliation with Russia a failure, 348; opposition to Russia at Conference of Paris, 357; rupture with France imminent, 358; compromises effected, 361—365; Austria and England contrasted, 377; fatal attitude on Italian Question, 379; her position on eve of war with Sardinia, ii. 25; internal reforms and change of system in administration of affairs throughout the Empire, 92; relaxation of laws affecting non-Catholics, 93; review of the Jewish difficulty, 93—95; the Imperial Patent, 95; review of the Protestant difficulty, 95—105; reasons for Hungary's refusal of the Patent, 105—107; policy of non-intervention with regard to the Italian Question, 110, 123; foreign relations at opening of 1860, 110, 111; declines suggestion of Napoleon to oppose invasion of Papal States, 122; visit of the Empress to Madeira facilitated by Queen Victoria, 142, 143; reorganisation of the Empire and reforms with regard to guilds and trades, 144; reforms with regard to Jewish disabilities, 144—146; with regard to constitutional government, 146, 147; national debt and finances, 147—149; the Hungarian difficulty, 149—155; relations with other provinces, 155. *See* HUNGARIAN QUESTION

Austria and France, Prince Bismarck's fears of a Franco-Austrian alliance, ii. 274, 275

Austria and Prussia: Count Bernstorff appointed Minister of Foreign Affairs, ii. 199; activity of the National Verein, 205; Count Beust's plan for the creation of a central power, 205, 206; objections raised, 206, 207; Bismarck's alternative policy of the sword, 207; Count Beust's politics, 207; origin of the German Question, 207; attitude of the different States with regard to it, 208, 209; Bismarck's statesmanship, 209, 210; Prussian proposals for Dietal reform, 217; alarm felt by the Confederation, 217; Prussia's aim, 217; identic notes of protest, 217, 218; conversation between Lord A. Loftus and King William I. on prevailing disunion, 218—220. *See* HESSIAN QUESTION. Value set by Prussia on Italian alliance, 243; Lord A. Loftus and Count Bernstorff on the relations of Austria and Prussia, 259—262; Bismarck on proposed Federal reform, 271; and relations of Austria and Prussia, 277; French neutrality secured, 280

Austro-French War, The. *See* FRANCO-AUSTRIAN WAR.

Austrian Revolution: State of country in 1848, i. 133; saved by the army, 134; Ministerial concessions, 134; withdrawal of the Emperor, 134; martial law proclaimed, 134; fresh insurrection in Vienna, 134; the capital taken by storm, 135; abdication of the Emperor, 135; general constitution proclaimed, and withdrawn, 135

B.

Babelsberg, the creation of Emperor Frederick II., ii. 267

Bacourt, M. de, character, ii. 190, 191; prediction regarding Bonapartism, 191

Baden, Grand Duchy of, The garden of Germany, i. 92; spirit of Liberalism, 93; revolution of 1849, 95—103

Baden-Baden, Life and society in 1861, ii. 194

Balabine, M. de, on improved relations of Austria and Russia, ii. 13, 80; character, 14; on peace of Villa Franca, 72; on right of nations to choose their own rulers, 79

Bamberg Coalition: Origin, i. 256; political motives, 257; conciliatory attitude towards France, 258; its representatives' visit to Paris, 258

Barrot, M. Odillon, opposed to Spanish marriages, i. 111

Batthyani, Count, loyalty and patriotism, i. 134

Bavaria, Riots at Munich, i. 137; abdication of King Louis, 137

Becher, Oscar—Attempt on life of King William I. of Prussia, ii. 178—180

Belgium, Question of fortresses, i. 33; and German Confederation or Customs union with France, 33; disarms French troops after Sedan, 33

Berlin: In 1837, i. 25; Court, 25; society, 26; curious police regulation, 26; Jewish difficulty at Court, 27; extension of capital, 38; causes of abstention of aristocracy from visiting the capital, 38; insurrection of 1848, 113—115; improvements in 1861, ii. 164, 165

Bernstorff, Count, favours maintenance of Ottoman Empire, i. 43; Minister of Foreign Affairs, ii. 199; on recognition of Kingdom of Italy, 220, 221; on commercial relations of England and Prussia, 250—251; on relations of Austria and Prussia, 259—262; resignation of office, 262

Beust, Count, Visit to Paris, i. 258

Bismarck, Prince von, "Blut und Eisen," i. 65, ii. 278; remarkable statement to Mr. Disraeli, i. 204; directs foreign policy of Prussia, 205; antipathy to Austria, 205; character, 206; jealousy of England, 207; and the "smoking" difficulty, 207; favours a policy of neutrality, 209; a Russo-Prussian-French alliance his ideal, 209, ii.

280; opposed by the king, i. 209, ii. 280; differences with Baron Manteuffel, i. 211; the object of his policy, 231; his opinion of England, 316; interview with Lord A. Loftus on foreign affairs, ii. 274—279
Blum, Robert, Execution of, i. 135
"Blut und Eisen," Real meaning of the term, i. 65, ii. 278
Bolgrad, Turkish garrison at, ii. 244; bombardment of, 245; the fortress ceded to Servia, 246
Bowring, Sir J., Report on the Zollverein, i. 32
Breadalbane, Marquis of, Charged with investiture of King of Prussia with Order of the Garter, ii. 167; himself invested with Order of the Black Eagle, 168; his satisfaction, 169
Bresson, Comte C. de, Intrigues and suicide, i. 29; estimate of death of Frederick William III., 41; efforts to bring about a Franco-Russian alliance, 48; expected recall, 50
Brighton in William IV.'s reign, i. 4
Brougham, Lord, on King of Würtemberg's stables, i. 79
Bruck, Baron, Suicide of, ii. 116
Brunswick, Duchy of, occupied by Prussia, i. 126
Budberg, Baron, Explanation of Marquis Wielopolski's resignation, ii. 202; favours independence of Christian provinces of Turkey, 252, 253; his character, 253
Bülow, Baron, and quadruple treaty against Mehemet Ali, i. 50; recalled from London, 73; appointed to Germanic Diet and Minister of Foreign Affairs, 73
Bunsen, Chevalier, appointed Minister at London, i. 74
Buol Schauenstein, Count, Character, i. 319; resignation of office and causes of it, ii. 35—41; Malmesbury's message of condolence, 41; no change in policy of Austria involved, 42; his views of Austrian foreign policy, 42

C.

Canning, Sir Stratford: Special Mission to European Courts on affairs of Greece: Brussels, i. 117; Hanover, 117; interview with King Ernest, 118; Brunswick, 125; Berlin, 126; sensitiveness of Lord Westmorland, 127; audiences of the king, 128; Dresden, 129; Vienna, 129; sensitiveness of Lord Ponsonby, 130; views on Austria, 136; and on Hungary, 137; Munich, 137; receipt of Lamartine's famous address, 138; character, 138, 139; Trieste, 139; threatened by Italian fleet, 140; narrow escape of Austrian fleet, 141; contemplated intervention at Venice, 142; Corfu, 144; Vostitza, 146; Corinth, 147; the Piræus, 147; unpleasant incident in regard to General Church, 149; differences with Sir Edmund Lyons, 151; illness, 153; Constantinople, 159; interview with the Sultan, 161
Carbonari, Origin and oath of Society, i. 352; relations of Orsini and Napoleon III. with, 353
Carlsbad Conference, Anti-democratic measures, i. 23
Cavour, Count, the author and prime mover of Austro-French war, ii. 26 objects of his policy, 27, 28; resignation of office, 71; death, 180
Charles X. approves Prince de Polignac's policy, i. 43, 47; ingratitude towards England, 47; dethroned, 47
Charlottenburg Mausoleum, i. 59
Chinese War, The: Its causes, ii. 88; burning of the Summer Palace at Pekin, 88; Peace of Tientsin, 88
Cholera: In Berlin, i. 14; Constantinople, 160
Clarendon, Lord, as Minister of Foreign Affairs, ii. 15; eulogy of Lord Malmesbury, 15
Constantinople, Description of, i. 159, 160; palace of Tcheragan, 161; mosque of Santa Sophia, 162; Sweet Waters of Asia, 163; progress and development, 164
Corfu, description of, i. 144
Cracow, Incorporated by Austria, i. 110
Crimean War, The: Occupation of the Danubian Principalities by Russia, i. 173, 184; war declared by the Porte, 173, 185; Austria summons Russia to evacuate the Principalities, 191; suggested basis of peace, 191; the evacuation agreed to, 192; the Russian forces retire be

yond the Pruth, 192; the Principalities occupied by Austria, 192; despatches, Appendix, i. 401—422; destruction of a Turkish squadron at Sinope, i. 196; Austria's ultimatum to Russia, 216; declaration of war by England and France, 216; council of war at Varna, 217; expedition to the Crimea, 217; naval campaign in the Baltic, 219; bombardment of Bomarsund, 219; impracticability of attacking Cronstadt, 219; blockade of Russian ports in the Baltic, 220; sufferings of the Allies, 225, 230; death of Lord Raglan, 225; battle of Inkerman, 227; "The Memory of our Dead," 228; treaty between England, France, and Austria, 231, and Appendix, i. 422; conferences at Vienna, 231; bombardment of Sevastopol, 234; Balaclava, 237; the campaign in Asia, 238; bombardment of Sveaborg, 240; fall of Sevastopol, 242; the Czar's order of the day, 244; prospects of peace, 246; terms of peace, 247; ultimatum from Austria, 248; accepted by Russia, 249; results of the war, 268

Cumberland, Duke of. *See* HANOVER

D.

Danish Question, The: Formation of a great Scandinavian State suggested, i. 284; reversion of the Duchies to Prussia, 284. *See* SCHLESWIG-HOLSTEIN

Danubian Principalities Question, The: Prince Napoleon's views, i. 282; Difficulty as to their union, 292; Baron Manteuffel's attitude, 293; differences between England and France, 294; satisfactorily settled by visit of Emperor Napoleon to Osborne, 294; Paris Conference, 357; Austria's opposition, 357; compromises effected and settlement, 360—365; subsequent autonomy, 366; union of the Danubian provinces, ii. 86; opposed by Count Rechberg, 124; with Lord John Russell's approval, 126; their union accomplished, 86

Dauphin, The, opposes Prince de Polignac's European policy, i. 45

Dino, Duchesse de. *See* SAGAN.

Drouyn de L'Huys, M., Policy of, ii. 269; succeeds M. de Thouvenel as Minister of Foreign Affairs, 269; effect of his appointment on South German States and on Bismarck, 269, 270

Dufferin, Lord, Appointed British Commissioner for Syria, ii. 89

E.

Eastern Question, The: Difficulty of the Holy Places raised by France, i. 171; demands of the Czar, 171; secret mission of Count Leiningen, 172; Countess Kisseleff on the imminence of war, 172; Vienna Conference and Note, 173, 185: accepted by Russia and declined by Turkey, 173, 185; modifications proposed by Turkey, 187; inaction of German Powers frustrates hopes of peace, 174; interview between Emperors of Austria and Russia at Olmutz, 178; correspondence between Emperor of Russia and King of Prussia, 178—180; the King's visit to Warsaw, 181; firmness of Baron Manteuffel, 181, 182; visit of the Czar to Berlin, 182; Lord Clarendon on the situation, 188; Russia's new proposal, 189; Lord Aberdeen's aversion to war and Ministerial crisis in England, 189; despatches, Appendix, i. 401—422; the King of Prussia supports Russia, i. 197; but eventually yields to Baron Manteuffel, 199; special mission of Count Albert Pourtales to London, 200; Lord Aberdeen replaced by Lord Palmerston, 230; proposed conference at Paris, 328—331; Turkey and Montenegro, 331—341; proposed cession of Danubian provinces declined by Russia, 343. *See* CRIMEAN WAR. Union of the Danubian Provinces, ii. 86; opposed by Count Rechberg and Lord John Russell, 124, 126; proposed change in law of succession to Turkish throne, 124; opposed by Count Rechberg and Lord John Russell, 124, 125; views of Prussia as to duration of foreign occupation of Syria, 165, 166; encounter between Turkish and Servian troops,

244, 245; Bolgrad bombarded, 245; conference of the Powers at Constantinople, 245; decisive action of the Porte, 245, 246; cession of fortress of Bolgrad to Servia, 246; encounter between Turkish and Montenegrin forces, 246; intervention of Prince Gortchacoff, 246; Turkish counter-proposals, 247; review of the situation, 247—249; armistice agreed to, 249; conference of the Powers at Constantinople, 249; Baron Budberg favours independence of the Christian provinces of Turkey, 252, 253. *See* DANUBIAN PRINCIPALITIES QUESTION

Edinburgh, Duke of, Question of wearing the fez at his marriage, i. 52

Education, State of, in Prussia and England, i. 223

Elizabeth, Queen, of Prussia, Conversion to Protestantism, i. 65

England, Policy of abstention from foreign alliances, i. 272; and Continental war, 273

England and France. *See* FRANCE AND ENGLAND

Eynathen, General, Suicide of, ii. 116

F.

Ferdinand, Emperor, of Austria, Abdication, i. 135

Fez, The, at religious ceremonies, i. 52

Fonblanque, M. de, Attack on and death of, i. 345

Forts *v.* Ships, i. 236

France and Austria. *See* AUSTRIA AND FRANCE

France and England: Prince Napoleon on alliance between, i. 281; indignation against England caused by Orsini's attempt on the Emperor's life, 312; Gortchacoff's policy to break up the Anglo-French alliance, ii. 276

France and Prussia: Negotiations for Commercial Treaty, ii. 249, 250; unfavourably received by Southern States of Germany and Austria, 249; Prince Bismarck on Franco-Prussian alliance, 275, 276

France and Russia, Prince Bismarck on rumoured alliance between Russia and France, ii. 276

Franco-Austrian War: Probable attitude of Prussia and German States,

1. 290; Napoleon's address to Baron Hübner ominous of war, 372; general panic, 372; Count Buol's indifference, 373; position of Sardinia, 374; public opinion in England, 375; crossing of the Ticino, ii. 26; original causes and motives of war, 26—28; declaration of war by Austria, 33, and Appendix, ii. 324; invasion of Modena by Sardinia, 33; the Austrian army in Italy, 34; departure of the French Embassy from Vienna, 35; actions at Palestro and Montebello, 43; battle of Magenta, 43; the Austrian generalissimo superseded, 44; retreat of Austrian army and occupation of Milan by the Allies, 44; crossing of the Mincio and battle of Solferino, 49, 55; evacuation of Villa Franca, 55; armistice, 56; meeting of the Emperors Napoleon III. and Franz Josef, 56, 66; preliminaries of peace, 63—66: terms agreed to, 67; further negotiations, 68—71; disappointment of King Victor Emanuel and Cavour, 71; resignation of Cavour, 71; Zürich chosen for meeting of Plenipotentiaries, 71; the indemnity difficulty, 75, 76; the treaties signed, 85

Franz Josef, Emperor, Accession to the throne, i. 135

Frederick III., Emperor, Burial-place, i. 59

Frederick the Great, First stone of his monument laid by Frederick William III., i. 41

Frederick William III.: His habits, i. 15; character, 16; humorous anecdote, 16; devotion to the interests of the State, 16; devotion of his people, 16; aversion to political change and reform, 16; belief in the Divine right of kings, 16; reliance on the military power of Prussia, 17; promises of free institutions unfulfilled, 17; the indissoluble union of the three Northern Powers the basis of his foreign and internal policy, 17, 20; change of policy since, 22; his last will, 18; his death prophesied by Mme. Le Norman, 36; secluded life, 40; morganatic marriage with Countess Harrach, 40; on marriage of Prince Albert, 41; last act of his reign, 41; his funeral, 58

F.

Frederick William IV.: Warnings and advice from his father, i. 19; his accession welcomed by the Liberal party, 42; and by Comte de Bresson in view of closer alliance between Russia and France, 42, 49, 50; his burial-place, 59; his character and peaceful disposition, 63—65; his interest in prison reform, 64; his consort, 65; visit to England, 76, 77; declines the Imperial Crown, 93; reconstitutes the Diet at Frankfort, 93; the revolution of 1849: riots at Dresden, 95; the Baden army goes over to the insurgents, 95; flight of the Grand Duke, 95; encounters at Waaghäusel and Wiesenthal, 96; battle of Gernsbach, 99; siege and surrender of Rastatt, 101; vacillating policy, 112; the revolution breaks out at Berlin, 113; withdrawal of the troops, 113; the King in the hands of the revolutionary party, 114; flight of the Prince of Prussia, 114; the King removes to Potsdam, 115; weakness and vacillation on the Eastern Question, 174; illness and establishment of Regency, 285; differences between the King and the Regent, 285

Fry, Mrs. Elizabeth, Visit to Berlin, i. 64

G.

Garibaldi, His character and influence on the Italian Question, i. 355—357; farewell address to his companions-in-arms, Appendix, ii. 327

Gortchacoff, Prince: Avowed hatred of Austria, ii. 49, 82

Granville, Lord, His character, i. 6

Guelph Fund, The. *See* HANOVER

Guizot, M., succeeds M. Thiers, i. 50; promotes the Spanish marriages, 111

Gurney, Miss, Visit to Berlin, i. 64

H.

Hanover, Court, i. 118; anecdotes relating to it, 119; injudicious policy of King George, 121; the indemnity sequestrated, 122; injudicious policy of present Duke of Cumberland, 123; a possible arrangement, 123; submission of the Duke, 124

Harrach, Countess. *See* LIEGNITZ

Hauser, Caspar, Strange story of, i. 84, 85, 104—109

Hessian Question, The: King William I. on, 219; its nature, 222; understanding between Austria and Prussia, 222; General V. Willisen's special mission to Cassel, 223; insulting reception accorded it, 223—225; Prussian ultimatum, 225; dangers of the situation, 226; diplomatic relations broken off, 227; the question referred to the Diet, 227, 228; concentration of Prussian troops, 228; the Elector yields to the demands of the Diet and dismisses his Ministry, 228

Holy Alliance, The, i. 17; Great Britain no party to it, 57; its closing scene, 58; proposed resuscitation, 181

Holy Places, The: Question of, raised by France, i. 171

Hortense, Queen, intercedes with Prince Metternich for life of her son, i. 56

Huldigung: Meaning of the term, ii. 185; that of Frederick William IV., 185; difficulty in connection with that of King William I., 185—187

Humboldt, Baron Alexander von, Admiration for Mrs. Fry, i. 64

Hungarian Question, The: Insurrection against Austria, i. 134; difficulties experienced in the Government of, 368, 369; popular feeling in, 369; parties in, 370; happy solution of the difficulties, 370; basis of agreement laid down by Hungary, ii. 149; failure of Protestant deputation to Emperor with regard to the Patent, 150, 151; the Imperial Patent in abeyance and amnesty proclaimed, 152; failure of a Liberal policy to conciliate Hungary, 152, 155; Count George Apponyi's policy, 153, 155; death of Baron Josika, 153; suicide of Count Stéphan Széchneyi, 154

I.

Isabella, Queen, of Spain, 34: not recognised by Austria and Prussia, 53

INDEX.

Italian Confederation, the wish of Napoleon, a danger to the peace of Europe, ii. 46, 56
Italian Question, The: at the Congress of Paris, i. 305; Mazzini and the political refugees in England, 305; correspondence on same between Lords A. Loftus and Clarendon, 305—308; Orsini's attempt against life of Napoleon decides him to join Sardinia against Austria, 350, 353; secret meeting of Cavour and Napoleon at Plombières, 350; Napoleon's intentions, 351, 355; the Carbonari, 352; proposed restoration of Austrian Archdukes, 354; the Moderate programme in Italy, 354; the Mazzinist programme, 355; Garibaldi's policy, 355, 356; Count Buol's denial of the question, 376; Mazzini the real arbiter of war, 374, 377; Lord Malmesbury's despatch, 389; Napoleon's aims and duplicity, 395; Lord Cowley's mission to Vienna, 395; Count Buol's view of French policy, 396; failure of Lord Cowley's mission, 398; Count Buol's delusive hopes, 399; Russian proposal for a Congress, ii. 1—3, 12; Napoleon's policy, 3—8; proposed Congress accepted by England, France, Prussia and Austria, 8; Lord Malmesbury's conditions the basis of negotiation, 9, 10; Count Cavour's attitude, 10; meeting of the Emperors of Austria and Russia at Warsaw, 12; difficulties raised by Austria, 14; exclusion of Sardinia agreed to, 16; the disarmament of Sardinia a *sine qua non*, 16, 17, 19, 20, 22; Count Buol on participation of Italian States in Congress, 18; explanation of Austria's attitude, 20—22; Austria's confidential mission to Prussia, 23; Austria's summons to Sardinia to disarm, 24; Austria's position, 25; evasive answer of Count Cavour, 26. *See* FRANCO AUSTRIAN WAR. Count Buol's resignation, 35—41; Prussian Mission to Vienna, 42; unsatisfactory state of Austro-Hungarian Empire, 44—46, 51, 57; change of ministry in England, 46; Count Karolyi's special mission to St. Petersburg, 48, 49; Austria's reasons for desiring peace, 50, 60; Napoleon desirous of peace, 56—59; King of Würtemberg on the peace, 73; Napoleon's cordial reception of Prince Metternich, 82; the Central Italy question solved, 83; flight and deposition of the King of Naples, 84; Napoleon's disapproval, 84; French and Russian Ministers at Turin recalled, 84; remonstrances of Prussia, 84; *See* "LE PAPE ET LE CONGRÈS"; Delay in meeting of European Congress, 116; attitude of Austria with regard to Papal States, 117; refusal of the Pope to be represented and collapse of Congress, 117; annexation of Savoy and Nice by France, 117—119; alleged agreement between M. Benedetti and Count Cavour with regard to Venetia, 119—121; Austria encouraged to oppose invasion of Papal States, 122; Napoleon anxious to prevent their alienation, 123; Count Rechberg's criticism of Lord John Russell's policy, 125; Lord Russell's memorandum in reply, 126—129; Garibaldi's landing at Palermo and entry into Naples, 133; Siege and surrender of Gaëta, 133; march on Rome prevented by King Victor Emanuel, 133; Garibaldi's inflammatory appeal to his followers on his retirement to Caprera, Appendix ii. 327; Sir Henry Elliott's report on same, 134; Umbria and the Marches occupied with consent of Napoleon, 135; the unification of Italy accomplished, 135; Lord A. Loftus's difficulties with the Irish Papal Brigade, 138—142; Prussia declines to recognise the Kingdom of Italy, 177; difficulties in the way of Prussia recognising the Kingdom of Italy, 215, 216; change of feeling in Prince Gortchacoff towards Italy, 216; Count Bernstorff's conditional promise to recognise the Kingdom, 220; circumstances that led to its recognition by Prussia and Russia, 235-238; Baron Ricasoli's views regarding the Papal States, 242; the Liberal Party in Prussia approve recognition, 242; value set by Prussia on Italian alliance, 243; her desire for the consolidation of Italy, 243, 244; Lord A. Loftus and Prince Bismarck on the Italian question, 274

K.

Karolyi, Count: Special Mission to St. Petersburg, ii. 48; adverse report on state of feeling in Russia towards Austria, 48
Kiamil Pacha appointed Turkish envoy at Berlin, i. 51; his character, 51
Kossuth, President of Provisional Government in Hungary, i. 133
Kotzebue assassinated by Georges Sand, i. 22

L.

Latour, Count, Murder of, i. 134
La Tour-d'Auvergne, Prince, approves of proposed partition of Schleswig, ii. 221; transferred from Berlin to Rome, 268; his character, 268; on M. de Thouvenel's policy on Roman question, 269; other appointments, 269
Laybach, Congress of, i. 58
Lebanon, The: Excesses of the Maronites and Druses, ii. 88; co-operation of Powers to quell disorders, 88, 89; complete pacification effected, 89; views of Prussia as to duration of foreign occupation of Syria, 165, 166
"L'Empereur et la Prusse": Pamphlet advocating rectification of French frontiers, ii. 129; attributed to Napoleon, 129; anxiety aroused in Germany, 129; meeting of Prince Regent of Prussia and Napoleon at Baden-Baden, 129; French pacific assurances, 130
Le Norman, Mme., prophesies death of Frederick William III., i. 36
"Le Pape et le Congrès": Pamphlet attributed to Napoleon, ii. 85; its disavowal required by Count Walewski, 85; resignation of Count Walewski, 85; cause of proposed Paris Congress lapsing, 85; Count Rechberg and, 108
Liegnitz, Princess, Morganatic marriage with Frederick William III., i. 40; her tact and devotion to him, 40
Lieven, Princess, her position in the fashionable and diplomatic world, i. 9
Loftus, Lord Augustus: Early life, i. 1; literary tastes, 1; introduction into society, 2; presented to the King, 3; death of his sister, 4; visit to Paris, 5; at dinner by Louis Philippe to the late Marquis and Marchioness of Londonderry, 8; at Prince Talleyrand's last ball, 8; intimacy with M. de Bacourt, 10; at Court ball at the Tuileries, 10; invitation to Versailles, 11; return to England, 12; death of William IV., 12; first appointment as attaché to Legation at Berlin, 3, 12; departure for Berlin, 14; funeral of Duke Charles of Mecklenburg-Strelitz, 15; coldness between General Muffling and British Legation, 15; General Muffling's courtesy, 15; at last reception by Frederick William III. to the diplomatic body, 41; sent with despatches to St. Petersburg, 66; fiançailles of the Czarewitch, 72; appointed paid attaché at Stuttgart, 78; visit to Baden-Baden, 82; marriage, 83; lines on a nun's grave, 86; visit to Mannheim, 88; Her Majesty's representative at the marriage of Prince Leiningen, 91; Carlsruhe Theatre destroyed by fire, 91; the Revolution of 1849, 95; encounters with soldiers of the Free Corps, 96, 97; Baden-Baden escapes the carnage, 99; adventure at Rastatt, 102; appointment to special mission of Sir Stratford Canning, 116; visit to Brussels and Hanover, 117; at Brunswick, 125; at Berlin, 126; "itinerant" ambassadors undesirable, 127; at Dresden and Vienna, 129; revolutionary scenes, 130; at Munich, 137; at Trieste, 139; dissuades Sir Stratford Canning from intervening at Venice, 142; at Corfu, 144; at Vostitza, 146; at Corinth, 147; at the Piræus, 147; differences between Sir Stratford Canning and Sir Edmund Lyons, 151; failure to effect a reconciliation, 152; hopes with regard to Turkey and its capital, 157; at Constantinople, 159; interview with the Sultan, 161; the Eastern and Slavonic questions, 166; returns to London with despatches, 167; interview with Lord Palmerston, 167; resumes duties at Carlsruhe, 169; entertains the Prince of Prussia, 169; birth of a son, 170; appointed

Secretary of Legation at Stuttgart, 170; transferred to Berlin, 171; presented as chargé d'affaires at Berlin, 175; first interview with Baron Manteuffel, 176; Note from Lord Clarendon, 188; proposal to relieve Russia of article of Treaty of Paris regarding the Black Sea, 213; commendatory letter from Lord Clarendon, 215; reports on the attitude of Prussia, 232, 233; charged by Count Vitzthum with purchasing secret information, 251; on the Bamberg Coalition, 256; memorandum on state of Germany in 1855, 259; on results of Crimean War, 268; mission to Coblentz, 275; interview with Prince of Prussia on the Neufchâtel question, 275; report on conditions of settlement of same, 279; report of private audience with Prince Napoleon, 280; further interview, 283; report of same, 284; conversation with Baron Manteuffel on Danubian Principalities, 293; report on visit of Emperor Alexander to Berlin, 295; report on contemplated visit of the Emperors of Russia and France, 296; on Russian aims for a French alliance, 297; correspondence with Lord Clarendon on Mazzini and the political refugees in England, 305—308; reports on British Consulates in the Baltic, and on commercial status of Baltic ports, highly approved of, 313; appointed Envoy Extraordinary to Vienna, 315, 317; interview with Baron Stockmar at Potsdam, 315; and with Count Buol, on relations of Austria and France, 320; on relations of Austria and Prussia, 321; audience of the Emperor Franz Josef, 324; successful efforts to remove the difficulties between Austria and France on Danubian Provinces question, 357—365; conversation with Count Buol on Italian affairs, 373; report of interview with Count Buol communicating Lord Malmesbury's despatch on Italy, 385; despatch on menacing aspect of affairs, 392; private letter to Count Buol, 397; interview with Count Buol on Italian States participating in the Congress, ii. 18; conversation with Emperor Franz Josef on proposed disarmament of Sardinia, 18—20; Count Rechberg embittered by England's abandonment of Austria, 60—63; illness of his daughter, 72; conversation with King of Würtemberg on peace of Villa Franca, 73; return to Vienna, 75; cordial interview with Count Rechberg on restoration of Archdukes, 76—78; Austrian mission to Russia and reconciliation of the two Powers, 79—81; visit of Queen Victoria, Prince Consort, and Lord John Russell to Coburg, 89; accident to the Prince, 89; interviews with the Prince, 90; visit to the Imperial Court at Schönbrünn, 107; criticism of Lord John Russell's policy in assenting to Congress re the Treaty of Zürich, 118; interview with Count Rechberg on Eastern and Italian questions, 124; Lord Russell's memorandum in reply to Count Rechberg, 125; instructions to negotiate a commercial treaty with Austria, 136, 137; Lord Russell's letter on proposed diplomatic changes, 137; strained relations between England and Prussia, 138; difficulties with the Irish Papal Brigade, 138—142; summoned to London to confer with Lord John Russell, 155; audience of Prince Consort on reforms in Austria and Hungary, 155—157; return to Vienna, and presentation of letters of recall, 157; offered the Grand Cross of the Imperial Order of Leopold, 158, 159; dinner of adieu at Baron Anselm Rothschild's, 159; appointment as Minister at Berlin, 160; interview with Prince of Hohenzollern, 166, 167; official visits to Strelitz, 169, 171, 172; to Schwerin, 172; and to Dessau, 173; favoured position of minor sovereigns of Germany, 174, 175; conversation with the king on Schleswig-Holstein question, 181, 182; grand military fête at Potsdam, 182—184; illness and death of his favourite daughter, 195, 196; despatch to Lord John Russell on resignation of Marquis Wielopolski, 202; despatch on state of Germany at close of 1861, 208, 209; death of the Prince Consort, 210—212; conversation with King of Prussia re disunion among German States,

218—220; interview with Count Bernstorff re the recognition of Italy, 220, 221; interview with Baron Ricasoli, 242; Count Bernstorff on the commercial relations of England and Prussia, 250, 251; Baron Budberg on the Eastern question, 252, 253; visit of the Queen and Lord John Russell to Coburg, 254; negotiations about interchange of embassies at London and Berlin, 255, 256; appointed Minister at Munich, 256, 257; conversation with Lord John Russell on relations of Germany and Denmark, 257; Lord Russell's proposals, 257—259; memorandum of conversation with Count Bernstorff on European politics, 259—262; interview with Bismarck on European affairs, 274—279; recalled from Berlin, 281

Londonderry, Marquis and Marchioness, Dinner in their honour by Louis Philippe, i. 8; curious breach of etiquette, 8

Louis, King, of Bavaria, Unpopularity and abdication, i. 139

Louis Philippe, Pacific dispositions, i. 50; and the Spanish marriages, 111

Louise, Queen, of Prussia, i. 15; Mausoleum at Charlottenburg, 18

Luck, General von, and education of Frederick William IV. of Prussia, i. 34

Luck, Mme. de, Head of Carlist coterie in Berlin, i. 34

M.

MacMahon, Marshal, saves Napoleon III. at Magenta, ii. 44

Malmesbury, Lord, efforts to maintain peace, ii. 14; eulogy of Lord Clarendon, 15

Manin elected president of Republic of Venice, i. 134

Manteuffel, General, Character, i. 175; views on the Eastern Question, 176; Duel with M. Twesten, ii. 177

Marliani, M. de, expelled from Austria, i. 53

Maximilian, King, of Bavaria, Accession of, i. 137

Mecklenburg-Schwerin, under Constitutional Government, ii. 173; its aristocracy, 173; the country, 173

Mecklenburg-Strelitz, Duke Charles of, His death, i. 14; and funeral, 15; description of country, ii. 169; general contentment, 170

Mehemet Ali, in rebellion, i. 49; encouraged by France, 49; quadruple treaty to arrest his advance, 49; exclusion of France from treaty, 49; war imminent, 49; resignation of M. Thiers, 50

Metternich, Prince, and the Carlsbad Conference, i. 23; influence on commercial relations of Germany, 32; proposal for partition of Ottoman Empire, 43; counteracts M. Zea Bermudez' Mission, 53; on creation of a Germanic Confederation, 54; saves life of Prince Louis Napoleon, 56; his admiration of Queen Hortense, 56; character and statesmanship, 56; on Napoleon's Italian policy, ii. 11; on proposed Congress, 11

Microlaffski, General, in command of Baden rebel army, i. 104; escape to Switzerland, 104

Mildmay, Captain Edmund, British Commissioner to Austrian army in Franco-Austrian War, ii. 33

Moltke, General von, ii. 285

Monasterio, Marquis de, Carlist agent at Berlin, i. 34

Montenegro: Its origin, i. 331; conflict with Turkey, 332; position of Russia in regard to, 332; negotiations with regard to, 332—341; settlement arrived at, 341; encounter between Turkish and Montenegrin forces, ii. 246; intervention of Prince Gortchacoff, 246; Turkish counter-proposals, 247; review of the situation, 247—249; armistice agreed to, 249; conference of the Powers at Constantinople, 249

Montez, Lola, Her ascendency over King Louis of Bavaria, i. 137 agitation against her, 137 her escape, 137

Moustier, Marquis de, Account of Napoleon's policy of rectification of French frontiers, ii. 113—115; corroborated in 1866 by M. Benedetti's proposals to Prussia, 116

Muffling, General, resents evidence of Duke of Wellington before Committee on Military Affairs, i. 15; his courtesy, 15

N.

Napoleon III., His life saved by Prince Metternich, i. 56; Eastern Policy antagonistic to England, ii. 3; his European Policy, 7, 8; prevents Cavour's resignation, 22; in danger of capture at Magenta, 44; opposed to a strong united Italy, 53; his reasons for desiring peace, 56; his wish for an Italian confederation under Presidency of Pope, 56; views as to rectification of French frontiers, 113—115; his failure to induce Austria to oppose invasion of Papal States, 122; lax observance of Constitutional oath, 122, 123; anxiety to prevent alienation of Papal States, 123. *See* "L'EMPEREUR ET LA PRUSSE," "LE PAPE ET LE CONGRÈS."

National Verein, Its great aim, i. 261
Neufchâtel Question, The, i. 274; Bismarck's visit to Paris, 274, 278; interview between Lord A. Loftus and the Prince of Prussia, 275; settlement arrived at, 279; Prince Napoleon's visit to Berlin, 279; private interview between Lord A. Loftus and Prince Napoleon, 280
Neu Strelitz and the Ducal Château, ii. 170
Nice. *See* SAVOY AND NICE
Nicholas, Emperor, of Russia: At death of Frederick William III., i. 42; his views on that event, 42: opinion of Turkey, 43; defeats Comte de Bresson's projected alliance between France and Russia, 48; character, 67; motives of his policy on the Eastern Question, 193—196; death, 221
"Non-Intervention," The policy of, adopted by Prince Metternich, i. 58

O.

Olmutz, Convention of, i. 174
Orsini: Attempt on life of Napoleon III., i. 309; French indignation against England in consequence, 310; results, 311; Lord Palmerston's Conspiracy Bill defeated, 311

P.

Palmerston, Lord, i. 3, 12, 56; and convention against Mohemet Ali, 49
Papal States, The, Proposed reforms in, i. 379; Napoleon III. urges Austria to oppose their invasion, ii. 122; his anxiety to prevent their alienation, 123. *See* "LE PAPE ET LE CONGRÈS"
Paris, At conclusion of the Crimean War, i. 266
Paris, Congress of: Meeting of plenipotentiaries, i. 263; admission of Prussia, 263; reception of the Russian plenipotentiaries by Napoleon III., 263; peace concluded, 264; secret treaty between England, France, and Austria, 264, and Appendix, i. 422; satisfaction of Napoleon III., 264
Paris, Treaty of: Article regarding the Black Sea repudiated by Russia, ii. 214; conference in conformity with, 357
Pfordten, Herr von der, Visit to Paris, i. 258
Polignac, Prince de: Views about reconstruction of Europe, i. 43—46; adverse policy to England in regard to fall of Ottoman Empire, 44; on relative value of Belgium to France as compared with the Rhine provinces, 45; opposed by the Dauphin, 45; his plans defeated by the Revolution, 47
Polish Question, The: Riots at Warsaw, ii. 175, 199; Russia's weak policy, 175; fears of revolution entertained at Berlin, 175, 199; Baron Schleinitz's views, 176; Polish attempt to bring the question under the notice of Europe, 176; statistics of population of Grand Duchy of Posen, 199, 200; cession of territory by Russia to Prussia 200; strategical importance of the Grand Duchy to Prussia, 200; Polish grievances, 200; conciliatory policy of Russia abortive, 201; appointment of Grand Duke Constantine and Marquis Wielopolski, 201; attempt on life of Grand Duke, 201; resignation of Grand Duke and Marquis, 201; Baron Budberg's explanation of Marquis Wielopolski's resignation, 202; feeble interposition of

England and France unavailing, 203; Russia, Prussia, and Austria bound to each other by their Polish interests, 203; Polish view of the question, 203, 204; the Polish question replaced by the Slavonic question, 204, 205; appointment of the Grand Duke Constantine disapproved of by King of Prussia, 233; Sir William White's views regarding it, 234
Ponsonby, Lord, Character of, i. 129.
Potsdam, the New Palace, Sans-Souci and the Marmor Palace, ii. 266; the Town Palace, 267
Prague, Riots at, i. 134
Prince Consort, The: Visit to Coburg, and accident, ii. 89; his greatness and nobility of mind, 90, 91
Prussia: Attitude on Spanish and Portuguese Succession questions, i. 34; satisfactory administration of finances, 39; war fund, increased by will of Frederick William III., 39; a party to quadruple alliance against Mehemet Ali, 49; favours maintenance of Ottoman Empire, 50; political position on death of Frederick William III., 61; attitude on Eastern Question, 174, 268; jealousy and ill-will towards Austria, 174; admitted to Congress of Paris, 266; alliance with Italy foretold by Cavour, 290; pacific policy on Italian question, ii. 29, 30; distrust of France, 30—32; mission to Vienna, 42; struggle between the King and the Parliament, 160; its origin, 161; abolition of "Stade Dues" on the Elbe, 167; anxiety as to state of Poland, 175; visit of the King to Napoleon at Compiègne, 178; attempt on King's life at Baden-Baden, 178—180; and the Schleswig-Holstein question, 181, 182; the Coronation difficulty, 185—188; Napoleon's invitation to King to Manœuvres at Châlons, 188; reasons for accepting, 188, 189; cause of refusal, 189; coronation ceremony and speech by the King, 196; principle of ministerial responsibility unknown in Prussia, 197; coronation expenses paid by the King, 197; meeting of the new Parliament: state of parties, 213; the landed aristocracy unrepresented, 214; constitutional struggle between the King and the Parliament, 214, 215; a new order of knighthood, 216; dissolution of Parliament and change of ministry, 228; Bismarck appointed Minister at Paris, 228; Prince Hohenlohe Ingelfingen on the state of affairs, 229; special Russian mission to Paris coincident with Bismarck's appointment, 229, 232; Bismarck's relations with the King, 230, 231; his ambitious programme, 231—233; visit of a Japanese embassy to Berlin, 234; and of President of Liberia, 235; relations with France and Russia, 238, 244; the King's position with regard to the Constitutional struggle, 238; her attitude with regard to Royal Families of Naples and Hanover contrasted, 239, 240; commercial treaty with France, 249, 250; difficulties in consequence with Southern States and Austria, 249—252, 261; England's commercial relations with, 250, 251; the Liberal Party in Prussia unyielding, 253, 254; Bismarck's advent to power, 254, 262; Lord A. Loftus and Count Bernstorff on the Constitutional struggle, 262; the Ministerial crisis explained, 263—265; reduction of the naval budget, 265; Count Arnim's interposition places the two Houses of Parliament in direct opposition, 271, 272; close of the Session, 272; resolute attitude of the Liberal Party, 272, 273; attitude of the Press, 273
Prussia, Prince of, How his palace was saved in the Revolution of 1848, i. 24. *See* REGENCY

R.

Rauch, Professor, i. 18, 41, 59
Rechberg, Count, appointed Foreign Minister on recommendation of Prince Metternich, i. 55; his appointment calculated to conciliate Russia, ii. 13; recommended by Prince Metternich, 41; on the right of nations to choose their sovereigns, 77, 78; and "Le Pape et le Congrès," 108
Regency, The, in Prussia: Its establishment, i. 287; dismissal of the Manteuffel Ministry, 287; the

"New Era," 287; how viewed in England and France, 288; in Austria and Russia, 291; Count Cavour on same, 289; re-organisation of the army, 287
Reptile Fund, The, Origin of the term, i. 123
Rheinbund, The, contrasted with the state of Germany in 1855, i. 259
Ricasoli, Baron, Visit to Berlin, ii. 241; and Cavour contrasted, 241, 242; his views regarding the Papal States, 242
Roon, General von, ii. 287
Russell, Lady William, Her success in society, i. 28
Russell, Lord George William, declines the Presidency of Bombay, i. 28
Russell, Lord John, in favour of Italian independence, ii. 46, 51, 53; despatch on right of nations to choose their rulers, 51, 52; his policy supported by national feeling of Italian people, 52
Russell, Lord William, Prophecy by, i. 23; distinguished career, 27, 28; unfortunate mistake over the Presidency of Bombay, 28; and Kiamil Pacha, 51; recalled from Berlin, 75
Russia: Attitude on Spanish and Portuguese Succession questions, i. 34; influence on Prussia during reign of Frederick William III., 42; a party to the quadruple alliance against Mehemet Ali, 49; seeking a rapprochement with France, 265; projects in the Danubian Provinces, ii. 5
Russo-Prussian-French alliance, ii. 279; basis for, 280; Prince Bismarck's dream, opposed by King of Prussia, 280
Rustem Pacha at marriage of the Duke of Edinburgh, i. 52

S.

Sagan, Duchesse de, Her position in the fashionable and diplomatic world, i. 9; literary executrix of Prince Talleyrand, 10
Sand, Georges, assassinates Kotzebue, i. 22
Savoy and Nice, Annexation by France, ii. 117; the convention ceding them not part of the public law of Europe, 118; Napoleon III.'s reasons for hastening annexation, 118
Schleswig-Holstein Question, The: Its origin and character, i. 298; war about, 301, 302; its results, 302; Bismarck's policy with regard to a dual Administration, 303; King William I. on, ii. 181, 182; its ending, 182: Prussia's interest in, 205; proposed partition of Schleswig by Count Bernstorff, approved by French ambassador, 221; M. de Thouvenel's and Baron Brünnow's views, 239; Lord John Russell's proposals for settlement of, 257—259; accepted by Count Bernstorff, 258; rejected by Denmark, 259; consequences, 259; Bismarck on the question, 278, 279
Schwerin, and the Ducal Château, ii. 173
Servia, Change of dynasty, ii. 87; union with Montenegro desired by Russia, 87; assassination of Prince Michel Obrenovitch, 88; erected into a kingdom, 88; Turkish garrison at Bolgrad, 244; bombardment of the capital, 245; the fortress ceded to Servia, 246
Ships v. Forts, i. 236
Sigismund, Prince, of Germany, His death and burial, i. 59
Spanish Marriages, The, the result of the dynastic policy of Louis Philippe, i. 111
"Steinreich," Origin of the proverb, i. 32
Stockmar, Baron, His belief in the break-up of the Ottoman Empire, i. 43; his account of Prince de Polignac's European policy, 46; his character, ii. 136
Stuttgart, Description of, i. 78; Lord Brougham on King's stables at, 79; court, society, and diplomatic body, 79, 80
Syria. See LEBANON
Széchneyi, Count Stéphan, Character, last days and suicide of, ii. 154

T.

Talleyrand, Baron, Transferred from Turin to Berlin, ii. 268

INDEX.

Talleyrand, Prince, His last ball, i. 8; his appearance, 9; death, 9; his papers, 10
Teesdale, Colonel Sir Christopher, His bravery, i. 239
Theft of Secret Correspondence from Berlin, i. 249
Thiers, M., His failure to gain allies, i. 50; resignation of office, 50; opposes the Spanish marriages, ii. 111
Thouvenel, M. de, Minister of Foreign Affairs, ii. 85, 110; character, 110
Tibell, Attempt on life of, i. 23
Tientsin, Peace of, ii. 88
Todleben, General, i. 218
Toeplitz, Meeting at, of Emperor of Austria and Regent of Prussia, ii. 130
Torpedo Boat, Early idea of, i. 25
Troppau, Congress of, i. 58
Turkey, Rivalry between the Latin and Greek Churches in, i. 171
Twesten, M., Duel with General Manteuffel, ii. 177

U.

Universities: Expediency of removing them from the pale of large capitals, i. 24
Upton, General Arthur, i. 8

V.

Venice, Proclamation of independence of the Republic of, i. 134
Verona, Congress of, i. 27; the closing scene of the Holy Alliance, 58
Victoria, Queen: Visit to Stolzenfels, i. 77
Vienna, Insurrection in, i. 134; taken by storm by Prince Windischgrätz, 135; court and aristocracy, 326; ii. 112; society, i. 327; its people, 328; mode of lighting state apartments, ii. 112
Villa Franca, Peace of: Preliminaries, ii. 63—66; terms agreed to, 67; further negotiations, 66—71; disappointment of King Victor Emanuel and Cavour, 71; meeting of plenipotentiaries at Zürich, 71; the indemnity difficulty, 75, 76; the treaties signed, 85; the King of Würtemberg on, 73

W.

Waldemar, Prince, of Germany, His burial-place, i. 59
Walewski, Count, Resignation of office in connection with "Le Pape et le Congrès," ii. 85
War Fund, Advantages of a, i. 39
Warsaw, Meeting at, of Emperors of Austria and Russia and Regent of Prussia, ii. 131; assurances with regard to same given by Count Rechberg, 131
Wellington, Duke of: His evidence before Committee on Military Affairs resented by General Muffling, i. 15; his belief in the break-up of the Ottoman Empire, 43
Werther, Baron, i 31
Westmorland, Earl of, appointed Envoy at Berlin, i. 75; his character, 75
White, Sir William, his views regarding the appointment of the Grand Duke Constantine as Viceroy of Russian Poland, ii. 234
"White Lady," The, Legend of, i. 37;
Wielopolski, Marquis, appointment to the Government of Russian Poland, ii. 201; resignation, 201; Baron Budberg's explanation, 202
William I., Emperor of Germany: Advice to his grandson on union of Prussia and Russia, i. 21; as Crown Prince a suspected Carlist, 34; invested with the Order of the Garter, ii. 167, 168; attempt on life of, at Baden-Baden, 178—180; coronation difficulty, 185—187; his simple life and character, 191; his consort, 192—194; character, ii. 283, 284
William II., Emperor of Germany, promotes union between Prussia and Russia, i. 21
William IV., King: Love of society, i. 2; his family by Mrs. Jordan, 3; called "The Sailor King," 3; his death, 12; his character, 13; action on the Reform Bill, 13; the Hanover revenues, 14
William, Prince, of Prussia, named "der Alte Wilhelm," i. 26

Windischgrätz, Prince, takes Vienna by storm, i. 135; his character, 136
Wittgenstein, Prince, i. 15, 31
Worth, M., escapes from Paris in a balloon, ii. 286
Wrangel, Field-Marshal, i. 60
Würtemberg an opponent of Prussian hegemony, i. 81; progress of the country, 81
Wyllie, Sir C. : His position at the Russian Court, i. 70; account of death of Emperor Alexander, 68

Z.

Zea Bermudez, M. : His failure to obtain recognition of Queen Isabella, i. 53
Zollverein, i. 32; the basis of German unity and Prussian supremacy, 53
Zürich, Treaty of, not part of the public law of Europe, ii. 118; criticism of Lord John Russell's policy in assenting to Congress re the Treaty of Zürich, 118

A SELECTED LIST

OF

ASSELL & COMPANY'S

PUBLICATIONS.

7 G—9.92

Selections from Cassell & Company's Publications

Illustrated, Fine Art, and other Volumes.

Abbeys and Churches of England and Wales, The: Descriptive, Historical, Pictorial. Series I. and II. 21s. each.
A Blot of Ink. Translated by Q and PAUL FRANCKE. 5s.
Across Thibet. By GABRIEL BONVALOT. With about 100 Illustrations and a large Route Map in Colours. In Two Vols. 32s.
Adventure, The World of. Fully Illustrated. Complete in Three Vols. 9s. each.
Africa and its Explorers, The Story of. By Dr. ROBERT BROWN, M.A., F.L.S., F.R.G.S., &c. With numerous Original Illustrations. Vol. I. 7s. 6d.
American Life. By PAUL DE ROUSIERS. 12s. 6d.
Anglomaniacs, The. By Mrs. BURTON HARRISON. 3s. 6d.
Animal Painting in Water Colours. With Coloured Plates. 5s.
Arabian Nights Entertainments (Cassell's). With about 400 Illustrations. 10s. 6d.
Architectural Drawing. By R. PHENÉ SPIERS. Illustrated. 10s. 6d.
Army, Our Home. Being a Reprint of Letters published in the *Times* in November and December, 1891. By H. O. ARNOLD-FORSTER, M.P. 1s.
Art, The Magazine of. Yearly Volume. With about 400 Illustrations, and Twelve Etchings, Photogravures, &c. 16s.
Artistic Anatomy. By Prof. M. DUVAL. *Cheap Edition.* 3s. 6d.
Atlas, The Universal. A New and Complete General Atlas of the World, with 117 Pages of Maps, handsomely produced in Colours, and a Complete Index to over 100,000 Names. Complete in One Volume, cloth, 30s. net; or half-morocco, 35s. net.
Bashkirtseff, Marie, The Journal of. Translated from the French by MATHILDE BLIND. With Portraits and an Autograph Letter. *Cheap Edition*, 7s. 6d.
Bashkirtseff, Marie, The Letters of. Translated by MARY J. SERRANO. 7s. 6d.
Beach of Falesá, and the Bottle Imp. By R. L. STEVENSON. Illustrated. 5s.
Beetles, Butterflies, Moths, and other Insects. With 12 Coloured Plates from "Der Insekten Sammler." 3s. 6d.
Biographical Dictionary, Cassell's New. Containing Memoirs of the Most Eminent Men and Women of all Ages and Countries. 7s. 6d.
Birds' Nests, Eggs, and Egg-Collecting. By R. KEARTON. Illustrated with 16 Coloured Plates of Eggs. 5s.
Blue Pavilions, The. By Q, Author of "Dead Man's Rock," &c. 6s.
Breechloader, The, and How to Use It. By W. W. GREENER. 2s.
British Ballads. 275 Original Illustrations. Two Vols. Cloth, 15s.
British Battles on Land and Sea. By JAMES GRANT. With about 600 Illustrations. Three Vols., 4to, £1 7s.; *Library Edition*, £1 10s.
British Battles, Recent. Illustrated. 4to, 9s. *Library Edition*, 10s.
Browning, An Introduction to the Study of. By ARTHUR SYMONS. 2s. 6d.
Butterflies and Moths, European. By W. F. KIRBY. With 61 Coloured Plates. Demy 4to, 35s.
Canaries and Cage-Birds, The Illustrated Book of. By W. A. BLAKSTON, W. SWAYSLAND, and A. F. WIENER. With 56 Fac-simile Coloured Plates, 35s.
Carnation Manual, The. Edited and Issued by The National Carnation and Picotee Society (Southern Section). 3s. 6d.
Cassell's Family Magazine. Yearly Volume. Illustrated. 9s.
Cathedrals, Abbeys, and Churches of England and Wales. Descriptive, Historical, Pictorial. Edited by Prof. T. G. BONNEY, D.Sc., LL.D., F.R.S. With nearly 500 Original Illustrations. *Popular Edition.* Two Vols. 25s.
Celebrities of the Century. Being a Dictionary of the Men and Women of the Nineteenth Century. *Cheap Edition*, 10s. 6d.
Chess Problem, The. With Illustrations by C. PLANCK and others. 7s. 6d.
China Painting. By FLORENCE LEWIS. With Sixteen Coloured Plates, and a Selection of Wood Engravings. With full Instructions. 5s.
Choice Dishes at Small Cost. By A. G. PAYNE. *Cheap Edition*, 1s.
Christianity and Socialism, Lectures on. By BISHOP BARRY. 3s. 6d.
Cities of the World. Four Vols. Illustrated. 7s. 6d. each.
Civil Service, Guide to Employment in the. *New and Enlarged Edition.* 3s. 6d.
Climate and Health Resorts. By Dr. BURNEY YEO. 7s. 6d.

Selections from Cassell & Company's Publications.

Clinical Manuals for Practitioners and Students of Medicine. (*A List of Volumes forwarded post free on application to the Publishers.*)
Clothing, The Influence of, on Health. By FREDERICK TREVES, F.R.C.S. 2s.
Cobden Club, Works published for the. (*A Complete List on application.*)
Colonist's Medical Handbook, The. By E. ALFRED BARTON, M.R.C.S. 2s. 6d.
Colour. By Prof. A. H. CHURCH. *New and Enlarged Edition.* 3s. 6d.
Columbus, The Career of. By CHARLES ELTON, Q.C. 10s. 6d.
Commercial Botany of the Nineteenth Century. By J. R. JACKSON, A.L.S. Cloth gilt, 3s. 6d.
Conning Tower, In a. By H. O. ARNOLD-FORSTER, M.P., Author of "The Citizen Reader," &c. With Original Illustrations by W. H. OVEREND. 1s.
Conquests of the Cross. Edited by EDWIN HODDER. With numerous Original Illustrations. Complete in Three Vols. 9s. each.
Cookery, A Year's. By PHYLLIS BROWNE. *New and Enlarged Edition.* 3s. 6d.
Cookery, Cassell's Dictionary of. Containing about Nine Thousand Recipes, 7s. 6d.; roxburgh, 10s. 6d.
Cookery, Cassell's Popular. With Four Coloured Plates. Cloth gilt, 2s.
Cookery, Cassell's Shilling. *95th Thousand.* 1s.
Cookery, Vegetarian. By A. G. PAYNE. 1s. 6d.
Cooking by Gas, The Art of. By MARIE J. SUGG. Illustrated. Cloth, 3s. 6d.
Countries of the World, The. By ROBERT BROWN, M.A., Ph.D., &c. Complete in Six Vols., with about 750 Illustrations. 4to, 7s. 6d. each.
Cremation and Urn-Burial; or, The Cemeteries of the Future. By W. ROBINSON. With Plates and Illustrations. 1s.
Cromwell, Oliver: The Man and His Mission. By J. ALLANSON PICTON, M.P. *Cheap Edition.* With Steel Portrait. 3s. 6d.
Cyclopædia, Cassell's Concise. Brought down to the latest date. With about 600 Illustrations. *New and Cheap Edition*, 7s. 6d.
Cyclopædia, Cassell's Miniature. Containing 30,000 Subjects. Cloth, 3s. 6d.; half roxburgh, 4s. 6d.
Dickens, Character Sketches from. FIRST, SECOND, and THIRD SERIES. With Six Original Drawings in each, by FREDERICK BARNARD. In Portfolio. 21s. each.
Dick Whittington, A Modern. By JAMES PAYN, Author of "By Proxy," &c. Two Vols. 21s.
Dictionaries. (For description see alphabetical letter.) Religion, Bible, Biographical, Celebrities, Encyclopædic, Mechanical, Phrase and Fable, English, English History, English Literature, Domestic, Cookery. (French, German, and Latin, see with *Educational Works.*)
Disraeli, Benjamin, Personal Reminiscences of. By HENRY LAKE. 3s. 6d.
Disraeli in Outline. By F. CARROLL BREWSTER, LL.D. 7s. 6d.
Dog, Illustrated Book of the. By VERO SHAW, B.A. With 28 Coloured Plates. Cloth bevelled, 35s.; half-morocco, 45s.
Dog, The. By IDSTONE. Illustrated. 2s. 6d.
Domestic Dictionary, The. An Encyclopædia for the Household. Cloth, 7s. 6d.
Doré Gallery, The. With 250 Illustrations by GUSTAVE DORÉ. 4to, 42s.
Doré's Dante's Inferno. Illustrated by GUSTAVE DORÉ. *Popular Edition.* With Introduction by A. J. BUTLER. Cloth gilt or buckram, 7s. 6d.
Doré's Milton's Paradise Lost. Illustrated by GUSTAVE DORÉ. 4to, 21s.
Dr. Dumány's Wife. A Novel. By MAURUS JÓKAI. 7s. 6d.
Earth, Our, and its Story. Edited by Dr. ROBERT BROWN, F.L.S. With 36 Coloured Plates and 740 Wood Engravings. Complete in Three Vols. 9s. each.
Edinburgh, Old and New, Cassell's. With 600 Illustrations. Three Vols. 9s. each; library binding, £1 10s. the set.
Egypt: Descriptive, Historical, and Picturesque. By Prof. G. EBERS. Translated by CLARA BELL, with Notes by SAMUEL BIRCH, LL.D., &c. Two Vols. 42s.
Electricity, Age of, from Amber Soul to Telephone. By PARK BENJAMIN, Ph.D. 7s. 6d.
Electricity, Practical. By Prof. W. E. AYRTON. Illustrated. 7s. 6d.
Electricity in the Service of Man. A Popular and Practical Treatise. With nearly 850 Illustrations. *Cheap Edition*, 9s.
"Eli Perkins." Thirty Years of Wit. By MELVILLE D. LANDON ("Eli Perkins"). 4s.
Employment for Boys on Leaving School, Guide to. By W. S. BEARD, F.R.G.S. 1s. 6d.

Selections from Cassell & Company's Publications.

Encyclopædic Dictionary, The. Complete in Fourteen Divisional Vols., 10s. 6d. each; or Seven Vols., half-morocco, 21s. each; half-russia, 25s. each.
England, Cassell's Illustrated History of. With 2,000 Illustrations. Ten Vols., 4to, 9s. each. *New and Revised Edition.* Vols. I. to V., 9s. each.
English Dictionary, Cassell's. Containing Definitions of upwards of 100,000 Words and Phrases. Demy 8vo, 1,100 pages, cloth gilt, 7s. 6d. *Cheap Edition,* 3s. 6d.
English History, The Dictionary of. *Cheap Edition,* 10s. 6d.; roxburgh, 15s.
English Literature, Library of. By Prof. HENRY MORLEY. Complete in Five Vols. 7s. 6d. each.
English Literature, Morley's First Sketch of. *Revised Edition,* 7s. 6d.
English Literature, The Dictionary of. By W. DAVENPORT ADAMS. *Cheap Edition,* 7s. 6d.; roxburgh, 10s. 6d.
English Literature, The Story of. By ANNA BUCKLAND. 3s. 6d.
English Writers. By HENRY MORLEY. Vols. I. to VIII. 5s. each.
Æsop's Fables. Illustrated by ERNEST GRISET. *Cheap Edition.* Cloth, 3s. 6d.; bevelled boards, gilt edges, 5s.
Etiquette of Good Society. 1s.; cloth, 1s. 6d.
Eye, Ear, and Throat, The Management of the. 3s. 6d.
Fairway Island. By HORACE HUTCHINSON. With Four Full-page Plates. 5s.
Faith Doctor, The. A Novel. By Dr. EDWARD EGGLESTON. 7s. 6d.
Family Physician. By Eminent PHYSICIANS and SURGEONS. *New and Revised Edition.* Cloth, 21s.; roxburgh, 25s.
Father Mathew: His Life and Times. By FRANK J. MATHEW. 2s. 6d.
Father Stafford. A Novel. By ANTHONY HOPE, Author of "A Man of Mark." 6s.
Fenn, G. Manville, Works by. Boards, 2s. each; or cloth, 2s. 6d.
  The Parson o' Dumford. } In boards only. | Poverty Corner. In boards only.
  The Vicar's People. | My Patients. In cloth only.
Field Naturalist's Handbook, The. By Rev. J. G. WOOD & THEODORE WOOD. 5s.
Figuier's Popular Scientific Works. With Several Hundred Illustrations in each. 3s. 6d. each.
  The Insect World. | Reptiles and Birds. | The Vegetable World.
  The Human Race. | Mammalia. | Ocean World.
  The World before the Deluge.
Figure Painting in Water Colours. With 16 Coloured Plates. 7s. 6d.
Flora's Feast. A Masque of Flowers. Penned and Pictured by WALTER CRANE. With 40 pages in Colours. 5s.
Flower Painting, Elementary. With Eight Coloured Plates. 3s.
Flower Painting in Water Colours. With Coloured Plates. 5s.
Flowers, and How to Paint Them. By MAUD NAFTEL. With Coloured Plates. 5s.
Football: the Rugby Union Game. Edited by Rev. F. MARSHALL. Illustrated. 7s. 6d.
Fossil Reptiles, A History of British. By Sir RICHARD OWEN, K.C.B., F.R.S., &c. With 268 Plates. In Four Vols. £12 12s.
France as It Is. By ANDRÉ LEBON and PAUL PELET. With Maps. 7s. 6d.
Garden Flowers, Familiar. By SHIRLEY HIBBERD. With Coloured Plates by F. E. HULME, F.L.S. Complete in Five Series. Cloth gilt, 12s. 6d. each.
Gardening, Cassell's Popular. Illustrated. Complete in Four Vols. 5s. each.
Geometrical Drawing for Army Candidates. By H. T. LILLEY, M.A. 2s. 6d.
Geometry, First Elements of Experimental. By PAUL BERT. 1s. 6d.
Geometry, Practical Solid. By Major ROSS. 2s.
George Saxon, The Reputation of. By MORLEY ROBERTS. 5s.
German Emperor, The, and his Eastern Neighbours. By POULTNEY BIGELOW. 3s.
Gilbert, Elizabeth, and her Work for the Blind. By FRANCES MARTIN. 2s. 6d.
Gleanings from Popular Authors. Two Vols. With Original Illustrations. 4to, 9s. each. Two Vols. in One, 15s.
Gulliver's Travels. With 88 Engravings. Cloth, 3s. 6d.; cloth gilt, 5s.
Gun and its Development, The. By W. W. GREENER. Illustrated. 10s. 6d.
Guns, Modern Shot. By W. W. GREENER. Illustrated. 5s.
Health at School. By CLEMENT DUKES, M.D., B.S. 7s. 6d.
Health, The Book of. By Eminent Physicians and Surgeons. Cloth, 21s.
Heavens, The Story of the. By Sir ROBERT STAWELL BALL, LL.D., F.R.S. With Coloured Plates and Wood Engravings. *Popular Edition,* 12s. 6d.

Selections from Cassell & Company's Publications.

Heroes of Britain in Peace and War. With 300 Original Illustrations. *Cheap Edition.* Two Vols. 3s. 6d. each, or two vols. in one, cloth gilt, 7s. 6d.
Historic Houses of the United Kingdom. With Contributions by the Rev. Professor BONNEY, F.R.S., and others. Profusely Illustrated. 10s. 6d.
History, A Footnote to. Eight Years of Trouble in Samoa. By ROBERT LOUIS STEVENSON. 6s.
Hors de Combat; or, Three Weeks in a Hospital. Founded on Facts. By GERTRUDE and ETHEL ARMITAGE SOUTHAM. Illustrated, crown 4to, 5s.
Horse, The Book of the. By SAMUEL SIDNEY. With 28 Fac-simile Coloured Plates. Demy 4to, 35s.; half-morocco, £2 5s.
Houghton, Lord: The Life, Letters, and Friendships of Richard Monckton Milnes, First Lord Houghton. By T. WEMYSS REID. Two Vols. 32s.
Household, Cassell's Book of the. Illustrated. Complete in Four Vols. 5s. each; or Four Vols., in two, half-morocco, 25s.
Hygiene and Public Health. By B. ARTHUR WHITELEGGE, M.D. 7s. 6d.
India, Cassell's History of. By JAMES GRANT. With 400 Illustrations. Two Vols., 9s. each, or One Vol., 15s.
In-door Amusements, Card Games, and Fireside Fun, Cassell's Book of. With numerous Illustrations. *Cheap Edition.* Cloth, 2s.
Industrial Freedom: a Study in Politics. By B. R. WISE. 5s.
Into the Unknown: a Romance of South Africa. By LAWRENCE FLETCHER. 4s.
Irish Leagues, The Work of the. The Speech of the Right Hon. Sir HENRY JAMES, Q.C., M.P., Replying in the Parnell Commission Inquiry. 6s.
Irish Union, The; Before and After. By A. K. CONNELL, M.A. 2s. 6d.
"I Saw Three Ships," and other Winter's Tales. By Q. Buckram, 6s.
Italy from the Fall of Napoleon I. in 1815 to 1890. By J. W. PROBYN. 3s. 6d.
"Japanese" Library, Cassell's. Consisting of 12 Popular Works bound in Japanese style. Covers in water-colour pictures, 1s. 3d. each, net.
Handy Andy. Oliver Twist. Ivanhoe. Ingoldsby Legends. The Last of the Mohicans. The Last Days of Pompeii. The Yellowplush Papers. The Last Days of Palmyra. Jack Hinton the Guardsman. Selections from the Works of Thomas Hood. American Humour. Tower of London.
Kennel Guide, Practical. By Dr. GORDON STABLES. Illustrated. *Cheap Edition*, 1s.
"La Bella," and Others. By EGERTON CASTLE. Buckram, 6s.
Ladies' Physician, The. By a London Physician. 6s.
Lady's Dressing Room, The. Translated from the French of BARONESS STAFFE by LADY COLIN CAMPBELL. 3s. 6d.
Lake Dwellings of Europe. By ROBERT MUNRO, M.D., M.A. Cloth, 31s. 6d.
Law, How to Avoid. By A. J. WILLIAMS, M.P. *Cheap Edition*, 1s.
Legends for Lionel. With Coloured Plates by WALTER CRANE. 5s.
Leona. By Mrs. MOLESWORTH. 6s.
Letts's Diaries and other Time-saving Publications are now published exclusively by CASSELL & COMPANY. (*A List sent post free on application.*)
Life in Our Villages. Paper, 1s.; cloth boards, 2s.
Little Minister, The. By J. M. BARRIE. In One Vol. 7s. 6d.
Local Option in Norway. By THOMAS M. WILSON, C.E. 1s.
Locomotive Engine, The Biography of a. By HENRY FRITH. 5s.
Loftus, Lord Augustus, P.C., G.C.B., The Diplomatic Reminiscences of (1837—1862). With Portrait. Two Vols. Demy 8vo, 32s.
London, Greater. By EDWARD WALFORD. Two Vols. With about 400 Illustrations. 9s. each. *Library Edition.* Two Vols. £1 the set.
London, Old and New. By WALTER THORNBURY and EDWARD WALFORD. Six Vols., with about 1,200 Illustrations. Cloth, 9s. each. *Library Edition*, £3.
London Street Arabs. By MRS. H. M. STANLEY (DOROTHY TENNANT). With Pictures printed on a Tint. 5s.
Mechanics, The Practical Dictionary of. Illustrated. Four Vols. 21s. each.
Medical Handbook of Life Assurance. By JAMES EDWARD POLLOCK, M.D., F.R.C.P., and JAMES CHISHOLM, Fellow of the Institute of Actuaries, London. 7s. 6d.
Medicine Lady, The. By L. T. MEADE. Three Vols. 31s. 6d.
Medicine, Manuals for Students of. (*A List forwarded post free on application.*)
Modern Europe, A History of. By C. A. FYFFE, M.A. Three Vols. 12s. each.
Mount Desolation. An Australian Romance. By W. CARLTON DAWE. 5s.
Musical and Dramatic Copyright, The Law of. By EDWARD CUTLER, THOMAS EUSTACE SMITH, and FREDERIC E. WEATHERLY. 3s. 6d.
Music, Illustrated History of. By EMIL NAUMANN. Edited by the Rev. Sir F. A. GORE OUSELEY, Bart. Illustrated. Two Vols. 31s. 6d.

Selections from Cassell & Company's Publications.

Napier, The Life and Letters of the Rt. Hon. Sir Joseph, Bart., LL.D., D.C.L., M.R.I.A., Ex-Lord Chancellor of Ireland. By ALEX. CHARLES EWALD, F.S.A. *New and Revised Edition.* 7s. 6d.
National Library, Cassell's. In Volumes. Paper covers, 3d.; cloth, 6d. (*A Complete List of the Volumes post free on application.*)
Natural History, Cassell's Concise. By E. PERCEVAL WRIGHT, M.A., M.D., F.L.S. With several Hundred Illustrations. 7s. 6d.; also kept half-bound.
Natural History, Cassell's New. Edited by Prof. P. MARTIN DUNCAN, M.B., F.R.S., F.G.S. Complete in Six Vols. With about 2,000 Illustrations. Cloth, 9s. each.
Nature's Wonder Workers. By KATE R. LOVELL. Illustrated. 5s.
Naval War, The Last Great. By A. NELSON SEAFORTH. With Maps. 2s.
Navy, Royal, All About the. By W. LAIRD CLOWES. Illustrated. 1s.
Nelson, The Life of. By ROBERT SOUTHEY. Illustrated with Eight Plates, 3s. 6d.
Nursing for the Home and for the Hospital, A Handbook of. By CATHERINE J. WOOD. *Cheap Edition*, 1s. 6d.; cloth, 2s.
Nursing of Sick Children, A Handbook for the. By CATHERINE J. WOOD. 2s. 6d.
O'Driscoll's Weird, and Other Stories. By A. WERNER. Cloth, 5s.
Odyssey, The Modern. By WYNDHAM F. TUFNELL. Illustrated. 10s. 6d.
Ohio, The New. A Story of East and West. By EDWARD EVERETT HALE. 6s.
Our Own Country. Six Vols. With 1,200 Illustrations. Cloth, 7s. 6d. each.
Out of the Jaws of Death. By FRANK BARRETT. Three Vols. 31s. 6d.
Painting, The English School of. By ERNEST CHESNEAU. *Cheap Edition*, 3s. 6d.
Paxton's Flower Garden. With 100 Coloured Plates. (*Price on application.*)
People I've Smiled With. By MARSHALL P. WILDER. 2s.
Peoples of the World, The. By Dr. ROBERT BROWN. Complete in Six Volumes. With Illustrations. 7s. 6d. each.
Perfect Gentleman, The. By the Rev. A. SMYTHE-PALMER, D.D. 3s. 6d.
Phillips, Watts. Artist and Playwright. By Miss E. WATTS PHILLIPS. With 32 Plates. 10s. 6d.
Photography for Amateurs. By T. C. HEPWORTH. *Enlarged and Revised Edition.* Illustrated, 1s.; or cloth, 1s. 6d.
Phrase and Fable, Dictionary of. By the Rev. Dr. BREWER. *Cheap Edition, Enlarged*, cloth, 3s. 6d.; or with leather back, 4s. 6d.
Picturesque America. Complete in Four Vols., with 48 Exquisite Steel Plates, and about 800 Original Wood Engravings. £2 2s. each.
Picturesque Australasia, Cassell's. With upwards of 1,000 Illustrations. Complete in Four Vols. 7s. 6d. each.
Picturesque Canada. With about 600 Original Illustrations. Two Vols. £6 6s. the set.
Picturesque Europe. Complete in Five Vols. Each containing 13 Exquisite Steel Plates, from Original Drawings, and nearly 800 Original Illustrations. £21; half-morocco, £31 10s.; morocco gilt, £52 10s. *Popular Edition*. In Five Vols. 18s. each.
Picturesque Mediterranean, The. With a Series of Magnificent Illustrations from Original Designs by leading Artists of the day. Two Vols. Cloth, £2 2s. each.
Pigeon Keeper, The Practical. By LEWIS WRIGHT. Illustrated. 3s. 6d.
Pigeons, The Book of. By ROBERT FULTON. Edited by LEWIS WRIGHT. With 50 Coloured Plates and numerous Wood Engravings. 31s. 6d.; half-morocco, £2 2s.
Pity and of Death, The Book of. By PIERRE LOTI, Member of the French Academy. Translated by T. P. O'CONNOR, M.P. Antique paper, cloth gilt, 5s.
Playthings and Parodies. Short Stories by BARRY PAIN. 5s.
Poems, Aubrey de Vere's. A Selection. Edited by JOHN DENNIS. 3s. 6d.
Poets, Cassell's Miniature Library of the. Price 1s. each Vol.
Political Questions of the Day, A Manual of. By SYDNEY BUXTON, M.P. *New and Enlarged Edition*. Paper Covers, 1s.; or cloth, 1s. 6d.
Polytechnic Series, The. Practical Illustrated Manuals specially prepared for Students of the Polytechnic Institute, and suitable for the Use of all Students. (*A List will be sent on application.*)
Portrait Gallery, The Cabinet. *First, Second, and Third Series*, each containing 36 Cabinet Photographs of Eminent Men and Women of the day. With Biographical Sketches. 15s. each.
Poultry Keeper, The Practical. By LEWIS WRIGHT. Illustrated. 3s. 6d.
Poultry, The Book of. By LEWIS WRIGHT. *Popular Edition*. Illustrated. 10s. 6d.
Poultry, The Illustrated Book of. By LEWIS WRIGHT. With Fifty Exquisite Coloured Plates, and numerous Wood Engravings. *Revised Edition*. Cloth, 31s. 6d.

Selections from Cassell & Company's Publications.

Public Libraries, Free. *New and Enlarged Edition.* By THOMAS GREENWOOD, Author of "Museums and Art Galleries." Illustrated. 2s. 6d.
Queen Summer; or, The Tourney of the Lily and the Rose. Penned and Portrayed by WALTER CRANE. With 40 pages in Colours. 6s.
Queen Victoria, The Life and Times of. By ROBERT WILSON. Complete in 2 Vols. With numerous Illustrations. 9s. each.
Rabbit-Keeper, The Practical. By CUNICULUS. Illustrated. 3s. 6d.
Raffles Haw, The Doings of. By A. CONAN DOYLE, Author of "Micah Clarke," &c. Antique paper, cloth gilt, 5s.
Railway Guides, Official Illustrated. With Illustrations on nearly every page. Maps, &c. Paper covers, 1s.; cloth, 2s.

Great Eastern Railway.	London and North Western Railway.
Great Northern Railway.	London and South Western Railway.
Great Western Railway.	Midland Railway.
London, Brighton, and South Coast Railway.	South Eastern Railway.

Railway Library, Cassell's. Crown 8vo, boards, 2s. each.

Metzerott, Shoemaker. By Katharine P. Woods.	The Phantom City. By W. Westall.
David Todd. By David Maclure.	Jack Gordon, Knight Errant. By W. C. Hudson (Barclay North).
The Astonishing History of Troy Town. By Q.	The Diamond Button: Whose Was It? By W. C. Hudson (Barclay North).
The Admirable Lady Biddy Fane. By Frank Barrett.	Another's Crime. By Julian Hawthorne.
Commodore Junk. By G. Manville Fenn.	The Yoke of the Thorah. By Sidney Luska.
St. Cuthbert's Tower. By Florence Warden.	Who is John Noman? By C. Henry Beckett.
The Man with a Thumb. By W. C. Hudson (Barclay North).	The Tragedy of Brinkwater. By Martha L. Moodey.
By Right Not Law. By R. Sherard.	An American Penman. By Julian Hawthorne.
Within Sound of the Weir. By Thomas St. E. Hake.	Section 558; or, The Fatal Letter. By Julian Hawthorne.
Under a Strange Mask. By Frank Barrett.	The Brown Stone Boy. By W. H. Bishop.
The Coombsberrow Mystery. By J. Colwall.	A Tragic Mystery. By Julian Hawthorne.
Dead Man's Rock. By Q.	The Great Bank Robbery. By Julian Hawthorne.
A Queer Race. By W. Westall.	
Captain Trafalgar. By Westall and Laurie.	

Redgrave, Richard, C.B., R.A. Memoir. By F. M. REDGRAVE. 10s. 6d.
Richard, Henry, M.P. A Biography. By CHARLES MIALL. With Portrait. 7s. 6d.
Rivers of Great Britain: Descriptive, Historical, Pictorial.
  The Royal River: The Thames from Source to Sea. With Several Hundred Original Illustrations. *Original Edition*, £2 2s. *Popular Edition*, 16s.
  Rivers of the East Coast. With highly finished Engravings, and Etching as Frontispiece. *Original Edition*, 42s. *Popular Edition*, 16s.
Robinson Crusoe. *Cassell's New Fine-Art Edition.* With upwards of 100 Original Illustrations. 7s. 6d.
Romance, The World of. With New and Original Illustrations. Complete in One Volume. cloth, 9s.
Ronner, Mme. Henriette, The Painter of Cat Life and Cat Character. Containing a Portrait and Twelve Full-Page Illustrations in Photogravure and Sixteen Typogravures. The Text by M. H. SPIELMANN. 4to Edition with Photogravures on India paper, £2 10s.; Folio Edition, £3 10s.
Russo-Turkish War, Cassell's History of. With about 500 Illustrations. Two Vols., 9s. each; library binding, One Vol., 15s.
Salisbury Parliament, Diary of the. By H. W. LUCY. Illustrated by HARRY FURNISS. Cloth, 21s.
Sanitary Institutions, English. By Sir JOHN SIMON, K.C.B., F.R.S. 18s.
Saturday Journal, Cassell's. Illustrated throughout. Yearly Volume, 7s. 6d.
Science for All. Edited by Dr. ROBERT BROWN, M.A., F.L.S., &c. *Revised Edition.* With 1,500 Illustrations. Five Vols. 9s. each.
Science, Year Book of, The, for 1892. Edited by Rev. Prof. BONNEY. 7s. 6d.
Sea, The: Its Stirring Story of Adventure, Peril, and Heroism. By F. WHYMPER. With 400 Illustrations. Four Vols. 7s. 6d. each.
Secret of the Lamas, The. A Tale of Thibet. Crown 8vo, 5s.
Sent Back by the Angels. By F. LANGBRIDGE, M.A. 1s.
Shaftesbury, The Seventh Earl of, K.G., The Life and Work of. By EDWIN HODDER. With Portraits. Three Vols., 36s. *Cheap Edition*, 3s. 6d.
Shakespeare, Cassell's Quarto Edition. Edited by CHARLES and MARY COWDEN CLARKE, and containing about 600 Illustrations by H. C. SELOUS. Complete in Three Vols., cloth gilt, £3 3s.—Also published in Three separate Volumes, in cloth, viz.:—The COMEDIES, 21s.; The HISTORICAL PLAYS, 18s. 6d.; The TRAGEDIES, 25s.

Selections from Cassell & Company's Publications.

Shakespeare, Miniature. Illustrated. In Twelve Vols., in box, 12s.; **or in** Red Paste Grain (box to match), with spring catch, lettered in gold, 21s.
Shakespeare, The Plays of. Edited by Prof. HENRY MORLEY. **Complete in** Thirteen Vols. Cloth, in box, 21s.; half-morocco, cloth sides, 42s.
Shakespeare, The England of. By E. GOADBY. Illustrated. *New Edition*, 2s. 6d.
Shakspere, The International. *Édition de luxe.*
"King Henry VIII." By Sir JAMES LINTON, P.R.I. (Price on application).
"Othello." Illustrated by FRANK DICKSEE, R.A. £3 10s.
"King Henry IV." Illustrated by Herr EDUARD GRÜTZNER. £3 10s.
"As You Like It." Illustrated by the late Mons. EMILE BAYARD. £3 10s.
"Romeo and Juliet." Illustrated by FRANK DICKSEE, R.A. Is now out of print.
Shakspere, The Leopold. With 400 Illustrations, and an Introduction by F. J. FURNIVALL. *Cheap Edition*, 3s. 6d. Cloth gilt, gilt edges, 5s.; roxburgh, 7s. 6d.
Shakspere, The Royal. With Exquisite Steel Plates and Wood Engravings. Three Vols. 15s. each.
Sketches, The Art of Making and Using. From the French f G. FRAIPONT. By CLARA BELL. With Fifty Illustrations. 2s. 6d.
Smuggling Days and Smuggling Ways; or, The Story of a Lost Art. By Commander the Hon. HENRY N. SHORE, R.N. Illustrated. Cloth, 7s. 6d.
Snare of the Fowler, The. By Mrs. "ALEXANDER." Three Vols. 31s. 6d.
Social Welfare, Subjects of. By the Rt. Hon. SIR LYON PLAYFAIR, M.P. 7s. 6d.
Sports and Pastimes, Cassell's Complete Book of. With more than 900 Illustrations. *Cheap Edition*, 3s. 6d.
Squire, The. By Mrs. PARR. Three Vols. 31s. 6d.
Standard Library, Cassell's. Stiff covers, 1s. each; cloth, 2s. each.

Shirley.
Coningsby.
Mary Barton.
The Antiquary.
Nicholas Nickleby. Two Vols.
Jane Eyre.
Wuthering Heights.
The Prairie.
Dombey and Son. Two Vols.
Night and Morning.
Kenilworth.
The Ingoldsby Legends.
Tower of London.
The Pioneers.
Charles O'Malley.
Barnaby Rudge.
Cakes and Ale.
The King's Own.
People I have Met.
The Pathfinder.
Evelina.
Scott's Poems.
Last of the Barons.
Adventures of Mr. Ledbury.
Ivanhoe.
Oliver Twist.
Selections from Hood's Works.
Longfellow's Prose Works.
Sense and Sensibility.
Lytton's Plays.
Tales, Poems, and Sketches (Bret Harte).
The Prince of the House of David.
Sheridan's Plays.
Uncle Tom's Cabin.
Deerslayer.
Eugene Aram.
Jack Hinton, the Guardsman.
Rome and the Early Christians.
The Trials of Margaret Lyndsay.
Edgar Allan Poe. Prose and Poetry, Selections from.
Old Mortality.
The Hour and the Man.
Washington Irving's Sketch Book.
Last Days of Palmyra.
Tales of the Borders.
Pride and Prejudice.
Last of the Mohicans.
Heart of Midlothian.
Last Days of Pompeii.
Yellowplush Papers.
Handy Andy.
Selected Plays.
American Humour.
Sketches by Boz.
Macaulay's Lays and Selected Essays.
Harry Lorrequer.
Old Curiosity Shop.
Rienzi.
The Talisman.
Pickwick. Two Vols.
Scarlet Letter.
Martin Chuzzlewit. Two Vols.

Star-Land. By Sir ROBERT STAWELL BALL, LL.D., &c. Illustrated. 6s.
Storehouse of General Information, Cassell's. Fully Illustrated with High-Class Wood Engravings, and with Maps and Coloured Plates. In Vols. 5s. each.
Story of Francis Cludde, The. A Novel. By STANLEY J. WEYMAN. 7s. 6d.
Successful Life, The. By W. H. WEBBER. 3s. 6d.
Sybil Knox; or, Home Again. A Story of To-day. By EDWARD E. HALE, Author of "East and West," &c. 7s. 6d.
Teaching in Three Continents. Personal Notes on the Educational Systems of the World. By W. C. GRASBY. 6s.
Thackeray, Character Sketches from. Six New and Original Drawings by FREDERICK BARNARD, reproduced in Photogravure. 21s.
The Short Story Library.
Noughts and Crosses. By Q. 5s.
Otto the Knight, &c. By OCTAVE THANET.
Fourteen to One, &c. By ELIZABETH STUART PHELPS. 6s.
Eleven Possible Cases. By various Authors. 5s.
A Singer's Wife. By Miss FANNY MURFREE. 5s.
The Poet's Audience, and Delilah. By CLARA SAVILE CLARKE. 5s.
"Treasure Island" Series, The. *Cheap Illustrated Edition.* Cloth, 3s. 6d. each.
King Solomon's Mines. By H. RIDER HAGGARD.
Kidnapped. By ROBERT LOUIS STEVENSON.
Treasure Island. By ROBERT LOUIS STEVENSON.
The Splendid Spur. By Q.
The Master of Ballantrae. By ROBERT LOUIS STEVENSON.
The Black Arrow: A Tale of the Two Roses. By ROBERT LOUIS STEVENSON.

Selections from Cassell & Company's Publications.

Treatment, The Year-Book of, for 1893. A Critical Review for Practitioners of Medicine and Surgery. Ninth Year of Issue. Greatly Enlarged. 500 pages. 7s. 6d.
Tree Painting in Water Colours. By W. H. J. BOOT. With Eighteen Coloured Plates, and valuable instructions by the Artist. 5s.
Trees, Familiar. By Prof. G. S. BOULGER, F.L.S., F.G.S. Two Series. With Forty full-page Coloured Plates by W. H. J. BOOT. 12s. 6d. each.
"Unicode": The Universal Telegraphic Phrase Book. Pocket or Desk Edition. 2s. 6d. each.
United States, Cassell's History of the. By EDMUND OLLIER. With 600 Illustrations. Three Vols. 9s. each.
Universal History, Cassell's Illustrated. With nearly ONE THOUSAND ILLUSTRATIONS. Vol. I. Early and Greek History.—Vol. II. The Roman Period.—Vol. III. The Middle Ages.—Vol. IV. Modern History. 9s. each.
University Extension, Past, Present, and Future. By Prof. H. J. MACKINDER and M. E. SADLER, M.A. With Maps and Plans. 1s. 6d.
Vaccination Vindicated. By JOHN C. MCVAIL, M.D., D.P.H. Camb. 5s.
Verdict, The. A Tract on the Political Significance of the Report of the Parnell Commission. By A. V. DICEY, Q.C. 2s. 6d.
Vernon Heath's Recollections. Large crown 8vo, cloth gilt, 10s. 6d.
Verses Grave and Gay. By ELLEN THORNEYCROFT FOWLER. 3s. 6d.
Vicar of Wakefield and other Works, by OLIVER GOLDSMITH. Illustrated. 3s. 6d.; cloth, gilt edges, 5s.
Water-Colour Painting, A Course of. With Twenty-four Coloured Plates by R. P. LEITCH, and full Instructions to the Pupil. 5s.
Waterloo Letters. Edited by MAJOR-GENERAL H. T. SIBORNE, Late Colonel R.E. With Numerous Maps and Plans of the Battlefield. 21s.
Wedlock, Lawful; or, How Shall I Make Sure of a Legal Marriage. By TWO BARRISTERS. 2s.
Wild Birds, Familiar. By W. SWAYSLAND. Four Series. With 40 Coloured Plates in each. 12s. 6d. each.
Wild Flowers, Familiar. By F. E. HULME, F.L.S., F.S.A. Five Series. With 40 Coloured Plates in each. 12s. 6d. each.
Wood, The Life of the Rev. J. G. By his Son, the Rev. THEODORE WOOD. With Portrait. Extra crown 8vo, cloth. *Cheap Edition.* 5s.
Work. An Illustrated Journal of Practice and Theory for all Workmen, Professional and Amateur. Yearly Volume, cloth, 7s. 6d.
World of Wit and Humour, The. With 400 Illustrations. Cloth, 7s. 6d.
World of Wonders, The. With 400 Illustrations. Two Vols. 7s. 6d. each.
Wrecker, The. By R. L. STEVENSON and LLOYD OSBOURNE. Illustrated. 6s.
Yule Tide. CASSELL'S CHRISTMAS ANNUAL. 1s.

ILLUSTRATED MAGAZINES.

The Quiver, for Sunday and General Reading. Monthly, 6d.
Cassell's Family Magazine. Monthly, 7d.
"Little Folks" Magazine. Monthly, 6d.
The Magazine of Art. Monthly, 1s.
Chums. The New Illustrated Paper for Boys. Weekly, 1d.; Monthly, 6d.
Cassell's Saturday Journal. Weekly, 1d.; Monthly, 6d.
Work. An Illustrated Journal of Practice and Theory for all Workmen, Professional and Amateur. Weekly, 1d.; Monthly, 6d.

⁎⁎⁎ Full particulars of CASSELL & COMPANY'S **Monthly Serial Publications** *will be found in* CASSELL & COMPANY'S COMPLETE CATALOGUE.

Catalogues of CASSELL & COMPANY'S PUBLICATIONS, which may be had at all Booksellers', or will be sent post free on application to the Publishers:—
  CASSELL'S COMPLETE CATALOGUE, containing particulars of upwards of One Thousand Volumes.
  CASSELL'S CLASSIFIED CATALOGUE, in which their Works are arranged according to price, from *Threepence to Fifty Guineas.*
  CASSELL'S EDUCATIONAL CATALOGUE, containing particulars of CASSELL & COMPANY'S Educational Works and Students' Manuals.

  CASSELL & COMPANY, LIMITED, *Ludgate Hill, London.*

Selections from Cassell & Company's Publications.

Bibles and Religious Works.

Bible, Cassell's Illustrated Family. With 900 Illustrations. Leather, gilt edges, £2 10s.; full morocco, £3 10s.
Bible Educator, The. Edited by E. H. PLUMPTRE, D.D. With Illustrations, Maps, &c. Four Vols., cloth, 6s. each.
Bible Student in the British Museum, The. By the Rev. J. G. KITCHIN, M.A. *Entirely New and Revised Edition*, 1s. 4d.
Biblewomen and Nurses. Yearly Volume, 3s.
Bunyan's Pilgrim's Progress, and the Holy War, Cassell's Illustrated Edition of. With 200 Original Illustrations. Demy 4to, cloth, 16s.
Bunyan's Pilgrim's Progress (Cassell's Illustrated). 4to. *Cheap Edition*, 3s. 6d.
Bunyan's Pilgrim's Progress. With Illustrations. *Cheap Edition*, 2s. 6d.
Child's Bible, The. With 200 Illustrations. Demy 4to, 830 pp. *150th Thousand. Cheap Edition*, 7s. 6d. *Superior Edition*, with 6 Coloured Plates, gilt edges, 10s. 6d.
Child's Life of Christ, The. Complete in One Handsome Volume, with about 200 Original Illustrations. *Cheap Edition*, cloth, 7s. 6d.; or with 6 Coloured Plates, cloth, gilt edges, 10s. 6d. Demy 4to, gilt edges, 21s.
"Come, ye Children." By the Rev. BENJAMIN WAUGH. Illustrated. 5s.
Commentary, The New Testament, for English Readers. Edited by the Rt. Rev. C. J. ELLICOTT, D.D., Lord Bishop of Gloucester and Bristol. In Three Volumes. 21s. each.
    Vol. I.—The Four Gospels.
    Vol. II.—The Acts, Romans, Corinthians, Galatians.
    Vol. III.—The remaining Books of the New Testament.
Commentary, The Old Testament, for English Readers. Edited by the Rt. Rev. C. J. ELLICOTT, D.D., Lord Bishop of Gloucester and Bristol. Complete in 5 Vols. 21s. each.
    Vol. I.—Genesis to Numbers.   Vol. III.—Kings I. to Esther.
    Vol. II.—Deuteronomy to Samuel II.   Vol. IV.—Job to Isaiah.
    Vol. V.—Jeremiah to Malachi.
Commentary, The New Testament. Edited by Bishop ELLICOTT. Handy Volume Edition. Suitable for School and general use.

St. Matthew. 3s. 6d.	Romans. 2s. 6d.	Titus, Philemon, Hebrews, and James. 3s.
St. Mark. 3s.	Corinthians I. and II. 3s.	Peter, Jude, and John. 3s.
St. Luke. 3s. 6d.	Galatians, Ephesians, and Philippians. 3s.	The Revelation. 3s.
St. John. 3s. 6d.	Colossians, Thessalonians, and Timothy. 3s.	An Introduction to the New Testament. 3s. 6d.
The Acts of the Apostles. 3s. 6d.		

Commentary, The Old Testament. Edited by Bishop ELLICOTT. Handy Volume Edition. Suitable for School and general use.

Genesis. 3s. 6d.	Leviticus. 3s.	Deuteronomy. 2s. 6d.
Exodus. 3s.	Numbers. 2s. 6d.	

Dictionary of Religion, The. An Encyclopædia of Christian and other Religious Doctrines, Denominations, Sects, Heresies, Ecclesiastical Terms, History, Biography, &c. &c. By the Rev. WILLIAM BENHAM, B.D. *Cheap Edition.* 10s. 6d.
Doré Bible. With 230 Illustrations by GUSTAVE DORÉ. *Original Edition.* Two Vols., best morocco, gilt edges, £15. *Popular Edition.* With Full-page Illustrations. In One Vol. 15s.
Early Days of Christianity, The. By the Ven. Archdeacon FARRAR, D.D., F.R.S.
    LIBRARY EDITION. Two Vols., 24s.; morocco, £2 2s.
    POPULAR EDITION. Complete in One Volume, cloth, 6s.; cloth, gilt edges, 7s. 6d.; Persian morocco, 10s. 6d.; tree-calf, 15s.
Family Prayer-Book, The. Edited by the Rev. Canon GARBETT, M.A., and the Rev. S. MARTIN. Extra crown 4to, cloth, 5s.; morocco, 18s.
Gleanings after Harvest. Studies and Sketches. By the Rev. JOHN R. VERNON, M.A. Illustrated. 6s.
Gospel of Grace, The. By a LINDESIE. Cloth, 2s. 6d.
"Graven in the Rock." By the Rev. Dr. SAMUEL KINNS, F.R.A.S., &c. &c. Illustrated. 12s. 6d.

Selections from Cassell & Company's Publications.

"Heart Chords." A Series of Works by Eminent Divines. Bound in cloth, red edges, 1s. each.

My Father. By the Right Rev. Ashton Oxenden, late Bishop of Montreal.
My Bible. By the Rt. Rev. W. Boyd Carpenter, Bishop of Ripon.
My Work for God. By the Right Rev. Bishop Cotterill.
My Object in Life. By the Ven. Archdeacon Farrar, D.D.
My Aspirations. By the Rev G. Matheson, D.D.
My Emotional Life. By Preb. Chadwick, D.D.
My Body. By the Rev. Prof. W. G. Blaikie, D.D.
My Soul. By the Rev. P. B. Power, M.A.
My Growth in Divine Life. By the Rev. Prebendary Reynolds, M.A.
My Hereafter. By the Very Rev. Dean Bickersteth.
My Walk with God. By the Very Rev. Dean Montgomery.
My Aids to the Divine Life. By the Very Rev. Dean Boyle.
My Sources of Strength. By the Rev. E. E. Jenkins, M.A.

Helps to Belief. A Series of Helpful Manuals on the Religious Difficulties of the Day. Edited by the Rev. TEIGNMOUTH SHORE, M.A., Canon of Worcester, and Chaplain-in-Ordinary to the Queen. Cloth, 1s. each.

CREATION. By the late Lord Bishop of Carlisle.
MIRACLES. By the Rev. Brownlow Maitland, M.A.
PRAYER. By the Rev. T. Teignmouth Shore, M.A.
THE MORALITY OF THE OLD TESTAMENT. By the Rev. Newman Smyth, D.D.
THE DIVINITY OF OUR LORD. By the Lord Bishop of Derry.

THE ATONEMENT. By William Connor Magee, D.D., Late Archbishop of York.

Hid Treasure. By RICHARD HARRIS HILL. 1s.

Holy Land and the Bible, The. A Book of Scripture Illustrations gathered in Palestine. By the Rev. CUNNINGHAM GEIKIE, D.D., LL.D. (Edin.). With Map. Two Vols. 24s. *Illustrated Edition.* One Vol. 21s.

Life of Christ, The. By the Ven. Archdeacon FARRAR, D.D., F.R.S., Chaplain-in-Ordinary to the Queen.
CHEAP ILLUSTRATED EDITION. Large 4to, cloth, 7s. 6d. Cloth, full gilt, gilt edges, 10s. 6d.
LIBRARY EDITION. Two Vols. Cloth, 24s.; morocco, 42s.
POPULAR EDITION, in One Vol. 8vo, cloth, 6s.; cloth, gilt edges, 7s. 6d.; Persian morocco, gilt edges, 10s. 6d.; tree-calf, 15s.

Marriage Ring, The. By WILLIAM LANDELS, D.D. Bound in white leatherette. *New and Cheaper Edition,* 3s. 6d.

Morning and Evening Prayers for Workhouses and other Institutions. Selected by LOUISA TWINING. 2s.

Moses and Geology; or, the Harmony of the Bible with Science. By the Rev. SAMUEL KINNS, Ph.D., F.R.A.S. Illustrated. Demy 8vo, 8s. 6d.

My Comfort in Sorrow. By HUGH MACMILLAN, D.D., LL.D., &c., Author of "Bible Teachings in Nature," &c. Cloth, 1s.

New Light on the Bible and the Holy Land. By B. T. A. EVETTS. Illustrated. Cloth, 21s.

Protestantism, The History of. By the Rev. J. A. WYLIE, LL.D. Containing upwards of 600 Original Illustrations. Three Vols., 27s.; *Library Edition,* 30s.

"Quiver" Yearly Volume, The. With about 600 Original Illustrations and Coloured Frontispiece. 7s. 6d. Also Monthly, 6d.

St. George for England; and other Sermons preached to Children. *Fifth Edition.* By the Rev. T. TEIGNMOUTH SHORE, M.A., Canon of Worcester. 5s.

St. Paul, The Life and Work of. By the Ven. Archdeacon FARRAR, D.D., F.R.S., Chaplain-in-Ordinary to the Queen.
LIBRARY EDITION. Two Vols., cloth, 24s.; calf, 42s.
ILLUSTRATED EDITION, complete in One Volume, with about 300 Illustrations, £1 1s.; morocco, £2 2s.
POPULAR EDITION. One Volume, 8vo, cloth, 6s.; cloth, gilt edges, 7s. 6d.; Persian morocco, 10s. 6d.; tree-calf, 15s.

Shall We Know One Another in Heaven? By the Rt. Rev. J. C. RYLE, D.D., Bishop of Liverpool. *New and Enlarged Edition.* Paper Covers, 6d.

Shortened Church Services and Hymns, suitable for use at Children's Services. Compiled by the Rev. T. TEIGNMOUTH SHORE, M.A., Canon of Worcester. *Enlarged Edition.* 1s.

Signa Christi: Evidences of Christianity set forth in the Person and Work of Christ. By the Rev. JAMES AITCHISON. 5s.

"Sunday:" Its Origin, History, and Present Obligation. By the Ven. Archdeacon HESSEY, D.C.L. *Fifth Edition,* 7s. 6d.

Twilight of Life, The: Words of Counsel and Comfort for the Aged. By JOHN ELLERTON, M.A. 1s. 6d.

Selections from Cassell & Company's Publications.

Educational Works and Students' Manuals.

Agricultural Text-Books, Cassell's. (The "Downton" Series.) Fully Illustrated. Edited by JOHN WRIGHTSON, Professor of Agriculture.
   Soils and Manures. By J. M. H. Munro, D.Sc. (London), F.I.C., F.C.S. 2s. 6d.
   Farm Crops. By Professor Wrightson. 2s. 6d.
   Live Stock. By Professor Wrightson. 2s. 6d.
Alphabet, Cassell's Pictorial. Size, 35 inches by 42½ inches. Mounted on Linen, with rollers. 3s. 6d.
Arithmetic:—Howard's Anglo-American Art of Reckoning. The Standard Teacher and Referee of Shorthand Business Arithmetic. By C. F. HOWARD. Paper, 1s.; cloth, 2s. *New Enlarged Edition*, 5s.
Arithmetics, The Modern School. By GEORGE RICKS, B.Sc. Lond. With Test Cards. (*List on application.*)
Atlas, Cassell's Popular. Containing 24 Coloured Maps. 2s. 6d.
Book-Keeping. By THEODORE JONES. FOR SCHOOLS, 2s.; or cloth, 3s. FOR THE MILLION, 2s.; or cloth, 3s. Books for Jones's System, Ruled Sets of, 2s.
Chemistry, The Public School. By J. H. ANDERSON, M.A. 2s. 6d.
Classical Texts for Schools, Cassell's. (*A list sent post free on application.*)
Cookery for Schools. By LIZZIE HERITAGE. 6d.
Copy-Books, Cassell's Graduated. Complete in 18 Books. 2d. each.
Copy-Books, The Modern School. Complete in 12 Books. 2d. each.
Drawing Copies, Cassell's "New Standard." Complete in 14 Books. 2d., 3d., and 4d. each.
Drawing Copies, Cassell's Modern School Freehand. First Grade, 1s. Second Grade, 2s.
Electricity, Practical. By Prof. W. E. AYRTON. 7s. 6d.
Energy and Motion: A Text-Book of Elementary Mechanics. By WILLIAM PAICE, M.A. Illustrated. 1s. 6d.
English Literature, A First Sketch of, from the Earliest Period to the Present Time. By Prof. HENRY MORLEY. 7s. 6d.
Euclid, Cassell's. Edited by Prof. WALLACE, M.A. 1s.
Euclid, The First Four Books of. *New Edition*. In paper, 6d.; cloth, 9d.
French, Cassell's Lessons in. *New and Revised Edition.* Parts I. and II., each, 2s. 6d.; complete, 4s. 6d. Key, 1s. 6d.
French-English and English-French Dictionary. *Entirely New and Enlarged Edition.* 1,150 pages, 8vo, cloth, 3s. 6d.
French Reader, Cassell's Public School. By GUILLAUME S. CONRAD. 2s. 6d.
Galbraith and Haughton's Scientific Manuals.
   Plane Trigonometry. 2s. 6d. Euclid. Books I., II., III. 2s. 6d. Books IV., V., VI. 2s. 6d. Mathematical Tables. 3s. 6d. Mechanics. 3s. 6d. Natural Philosophy. 3s. 6d. Optics. 2s. 6d. Hydrostatics. 3s. 6d. Steam Engine. 3s. 6d. Algebra. Part I., cloth, 2s. 6d. Complete, 7s. 6d. Tides and Tidal Currents, with Tidal Cards, 3s.
Gaudeamus. Songs for Colleges and Schools. Edited by JOHN FARMER. 5s. Words only, paper, 6d.; cloth, 9d.
Geometry, First Elements of Experimental. By PAUL BERT. Illustrated. 1s. 6d.
Geometry, Practical Solid. By Major ROSS, R.E. 2s.
German Dictionary, Cassell's New. German-English, English-German. *Cheap Edition*, cloth, 3s. 6d.
German of To-Day. By Dr. HEINEMANN. 1s. 6d.
German Reading, First Lessons in. By A. JAGST. Illustrated. 1s.
Hand-and-Eye Training. By G. RICKS, B.Sc. Two Vols., with 16 Coloured Plates in each Vol. Crown 4to, 6s. each.
"Hand-and-Eye Training" Cards for Class Work. Five sets in case. 1s. each.
Historical Cartoons, Cassell's Coloured. Size 45 in. × 35 in. 2s. each. Mounted on canvas and varnished, with rollers, 5s. each. (Descriptive pamphlet, 16 pp., 1d.)
Historical Course for Schools, Cassell's. Illustrated throughout. I.—Stories from English History, 1s. II.—The Simple Outline of English History, 1s. 3d. III.—The Class History of England, 2s. 6d.
Latin Dictionary, Cassell's New. (Latin-English and English-Latin). Revised by J. R. V. MARCHANT, M.A., and J. F. CHARLES, B.A. 3s. 6d.
Latin Primer, The New. By Prof. J. P. POSTGATE. 2s. 6d.
Latin Primer, The First. By Prof. POSTGATE. 1s.
Latin Prose for Lower Forms. By M. A. BAYFIELD, M.A. 2s. 6d.
Laundry Work (How to Teach It). By Mrs. E. LORD. 6d.

Selections from Cassell & Company's Publications.

Laws of Every-Day Life. For the Use of Schools. By H. O. ARNOLD-FORSTER, M.P. 1s. 6d. *Special Edition* on green paper for those with weak eyesight, 2s.
Little Folks' History of England. By ISA CRAIG-KNOX. Illustrated. 1s. 6d.
Making of the Home, The. By Mrs. SAMUEL A. BARNETT. 1s. 6d.
Map-Building Series, Cassell's. Outline Maps prepared by H. O. ARNOLD-FORSTER, M.P. Per set of 12, 1s.
Marlborough Books:—Arithmetic Examples. 3s. Arithmetic Rules. 1s. 6d. French Exercises. 3s. 6d. French Grammar. 2s. 6d. German Grammar. 3s. 6d.
Mechanics for Young Beginners, A First Book of. By the Rev. J. G. EASTON, M.A. 4s. 6d.
Mechanics and Machine Design, Numerical Examples in Practical. By R. G. BLAINE, M.E. With Diagrams. Cloth, 2s. 6d.
"Model Joint" Wall Sheets, for Instruction in Manual Training. By S. BARTER. Eight Sheets, 2s. 6d. each.
Natural History Coloured Wall Sheets, Cassell's New. Consisting of 18 subjects. Size, 39 by 31 in. Mounted on rollers and varnished. 3s. each.
Object Lessons from Nature. By Prof. L. C. MIALL, F.L.S., F.G.S. Fully Illustrated. Half cloth, paper boards, 2s.; or cloth, 2s. 6d.
Physiology for Schools. By ALFRED T. SCHOFIELD, M.D., M.R.C.S., &c. With Wood Engravings and Coloured Plates. 1s. 9d. Three Parts, paper covers, 5d. each; or cloth limp, 6d. each.
Poetry Readers, Cassell's New. Illustrated. 12 Books. 1d. each. Cloth, 1s. 6d.
Popular Educator, Cassell's New. With Revised Text, New Maps, New Coloured Plates, New Type, &c. Complete in Eight Vols. 5s. each; or Eight Volumes in Four, half-morocco, 50s.
Reader, The Citizen. By H. O. ARNOLD-FORSTER, M.P. Cloth, 1s. 6d.; also a Scottish Edition, Cloth, 1s. 6d.
Reader, The Temperance. By Rev. J. DENNIS HIRD. Crown 8vo, 1s. 6d.
Readers, Cassell's "Higher Class." (*List on application.*)
Readers, Cassell's Historical. Illustrated. (*List on application.*)
Readers, Cassell's Readable. Illustrated. (*List on application.*)
Readers for Infant Schools, Coloured. Three Books. 4d. each.
Readers, The Modern Geographical. Illustrated throughout. (*List on application.*)
Readers, The Modern School. Illustrated. (*List on application.*)
Reading and Spelling Book, Cassell's Illustrated. 1s.
Round the Empire. By G. R. PARKIN. With a Preface by the Rt. Hon. the Earl of Rosebery, K.T. Fully Illustrated. 1s. 6d.
School Bank Manual, A. By AGNES LAMBERT. 6d.
School Certificates, Cassell's. Three Colours, 6¼ × 4⅞ in., 1d.; Five Colours, 11¾ × 9¼ in., 3d.; Seven Colours and Gold, 9⅞ × 6⅞ in., 3d.
Science Applied to Work. By J. A. BOWER. Illustrated. 1s.
Science of Every-Day Life. By J. A. BOWER. Illustrated. 1s.
Sculpture, A Primer of. By E. ROSCOE MULLINS. Illustrated. 2s. 6d.
Shade from Models, Common Objects, and Casts of Ornament, How to. By W. E. SPARKES. With 25 Plates by the Author. 3s.
Shakspere's Plays for School Use. Illustrated. 5 Books. 6d. each.
Spelling, A Complete Manual of. By J. D. MORELL, LL.D. 1s.
Technical Educator, Cassell's. Illustrated throughout. *New and Revised Edition.* Four Vols. 5s. each.
Technical Manuals, Cassell's. Illustrated throughout. 16 Vols., from 2s. to 4s. 6d. (*List free on application.*)
Technology, Manuals of. Edited by Prof. AYRTON, F.R.S., and RICHARD WORMELL, D.Sc., M.A. Illustrated throughout.

The Dyeing of Textile Fabrics. By Prof. Hummel. 5s.	Design in Textile Fabrics. By T. R. Ashenhurst. 4s. 6d.
Watch and Clock Making. By D. Glasgow, Vice-President of the British Horological Institute. 4s. 6d.	Spinning Woollen and Worsted. By W. S. McLaren, M.P. 4s. 6d.
	Practical Mechanics. By Prof. Perry, M.E. 3s. 6d.
Steel and Iron. By Prof. W. H. Greenwood, F.C.S., M.I.C.E., &c. 5s.	Cutting Tools Worked by Hand and Machine. By Prof. Smith. 3s. 6d.

Test Cards, Cassell's Combination. In sets, 1s. each.
Test Cards, Cassell's Modern School. In sets, 1s. each.
World of Ours, This. By H. O. ARNOLD-FORSTER, M.P. Fully Illustrated. 3s. 6d.

Selections from Cassell & Company's Publications.

Books for Young People.

"Little Folks" Half-Yearly Volume. Containing 432 pages of Letterpress, with Pictures on nearly every page, together with Two Full-page Plates printed in Colours and Four Tinted Plates. Coloured boards, 3s. 6d.; or cloth gilt, gilt edges, 5s.
Bo-Peep. A Book for the Little Ones. With Original Stories and Verses. Illustrated with beautiful Pictures on nearly every page, and Coloured Frontispiece. Yearly Volume. Elegant picture boards, 2s. 6d.; cloth, 3s. 6d.
Bashful Fifteen. By L. T. MEADE. Illustrated. 3s. 6d.
Peep of Day. An Old Friend in a New Dress. Illustrated. 2s. 6d.
Maggie Steele's Diary. By E. A. DILLWYN. 2s. 6d.
A Bundle of Tales. By MAGGIE BROWNE, SAM BROWNE, & AUNT ETHEL. 3s. 6d.
Fairy Tales in Other Lands. By JULIA GODDARD. Illustrated. 3s. 6d.
Story Poems for Young and Old. By E. DAVENPORT. 6s.
Pleasant Work for Busy Fingers. By MAGGIE BROWNE. Illustrated. 5s.
Born a King. By FRANCES and MARY ARNOLD-FORSTER. Illustrated. 1s.
The Marvellous Budget: being 65,536 Stories of Jack and Jill. By the Rev. F. BENNETT. Illustrated. Cloth gilt, 2s. 6d.
Magic at Home. By Prof. HOFFMAN. Fully Illustrated. A Series of easy and startling Conjuring Tricks for Beginners. Cloth gilt, 5s.
Schoolroom and Home Theatricals. By ARTHUR WAUGH. With Illustrations by H. A. J. MILES. Cloth, 2s. 6d.
Little Mother Bunch. By Mrs. MOLESWORTH. Illustrated. Cloth, 3s. 6d.
Heroes of Every-Day Life. By LAURA LANE. With about 20 Full-page Illustrations. 256 pages, crown 8vo, cloth, 2s. 6d.
Ships, Sailors, and the Sea. By R. J. CORNEWALL-JONES. Illustrated throughout, and containing a Coloured Plate of Naval Flags. *Cheap Edition*, 2s. 6d.
The Tales of the Sixty Mandarins. By P. V. RAMASWAMI RAJU. 5s.
Gift Books for Young People. By Popular Authors. With Four Original Illustrations in each. Cloth gilt, 1s. 6d. each.

The Boy Hunters of Kentucky. By Edward S. Ellis.
Red Feather: a Tale of the American Frontier. By Edward S. Ellis.
Fritters; or, "It's a Long Lane that has no Turning."
Trixy; or, "Those who Live in Glass Houses shouldn't throw Stones."
The Two Hardcastles.
Seeking a City.
Rhoda's Reward.
Jack Marston's Anchor.
Frank's Life-Battle.
Major Monk's Motto; or, "Look Before you Leap."
Tim Thomson's Trial; or, "All is not Gold that Glitters."
Ursula's Stumbling-Block.
Ruth's Life-Work; or, "No Pains, no Gains."
Rags and Rainbows.
Uncle William's Charge.
Pretty Pink's Purpose.

"Golden Mottoes" Series, The. Each Book containing 208 pages, with Four full-page Original Illustrations. Crown 8vo, cloth gilt, 2s. each.

"Nil Desperandum." By the Rev. F. Langbridge, M.A.
"Bear and Forbear." By Sarah Pitt.
"Foremost if I Can." By Helen Atteridge.
"Honour is my Guide." By Jeanie Hering (Mrs. Adams-Acton).
"Aim at a Sure End." By Emily Searchfield.
"He Conquers who Endures." By the Author of "May Cunningham's Trial," &c.

"Cross and Crown" Series, The. With Four Illustrations in each Book. Crown 8vo, 256 pages, 2s. 6d. each.

Heroes of the Indian Empire; or, Stories of Valour and Victory. By Ernest Foster.
Through Trial to Triumph; or, "The Royal Way." By Madeline Bonavia Hunt.
In Letters of Flame; A Story of the Waldenses. By C. L. Mateaux.
Strong to Suffer; A Story of the Jews. By E. Wynne.
By Fire and Sword; a Story of the Huguenots. By Thomas Archer.
Adam Hepburn's Vow; A Tale of Kirk and Covenant. By Annie S. Swan.
No. XIII.; or, the Story of the Lost Vestal. A Tale of Early Christian Days. By Emma Marshall.
Freedom's Sword; A Story of the Days of Wallace and Bruce. By Annie S. Swan.

Five Shilling Books for Young People. With Original Illustrations. Cloth gilt, 5s. each.

Under Bayard's Banner. By Henry Frith.
The Champion of Odin; or, Viking Life in the Days of Old. By J. Fred. Hodgetts.
Bound by a Spell; or, the Hunted Witch of the Forest. By the Hon. Mrs. Greene.

Albums for Children. Price 3s. 6d. each.

The Chit-Chat Album. Illustrated.
The Album for Home, School, and Play. Set in bold type, and Illustrated throughout.
My Own Album of Animals. Illustrated.
Picture Album of All Sorts. Illustrated.

"Wanted a King" Series. Illustrated. 3s. 6d. each.

Robin's Ride. By Ellinor Davenport Adams.
Great-Grandmamma. By Georgina M. Synge.
Wanted—a King; or, How Merle set the Nursery Rhymes to Rights. By Maggie Browne.

Selections from Cassell & Company's Publications.

Crown 8vo Library. Cheap Editions. 2s. 6d. each.

Rambles Round London. By C. L. Matéaux. Illustrated.
Around and About Old England. By C. L. Matéaux. Illustrated.
Paws and Claws. By one of the Authors of "Poems Written for a Child." Illustrated.
Decisive Events in History. By Thomas Archer. With Original Illustrations.
The True Robinson Crusoes. Cloth gilt.
Peeps Abroad for Folks at Home. Illustrated throughout.
Wild Adventures in Wild Places. By Dr. Gordon Stables, R.N. Illustrated.
Modern Explorers. By Thomas Frost. Illustrated. New and cheaper Edition.
Early Explorers. By Thomas Frost.
Home Chat with our Young Folks. Illustrated throughout.
Jungle, Peak, and Plain. Illustrated throughout.
The England of Shakespeare. By E. Goadby. With Full-page Illustrations.

Three and Sixpenny Books for Young People. With Original Illustrations. Cloth gilt, 3s. 6d. each.

The King's Command. A Story for Girls. By Maggie Symington.
A Sweet Girl Graduate. By L. T. Meade.
The White House at Inch Gow. By Mrs. Pitt.
Lost in Samoa. A Tale of Adventure in the Navigator Islands. By E. S. Ellis.
Tad; or, "Getting Even" with Him. By H. S. Ellis.
Polly. By L. T. Meade.
The Palace Beautiful. By L. T. Meade.
"Follow my Leader."
For Fortune and Glory.
The Cost of a Mistake. By Sarah Pitt.
Lost among White Africans.
A World of Girls. By L. T. Meade.

Books by Edward S. Ellis. Illustrated. Cloth, 2s. 6d. each.

The Hunters of the Ozark.
The Camp in the Mountains.
Ned in the Woods. A Tale of Early Days in the West.
Down the Mississippi.
The Last War Trail.
Ned on the River. A Tale of Indian River Warfare.
Footprints in the Forest.
Up the Tapajos.
Ned in the Block House. A Story of Pioneer Life in Kentucky.
The Lost Trail.
Camp-Fire and Wigwam.
Lost in the Wilds.

Sixpenny Story Books. By well-known Writers. All Illustrated.

The Smuggler's Cave.
Little Lizzie.
The Boat Club.
Luke Barnicott.
Little Bird.
Little Pickles.
The Elchester College Boys.
My First Cruise.
The Little Peacemaker.
The Delft Jug.

Cassell's Picture Story Books. Each containing 60 pages. 6d. each.

Little Talks.
Bright Stars.
Nursery Joys.
Pet's Posy.
Tiny Tales.
Daisy's Story Book.
Dot's Story Book.
A Nest of Stories.
Good Night Stories.
Chats for Small Chatterers.
Auntie's Stories.
Birdie's Story Book.
Little Chimes.
A Sheaf of Stories.
Dewdrop Stories.

Illustrated Books for the Little Ones. Containing interesting Stories. All Illustrated. 1s. each; or cloth gilt, 1s. 6d.

Firelight Stories.
Sunlight and Shade.
Rub-a-dub Tales.
Fine Feathers and Fluffy Fur.
Scrambles and Scrapes.
Tittle Tattle Tales.
Dumb Friends.
Indoors and Out.
Some Farm Friends.
Those Golden Sands.
Little Mothers and their Children.
Our Pretty Pets.
Wandering Ways.
Our Schoolday Hours.
Creatures Tame.
Creatures Wild.
Up and Down the Garden.
All Sorts of Adventures.
Our Sunday Stories.
Our Holiday Hours.

Shilling Story Books. All Illustrated, and containing Interesting Stories.

Seventeen Cats.
Bunty and the Boys.
The Heir of Elmdale.
The Mystery at Shoncliff School.
Claimed at Last, and Roy's Reward.
Thorns and Tangles.
The Cuckoo in the Robin's Nest.
John's Mistake.
Diamonds in the Sand.
Surly Bob.
The History of Five Little Pitchers.
The Giant's Cradle.
Shag and Doll.
Aunt Lucia's Locket.
The Magic Mirror.
The Cost of Revenge.
Clever Frank.
Among the Redskins.
The Ferryman of Brill.
Harry Maxwell.
A Banished Monarch.

"Little Folks" Painting Books. With Text, and Outline Illustrations for Water-Colour Painting. 1s. each.

Fruits and Blossoms for "Little Folks" to Paint.
The "Little Folks" Proverb Painting Book. Cloth only, 2s.
The "Little Folks" Illuminating Book.

Eighteenpenny Story Books. All Illustrated throughout.

Wee Willie Winkie.
Ups and Downs of a Donkey's Life.
Three Wee Ulster Lassies.
Up the Ladder.
Dick's Hero; & other Stories.
The Only Boy.
Raggles, Baggles, and the Emperor.
Roses from Thorns.
Faith's Father.
By Land and Sea.
The Young Berringtons.
Jeff and Leff.
Tom Morris's Error.
Worth more than Gold.
"Through Flood—Through Fire."
The Girl with the Golden Locks.
Stories of the Olden Time.

Selections from Cassell & Company's Publications.

The "World in Pictures" Series. Illustrated throughout. 2s. 6d. each.

A Ramble Round France.
All the Russias.
Chats about Germany.
The Land of the Pyramids (Egypt).
Peeps into China.
The Eastern Wonderland (Japan).
Glimpses of South America.
Round Africa.
The Land of Temples (India).
The Isles of the Pacific.

Cheap Editions of Popular Volumes for Young People. Illustrated. 2s. 6d. each.

In Quest of Gold; or, Under the Whanga Falls.
On Board the *Esmeralda*; or, Martin Leigh's Log.
The Romance of Invention: Vignettes from the Annals of Industry and Science.
Esther West.
Three Homes.
For Queen and King.
Working to Win.
Perils Afloat and Brigands Ashore.

Two-Shilling Story Books. All Illustrated.

Stories of the Tower.
Mr. Burke's Nieces.
May Cunningham's Trial.
The Top of the Ladder: How to Reach it.
Little Flotsam.
Madge and her Friends.
The Children of the Court.
A Moonbeam Tangle.
Maid Marjory.
The Four Cats of the Tippertons.
Marion's Two Homes.
Little Folks' Sunday Book.
School Girls.
Two Fourpenny Bits.
Poor Nelly.
Tom Heriot.
Aunt Tabitha's Waifs.
In Mischief Again.
Through Peril to Fortune.
Peggy, and other Tales.

Half-Crown Story Books.

Little Hinges.
Margaret's Enemy.
Pen's Perplexities.
Notable Shipwrecks.
Golden Days.
Wonders of Common Things.
At the South Pole.
Truth will Out.
Pictures of School Life and Boyhood.
The Young Man in the Battle of Life. By the Rev. Dr. Landels.
Soldier and Patriot (George Washington).

Cassell's Pictorial Scrap Book. In Six Sectional Volumes. Paper boards, cloth back, 2s. 6d. per Vol.

Our Scrap Book.
The Seaside Scrap Book.
The Little Folks' Scrap Book.
The Magpie Scrap Book.
The Lion Scrap Book.
The Elephant Scrap Book.

Library of Wonders. Illustrated Gift-books for Boys. Cloth, 1s. 6d.

Wonderful Adventures.
Wonderful Balloon Ascents.
Wonders of Bodily Strength and Skill.
Wonderful Escapes.
Wonders of Animal Instinct.

Books for the Little Ones. Fully Illustrated.

Rhymes for the Young Folk. By William Allingham. Beautifully Illustrated. 3s. 6d.
The Sunday Scrap Book. With Several Hundred Illustrations. Boards, 3s. 6d.; cloth, gilt edges, 5s.
The History Scrap Book. With nearly 1,000 Engravings. 5s.; cloth, 7s. 6d.
Cassell's Robinson Crusoe. With 100 Illustrations. Cloth, 3s. 6d.; gilt edges, 5s.
Fairy Tales. Illustrated. 3s. 6d.
The Old Fairy Tales. With Original Illustrations. Boards, 1s.; cloth, 1s. 6d.
My Diary. With Twelve Coloured Plates and 366 Woodcuts. 1s.
The Pilgrim's Progress. With Coloured Illustrations. 2s. 6d.
Cassell's Swiss Family Robinson. Illustrated. Cloth, 3s. 6d.; gilt edges, 5s.

The World's Workers. A Series of New and Original Volumes by Popular Authors. With Portraits printed on a tint as Frontispiece. 1s. each.

Charles Haddon Spurgeon. By G. Holden Pike.
Dr. Arnold of Rugby. By Rose E. Selfe.
The Earl of Shaftesbury.
Sarah Robinson, Agnes Weston, and Mrs. Meredith.
Thomas A. Edison and Samuel F. B. Morse.
Mrs. Somerville and Mary Carpenter.
General Gordon.
Charles Dickens.
Florence Nightingale, Catherine Marsh, Frances Ridley Havergal, Mrs. Ranyard ("L. N. R.").
Dr. Guthrie, Father Mathew, Elihu Burritt, Joseph Livesey.
Sir Henry Havelock and Colin Campbell Lord Clyde.
Abraham Lincoln.
David Livingstone.
George Müller and Andrew Reed.
Richard Cobden.
Benjamin Franklin.
Handel.
Turner the Artist.
George and Robert Stephenson.
Sir Titus Salt and George Moore.

⁂ The above Works (excluding Richard Cobden and C. H. Spurgeon) can also be had Three in One Vol., cloth, gilt edges, 3s.

CASSELL & COMPANY, Limited, Ludgate Hill, London;
Paris & Melbourne.

Lightning Source UK Ltd.
Milton Keynes UK
UKHW022230200519
343021UK00006B/173/P